Edges, Peaks, and Vales

A Mythocartography of California at the Margins

Craig Chalquist, PhD

Book Three of the *Animate California Trilogy*

World Soul Books
worldsoulbooks.com

Printed in the United States of America
ISBN 978-0-9826279-2-1

Front cover photograph by Mike Hows.

Table of Contents

The Animate California Trilogy

The capacity to exploit and destroy entire landscapes has loomed in step with the loss of the sense of the world as alive and ensouled. We will not appreciate or protect what we do not love, have not gotten to know in depth, and cannot perceive apart from our industrially amplified cravings to conquer or consume.

The Animate California Trilogy offers heartfelt and reflectively researched studies, sketches, and experiential snapshots that behold the land of California not as an object to be marked off, measured out, or used up, but as a living subject worthy of understanding, safeguarding, and care. To that end the focus lingers with stories, images, and recurring motifs that join this fabled and edgy land, in sickness and in health, to the "inner" life of its inhabitants.

World Soul Books hopes that by introducing and illustrating the "personhood" of the Golden State, the Animate California Trilogy will invite the reader into richer contact with the subjectivity of the land, its creatures, its sea, its sky, and even the matter composing them. In the end, perhaps we are only as humane as we choose to cherish and feel at home in the places that nurture us.

ACKNOWLEDGMENTS

My gratitude for assistance provided by Lola McCrary, Janelle Boatright, Michael Magnuson, and Frank Tuttle.

DEDICATION

To the first people of California--the original
mythographers--and to their hardy descendants.

INTRODUCTION:
California's Inward Turn

To know a place, like a friend or lover, is for it to become familiar; to know it better is for it to become strange again.

— Rebecca Solnit

Storytelling in America has always grown out of the land. It is hard to imagine Henry Thoreau without Walden, John Ford without Monument Valley, Black Elk without the Black Hills. Storytelling brings a place into being. Without stories, a landscape is just so much rocks and sand and gravel, so many board feet. The same is true for us. Without stories, we ourselves are incomplete, *on* the land, not *of* it.

— Phillip Round

California: over a hundred and sixty-three thousand square miles of coast, mountain, forest, desert, cropland, river, and urban sprawl. By contrast, all of Japan takes up a hundred and forty-five thousand square miles. Southern California would contain Switzerland without recourse to a shoehorn.

Car: an old blue Ford Escort hatchback dented but compact and reliable.

Me: a terrapsychologist still possessed in his late forties by the desire to study as much of his homeland as possible, if not by the wit to know when to quit.

It started in 2000, when a woman in a dream called herself San Diego and frowned like the city of the downward-turning bay seems to when glimpsed from above. This dream awakened me to how deeply the lands we occupy reach into us. Landscapes, storms, earthquakes, fires; rivers, forests, tree lines, marshes: all of it a reality psychical as well as geological or ecological.

I live in the San Francisco Bay Area, for example, having moved here in 2005. Around me teems the largest estuary on the Pacific Coast. An estuary is a sheltered transition zone where fresh water joins salt water, nutrients gather, and species meet. Ecosystems here produce rich biodiversity, an enormous quantity of organic matter, erosion-resisting grass, water purified of manmade toxins, a wide habitat range, and a variety of spawning grounds. All these services of creation and connection find their human parallels in the edgy, cosmopolitan Bay Area, birth place of the Golden Gate Bridge, blue jeans, the cable car, naval aviation, stop-action photography (setting the stage for motion pictures), the Free Speech Movement, Stanford University, the University of California, the vacuum tube, the klystron, the television (on Telegraph Hill no less), the silicon semiconductor, the personal computer, hypertext, part of the Internet, the Dotcom boom, gene splicing, ecopsychology, bioregionalism, and transpersonal psychology. It makes sense that the Lick Observatory east of San Jose detected Amalthea, Jupiter's fifth moon, named from the generous goat whose milk fed baby Zeus. The Bay Area is not only an ecological estuary, then, but a cultural, psychological, and spiritual one too, nourishing us on many levels.

The Tears of Llorona: A Californian Odyssey of Myth, Place, and Homecoming (2009) examined these person-place-thing interdependencies through stories, legends, plot lines, and myths recurring along El Camino Real from San Diego to Sonoma. These Imagination-based tools, I had found, ground out finer pictures of activated *ecological complexes*--recurrent traumas we share with our surroundings--than dualistic research stuck in a delusion of objectivity ever could. *Ventral Depths: Alchemical Themes and Mythic Motifs of the Great Central Valley of California* (2011) introduced the Valley as a vast retort cooking perennial transmutations of landscape, culture, and technology.

That left the interior edge of the state to explore: the Inland Empire and the southern, eastern, and northern border regions, followed by the northwest coast and counties just south of the Mendocino National Forest. Was I up for the challenge of listening to what they had to say?

I was. I needed to know more about alchemical California. I had never visited Mount Shasta, our state's pearly Philosopher's Stone glowing north of the Great Central Valley. Memories of family roots had grown in San Bernardino County. I did not understand the Salton Sea or why anyone would live in its sour stench. The date tree factories of Coachella Valley made no sense to me. I had not set eyes on the Owens Valley since boyhood, or on the towering coast redwoods for a decade.

If geography is psychology, then these inland segments of edges, peaks, and vales represent California's seldom-remarked introversion. Most outsiders know the Golden State through manically juxtaposed images of palm trees and neon signs beamed from our busy coast, but then extraverts get all the attention. Some of my journeys of soulseeing would move among land features less frequently advertised.

Every series of investigations changed my relationship to California, and I knew already that this one would too. Before that San Diego dream in 2000, I had thought of nature, place, and Earth as others of my culture do: as backdrops to and resources for more urgent human concerns. By the time I reached Sonoma, I understood myself as one slender thread—my last name refers to a "small branch"—in the eco-historical network of California's geographic mind. I had also moved from a dead universe into a living, animated cosmos in which I felt at home. My first name refers to a secured "outcropping of stone."

The Great Central Valley taught me of my homeland's quintessentially alchemical being, with the heart of the state a site of continual and, on the human side, primarily unconscious transformation. Now that I had sampled this mixture I would inspect the vessel itself.

The problem, however, was time. Not only was I teaching a lot more than I had contracted for, and at more than one school, I was tutoring students doing master's and doctoral work, designing a graduate-level ecotherapy program, writing and publishing journal articles and books, trying to stay current in the fields I taught, speaking at conferences and in interviews to promote *Ecotherapy*, the book I co-edited with Linda Buzzell.... and now facing a series of road trips that would cover more of California's animated expanse than two books' worth had already described.

Some of that territory was lightly inhabited, however, and because my chief interest remained on sites heavy with interaction between people and places, I would not need to linger in, or add much to what had been written about, the Mojave, Yosemite, Kings Canyon, Klamath-Trinity, or other national parks within California. That work properly belonged to thoughtful, poetic naturalists, not to a terrapsychologist scouting for active ecological complexes. Still, I could add some impressions of my visits....

Too, I was familiar with some of the territory already, especially in Southern California. Idyllwild, where I followed creeks as a boy; the Inland Empire, where my mother's side of my birth family lived; San Diego County, where I grew up; the Coachella Valley, and the long, unhealed scar of the international border...My visits there would be updates to impressions previously collected.

Even so, I would leave vast portions of California unexplored, and this troubled me. But in the time allowed, there was nothing I could do except cover as much ground as possible, watch and listen as thoughtfully as I could, take some photographs, write things down, and then leave the rest to whomever might come later. After all, even those areas well known and lived in by me hid secrets I would never discover. A deep dweller could stay in one valley or neighborhood all his life and never finish with getting to know it.

Like getting to know a person offers a tempting analogy, but places are far more complex because, as old Thales observed long ago, they contain everything we know of, including human beings and other living creatures, within their transhuman compass.

By the time I finished this last round of exploratory forays, eleven mobile years of absorption, reflection, digestion, and inward transmutation would be behind me. First, San Diego northward along El Camino Real up to Sonoma, the last mission outpost (*The Tears of Llorona*). Second, the Great Central Valley from Fort Tejon to Redding and back southward again (*Ventral Depths*). Third and last would involve San Bernardino and Riverside County, the southern border region through the Imperial Valley, northward along the Colorado River through the Mojave and its Death Valley, then along I-395 to and beyond Owens Valley to Lake Tahoe, out through Lassen onto the Modoc Plateau and across through Klamath National Forest, then south again along the west coast, through Humboldt and Mendocino Counties, and, turning inward again, through Lake County to Napa and down to bayside Benicia, where our state capital met briefly before its sudden and probably illegal relocation to a floodplain called Sacramento.

Upon finishing I still would not have seen and heard everything there was to find in the realm of Queen Calafía. But for the first time in my adult life, perhaps my entire life, I would feel a sense of completion about what I had felt called to involve myself in here.

Part One: Eastward

Inland Empire of
Hesperidean Outcasts

> My California is the shadowland of the glamorous
> coast, an inland, raw, dramatic place of rugged, del-
> icate landscapes and equally outrageous human
> dissatisfactions and hopes....In time I have come to
> love this place, would be lost anywhere else. I have,
> I hope, become its voice, of the precipitous, craggy
> slopes of Cajon Pass where I live, with its fierce
> winds tossing semi-trailers like cardboard boxes;
> the desperaate power of its citizens, who will try
> anything; yes, even the freeway, that reckless, won-
> derful, perverse river of life. I have found here what
> I most wanted, myself—a terrain twisted by
> immense forces of wind, water, and fault, folded,
> upthrusted, fantastic, a desertous landscape,
> strangely sweet-scented, of desire and love.
>   — Larry Kramer

From Bakersfield, I took Interstate 58 through Tehachapi, where
Northern California's water has been forced to flow uphill before
irrigating Southern California, down through the Antelope Valley:

Mojave, Rosamond ("Land of the Free, Home of the Brave"), Lancaster (where Mayor Parris invokes Jesus at city council meetings despite the church/state separation bother), and Palmdale, passing Edwards Air Force Base as I proceeded south. In Acton, a few miles southwest of Palmdale, the City of Los Angeles was demolishing Phonehenge West, a large collection of junk—old telephone poles, an antique railroad car, part of a Viking dwelling—connected by wooden bridges and assembled into a sculpture once inhabited by its builder, retired phone service technician Alan Kimble Fahey, before he was forced to move to Tehachapi.

Like so much of the Californian desert, as I would see close up in the Coachella Valley and Death Valley, I was passing briefly through Trickster territory. Mojave, for example, where ninety cases of blasting powder blew up a railroad depot in 1884. Palmdale got its name from German-Swiss settlers who mistook the Joshua trees for palms. Early names for the town also included Harold (sounding like "herald," the role of Hermes) and Trego, from Tregony, an ancient Cornish trading village of the kind visited by the tricky commerce god. Settler John Munz was attacked by coyotes while walking to Alpine to pick up his mail. Jackrabbits swarmed over the crops. During Prohibition, bootleggers dug an underground tunnel near Palmdale Boulevard to smuggle liquor distilled in the foothills near Littlerock.

Palmdale was not the only colony here. In the early 1900s an old Quaker colony went up and then went away. In 1914, a union organizer named Harriman with the unfortunate first name of Job founded Llano del Rio ("River Plain") Colony. For a few years the colony of fifty flourished, equipping itself with a rug factory, sawmill, aqueduct, Montessori school, hotel, printer, and even an Esperanto language club. Colonists did not use cash; instead, they put their wages toward food, clothing, shelter, and stock shares they purchased on credit. By 1918, their colony was the largest town in the Antelope Valley, but not for long. Under Harry Chandler, the *Los Angeles Times* ran a Red scare campaign against unpatriotic Socialists that cut off the colony's funding; meanwhile, the California Commissioner of Corporations denied the colony permission to build a reservoir. These outer assaults combined with internal divisions to render

Llano del Rio a ghost town, one of many left to decompose in the shadow of the Golden State.

I had been down Highway 14 before, down past its huge electronic gambling sign--"Antelope Valley Fairgrounds Satellite Wagering"--through the suburban sprawl of boxy Santa Clarita and on to the San Fernando Valley. Instead, I turned east and proceeded down 138 and, passing the Angeles National Forest on my right (south), entered Victorville, named after a railroad construction superintendent. Victorville got by on two industries: cement, and the Roy Rogers Museum near the courthouse. The Museum, a sort of hunter's Chuck E. Cheese, contains a large, plastic sculpture of Roy's horse Trigger, the horse himself, stuffed, Bullet the Wonder Dog, also stuffed, and various other animals and animal parts collected by Rogers on his numerous hunting expeditions: a stuffed antelope, wolves, foxes, hippo tusks, elephant feet, heads of wildebeest, gazelle, baboon....

Barstow was about twenty miles to the northeast, which put it a few miles east of Hinkley, where Erin Brockovich had fought to expose Pacific Gas and Electric's pollution of the groundwater with chromium, and twenty miles east of Boron, where half the world's borax was mined. Switching to I-15, I drove southwest through Hesperia on my way to San Bernardino, Riverside, and points beyond. Before 15 could sweep me into Rancho Cucamonga I caught Highway 215 and entered Berdoo from the north at nightfall.

Long before the advent of road signs, billboards, or Route 66, a giant arrowhead pointed the way.

According to Cahuilla legends, the large, downward-pointing mark in the foothills above what is now the San Bernardino Valley appeared in order to guide the people toward new hunting grounds and warm mineral springs. For some reason white sage growing within it contrasts with darker surrounding vegetation. The Cahuilla came here from the hot summers in the Mojave Desert to harvest berries, nuts, and acorns....until the missionaries arrived, starting with Francisco Dumetz in 1810. It was he who named the place after St. Bernard, whose name graces Swiss Alps passes whose hospices were noted for their hospitality. Pilgrims on their way to Rome often stopped at the saint's monastery high in the mountains to refresh themselves for the journey.

Of course, the *meaning* of a high pass--of any exalted threshold-- is that you attain it, rest if necessary, and move on. When the Spaniards decided to stay, the dried-up springs and unusual earth- quakes of 1812 convinced the Cahuilla that the spirits of the land were angry at the newcomers for their intrusion. When the intrud- ers set up an *assistencia* (mission branch) at San Bernardino Rancho in 1929, the Cahuilla attacked it and stole cattle In 1834, they sacked the building and burned it, and that was that for the missionaries.

Those missionaries, anyway. By 1851, incoming Mormons were building roads into the mountains to harvest timber and set up sawmills. So many trees fell that settlers called lumber "Mormon banknotes." (Later mills would provide much of the wood that raised up San Bernardino and Los Angeles.) Some of the banknotes built a fort against Ute raiders who swept through looking for cat- tle.

The original Mormon party consisted of four hundred and thir- ty-seven wayfarers, including twenty-six black slaves (half the party hied from the Deep South). The theocracy they set up in the San Bernardino Valley was lead by Amasa Lyman, who eventually left the church, and Charles Rich, who fathered fifty-one children and ended his days in Idaho. Lyman had been close to Joseph Smith; both had shed blood for the cause. One of Lyman's many wives was a sixteen-year-old named Priscilla. Rich was a member of Smith's secret Council of Fifty. On land purchased with money made in Utah by charging gold-seekers colossally inflated prices for food and supplies, Henry Sherwood, who had laid out Salt Lake City, surveyed a one-mile-square grid for a townsite.

The Mormons rode in on a reputation for industry, honesty, and integrity, but within a year their town ran under martial law, they remained in debt for the rancho they had bought, and internal con- flicts in their ideal society ripped open to reveal seamy secrets: sur- veyor Henry Sherwood's claim that Brigham Young had ordered him to assassinate a man in Nauvoo, Illinois; councilman Charles Crismon's refusal to tithe; Dr. Woodville Andrews' fake medical degree, abandoned wife and child, seduction of another woman, and theft of watches; attorney Quartus Sparks's fiery divorce after his own illicit affair surfaced.

As inner tensions thickened, and as colonists fleeing the authoritarianism of Utah arrived unannounced, prompting Young to write off the colony as "a haven for the disaffected," rust cut into the wheat crop (planted as both food source and Biblical metaphor), floods alternated with droughts, summer storms ruined newly raised adobe homes, plants came up shorter, and illnesses, accidents, and deaths mounted. In 1857, Lyman and Rich quit and two-thirds of the colonists departed, some to Utah, others to Northern California. Such is the fate of every institution founded on the premise that some people are wheat and others are chaff. The rancho was sold off to the chaff at a loss.

Young had been partly right: well-named San Bernardino (had the place somehow named itself?) has always been a haven for nomads and travelers; later, for gunslingers like Wyatt Earp, gamblers, barkeeps, and hookers; still later, for health-seekers headed for Arrowhead and Big Bear; and still later for bikers (the Hells Angels were founded here), drive-through tourists (the first McDonalds opened at 14th and E), and outlaws, and exiles of every stripe, hue, and inclination. Had not Antonio Luga sold his ranch to the Mormons because outlaws and raiders overran it at will? Had not the place once been called El Campo? As visitors the Mormons had done well for two years, but by the quiet timetable kept by the place itself, they overstayed their welcome.

On a Sunday morning, having spent the night in Colton, I stood considering San Bernardino's City Hall: a building with columns for legs, as though ready to get up and travel. A Vanir Tower stood next door, the Vanir having been, mythologically anyway, the Titans of Norse legend. Other giants gathered nearby: Wells Fargo, Bank of America, Chase.... Two young homeless men sat on the steps of the B of A building, both in black; one man's shirt had skulls all over it. On the corner of Mill and E, Spiderman spun forth a haircut ad. "We Support Heroes," a sign had proclaimed at the Martin Luther King Jr. statue looking out over Civic Center.

Around the center the poverty was appalling. The city's latest passersby through included Latinos and African Americans driving low-slung Oldsmobiles or waiting on street corners for employment or trouble. The cityscape around them was shabby and run down. A dry aqueduct. Billboards advertising tough lawyers. At Tippecanoe and Mill, a miles-long business park of blocky white buildings bore a blue star emblem. A tall fence around the Jewish cemetery. Grief Embers, a slave in the first Mormon party, had held the task of blowing a six-foot bishop's horn in case of an emergency, but his Heimdall signal had rung out too early or too late. Car horns now instead, and disheveled men clutching bottle-shaped paper bags.

The San Bernardino County Government Center stood where Jose Lugo's house had been and, later, a fort. The Historic Site Marker for the "Mormon Stockade" said it had been "built 1851 for projection [!} against Indians." The building, I noted, was shaped like a tombstone. As I shot pictures of the Jedediah Smith memorial, a homeless woman with black, scraggy hair, a gray shirt, and black pants asked me in a faltering, crazy tone if all this were a cemetery.

Back in my car again, I nearly ran a red light after glimpsing the Orange Raceway. Yes. No street named Bifrost, perhaps, but what a long history of transits and throughways: Cajon Pass, Mojave Trail, the Old Spanish Trail, another running to Los Angeles, a California Hotel equipped with a radio station, even Joe and Evelyn Brier living at the Tri-City Airport. Castaway Restaurant, Carousel Mall, Wigwam Motel ("Do It in a Tee Pee"), a baseball team named Stampede, Sage's for the first-ever one-stop retail shopping. The oldest commercial structure in town, the Garner Building at 4th and Court, had been a stage stop. The Santa Fe Depot at 3rd and J was the largest of its kind west of the Mississippi. Before then, New Mexicans had come here to buy horses from the Californios.

Painted below a downtown walkway:

Route 66 Rendezvous
Cruisin' Hall of Fame

This white wall displayed a map of "America's Main Street" and plaques of outstanding "cruisers," which meant locally established businesses like Pep Boys, Revell, *Popular Mechanics Magazine*, and Kustom Kars of California. The wall had been raised by the Visitors

Bureau, the city, and various corporate sponsors like Ford.

What John Steinbeck had dubbed the Mother Road, and Dust Bowl refugees the Glory Road, ran twenty-four hundred miles from Chicago to Santa Monica. Crossing eight states and three time zones, Route 66 was commissioned November 11, 1926 to pick up as many pieces possible of existing roadway. Although the Federal Aid Road Act of 1916 made funds available road-building, few states made use of them--mainly because most citizens rode trolleys or trains--until required by the Federal Highway Act of 1921 to set aside 7% of their roads as national highways. In 1923, Cy Avery was appointed state highway commissioner to oversee construction of this national system, with highways designated by numbers rather than by names. The eventual Route 66 was one of these highways. In 1926, Ford lowered the price of motorcars to ignite a driving surge.

However, it took until 1937 to pave all of 66. To advertise 66, a "Bunion Derby" foot race along its entire length included runners of every persuasion, including those in overalls, boots, moccasins, barefoot, cane-bearing, and ukulele-toting An unemployed actor showed up in a biblical robe.

If we reimagine roads as living beings retaining something of the spirit of those who walk, hobble, wheel, trot, and drive along them, then perhaps absorbing so many routes--Pontiac Trail, Osage Indian Trail, Wire Road, Postal Highway, Ozark Trail, Grand Canyon Route, National Old Trails Highway, Mormon Trail, Will Rogers Highway--left Route 66 one 6 short of a three-pack, a wild, meandering, two-dimensional monument to restlessness, reckless-ness, and kitsch.

> Route 66 is Steinbeck and Will Rogers and Woody Guthrie and Merle Haggard and Dorothea Lange and Mickey Mantle and Jack Kerouac. It's thou-sands of waitresses, service station attendants, fry cooks, truckers, grease monkeys, hustlers, state cops, wrecker drivers, and motel clerks. Route 66 is a soldier thumbing home for Christmas; an Okie family looking for a better life...It's yesterday, today,

and tomorrow. Truly a road of phantoms and
dreams, 66 is the romance of traveling the open
highway.

— Michael Wallis

What's out there on 66? From east to west, or water (Lake
Michigan) to water (Pacific Ocean): maple syrup at Funk's Grove,
Our Lady of the Highways statue of Mary just west of Raymond,
Ted Drewes Frozen Custard in St. Louis, the Meramec Caverns
where Jesse James hid out, Red Chaney's simple drive-through ham-
burger stand in Springfield, fields of grain waving in Kansas, the
gargoyled Coleman Theater in Miami ("My-am-uh"), Oklahoma, the
Big Blue Whale in Catoosa, the Tulsa Monument Company, Lloyd
Cook's replica-gorilla-guarded hubcap shop in Elk City, the Regal
Reptile Ranch in Alanreed, Cadillac Ranch (ten of them buried
nose-first in the dirt) in Amarillo, the Blue Swallow Motel in
Tucumcari, where the owner, Lillian Redman, hands out guest
cards ("We are all travelers. From "birth till death" we travel
between the eternities"), Club Cafe and its sourdough biscuits and
100% beef hamburgers in Santa Rosa along the Pecos, El Vado Motel
in Albuquerque, the New Mexican badlands, the Perpetual Ice
Caves, the Continental Divide, the Grand Canyon, Painted Desert,
Petrified Forest, and Meteor Crater, the Route 66 Museum at the
site of the original McDonalds in San Bernardino, the Wigwam
Motel, the Aztec Hotel in Monrovia (actually a Mayan look, but
named "Aztec" to sound evenmore exotic), the Jack Rabbit Trading
Post in Joseph City, and finally Santa Monica Boulevard and Pacific
Coast Highway, where the last 66 sign was removed and then van-
ished to travel elsewhere.

The sign was removed because Eisenhower, who came back
from Germany impressed by Hitler's Autobahn, pushed for a new
highway system via the Federal Aid Highway Act of 1956.

By the time the interstate system was fully under
construction and the Mother Road was being
phased out, fast-food corporations had managed to
smother many neighborhood beaneries, highway

food stands, and drive-ins owned by individuals. It
seemed the nation was determined to clone itself
and become uniform when it came to food, drink,
lodging, clothing, cologne, shoes, or just about anything else.

— Michael Wallis

Richard and Maurice McDonald left New Hampshire at the
start of the Depression to look for jobs in Hollywood. They worked
as set builders on the Columbia lot, then bought a movie theater in
Glendale that never succeeded. In 1937, they opened a Pasadena
drive-in restaurant, moved a few years later to a larger building on E
Street in Santa Barbara, and opened the McDonald Brothers Burgar
Bar Drive-In. It did so well the brothers bought a hillside mansion
with a tennis court and pool. In 1948, they fired all their carhops and
closed their restaurant for three months to retool. When it opened
again, the menu items had been cut to food that could be prepared
a task at a time, cooked quickly, and served without utensils. Paper
and plastic replaced dishes and glassware. As an old ad of theirs
explains, "Imagine--No Carhops--No Waitresses--No Dishwashers
--No Bus Boys--The McDonald's System is Self-Service!"

After visiting, Carl Karcher opened his own restaurant, Carl's
Junior, in 1956, the year of the Interstate Highway Act. Jack-in-the-
Box opened in San Diego. The waistline of the suburbs expanded.
Highways filled like choked arteries.

America's fast food chains were not launched by
large corporations relying upon focus groups and
market research. They were started by door-to-
door salesmen, short-order cooks, orphans, and
dropouts, by eternal optimists looking for a piece of
the next big thing.

— Eric Schlosser

Case in point: "Colonel" Harland Sanders, orphan and farm hand,
who practiced law without a law degree, delivered babies without
having a medical degree, sold insurance and Michelin tires, ran a gas

station, cooked, and went on the road again dressed like a Kentucky colonel. Hollywood held no monopoly on wearing costumes.

Although eclipsed by high-speed routes down which the traveler could drive without stopping to see anything, Route 66 led an underground life more neglected but not fundamentally different from its disreputable run in an earlier day. By the time Route 66 fan clubs sprang up like roadside weeds to repost signs, take photographs of crumbling Modernist cafes, and dust off stretches of the old Mother Road, a new generation of wayfarers found some of the old sites still available: a burlesque museum, concrete totem poles, a tree filled with pairs of shoes, a Jesse James statue, the oldest house and church in the U.S., the longest pedestrian bridge in the world, a round barn, the largest catsup bottle in the world, an enormous fish tank, a huge steel cross, many neon signs, a giant spaceman, Mickey Mantle's first ballpark, a museum of barbed wire housed in an old bra factory, and Elvis Presley's favorite Route 66 motel suite.

If a roadway were to dream of the post-frontier crumbling of American Modernity, such places--actual places, however symptomatic and bizarre--just might, like the eccentrics who maintain them and the tourists who visit them, serve as its animated, time-warped emblems, landscapes, and passersby of dream symbols caught up in a timeless imaginal procession.

THE LARGEST COUNTY IN the nation, large enough in fact to pack nine small states into its twenty thousand square miles of land ranging from below sea level (Death Valley) to the summit of San Gorgonio, is divided down the middle by the San Gabriels and San Bernardinos, mountains that separate the western valley from the eastern desert, and by the San Andreas Fault running diagonally through them. The San Bernardinos harbor Lake Arrowhead and Big Bear Lake.

Businessmen from Cincinnati formed the Arrowhead Reservoir Company to dam a lake named Little Bear and divert the water to citrus crops to the south. Their plan was for six lakes connected by tunnels, but the ancient arrowhead on the hillside pointed downward toward insurmountable obstacles, including dipping rails after rain damaged cement laid for a cable and rail system from Waterman Canyon to Skyland, earning its short life the nickname Incline Railroad (echoed by cars backing up the steep Arrowhead Road to keep gasoline flowing in their engines), and a lawsuit by Mojave Desert communities protesting the planned diversion of water. The project halted around the time that James Mooney, investor and general manager, ended six feet under.

Still, the arrowhead did seem a summons for some kind of attention. The reservoir was sold to an investment group under J. Benton Van Nuys, who built a members-only French Normal village on the lake shore for wealthy golfers and fishers. In 1946, the village was bought by the Los Angeles Turf Club (owners of the Santa Anita Race Track) for a Depressed $2 million, did not flourish, and sold out in 1960 to the first of a series of developers. George Coult Properties took over Lake Arrowhead Village in 1978 and, to make way for a resort and shopping arcade, allowed fire departments to conduct "burn and learn" lessons on everything but the original dance pavilion. In 2000, the Narrows was closed by a mudslide that dropped a huge rock into the roadway, prompting locals to hold a "Rock Out" party. Another flood closed the road in 2003. If the motto of New York is "Ever Upward," perhaps that of Lake Arrowhead points in the other direction.

Like everything that happens in a particular place, films shot there can hint at the place's character. In the case of Lake Arrowhead, the movie montage echoed young, once-shy goddesses and heroines in radical transformation, like the lake itself, starting in 1918 with Louise Glaum starring in *The Goddess of Lost Lake* as a Caucasian pretending to be an Indian princess. After that came the talkie *Sunrise*; *Eight Girls in a Boat*; *Now and Forever* with Shirley Temple, who also starred in *Heidi* and *The Blue Bird*; *Now, Voyager*, with Bette Davis blossoming into extraversion; *Boy Did I Get A Wrong Number* with Bob Hope and Elke Sommer; and *I'll Take Sweden*, with Arrowhead resident Frankie Avalon and a bevy of bathing beauties. Did the lake want attention? Did the downward-pointing arrowhead command, "Look At Me"? How many who came here had noticed the aspens, California bluebells, prickly poppies, lupines, oaks, ponderosa pine, incense cedar, Jeffrey pines, mountain sage, monkeyflower, manzanita, Indian paintbrush, chinquapin, baby blue-eyes, ranger's buttons, lemon lilies, columbine...

I looked around when I arrived, but what scenery remained--cold blue sky, snow-topped pines, ducks seated on sheaths of ice on the lake--peeked out from around fast food joints, boat tour landings pointed out by carved bears, and junk shops jammed into a big red-roofed arcade with a SHOPPING AND DINING sign on it. An upended stump with a McDonald's behind it announced some Lake Arrowhead Facts. Logging, of course, had been one of them.

I looked down at a McDonald's burger wrapper discarded in a parking lot next to the lake. Resorts and boutiques surrounded blue water in a tightening noose of commerce.

When you ask the men (it's usually men) responsible for this kind of commercialistic desolation why they have built to the point of overbuilding, they usually reply--in defensive, defiant tones, in studied, sociopathic apathy, or in the hush of former executioners and prison wardens looking back in guilt--that they have a right to make a decent living. But a living that mows down entire forests, turns rivers to toxic mud, blows tops off mountains, or turns lakes like this one into a cheap, overcrowded circus is neither decent nor really a "living." It is an indecent dying, a somnambulistic feeding of insatiable Moloch, a melting down of everything living into a cold, hard, golden calf. Happy Meal? Given the emotional and ecological consequences, it should be called the Misery Meal. And like any fast food, consuming it only enlarges the empty sense of hunger. Especially in a county with low median income, high unemployment, one in five kids in poverty, one in ten at risk of abuse or neglect, teen girls having babies, high infant mortality, and a 25% high school dropout rate.

In 1845, Benjamin Wilson of Tennessee was searching for the outlaw Joaquin Murietta when he stumbled into a valley, saw grizzly bears, shot twenty-two of them, added all this up, and named the place Big Bear Valley. William Holcomb set off a brief boom in 1860 by finding gold in the valley named after him; by 1884 a dam had materialized a large lake. Work stopped on the Bear Valley Dam in 1884 because Frank Brown, who added extra height to it, got nervous about it falling over, but in 1912, John Eastwood designed a multiple-arch dam there before drowning two years later in the King River. In 1916, the Bear Valley Development Company sold lots around the bear-claw-shaped lake.

Hotels followed, and fifty-two resorts by 1921, and a ski operation by 1949. One developer, Henry Keiner, built a Peter Pan Woodland Club that burned, to be replaced by an airport ("I can fly, I can fly!"). Film crews arrived as well to shoot the racist film *The Birth of a Nation* (at the end of which the heroine reenacted an old legend found at Castle Rock by plunging into the lake), *Gone with the Wind*, and *The Last of the Mohicans*.

Wildlife managers fear that the entire San Bernardino National Forest might be gone with the wind some day because higher temperatures brought by climate change encourage bark beetles to be fruitful and multiply. The trees they chew through burn in wildfires like matches dipped in gasoline.

Fay Trowbridge Legg, my birth mother's mother, lived in a house in Forest Falls ten miles south of Big Bear Lake as the crow flies but an hour away by road. She had been a private duty nurse while married to Edwin Murdock Legg, my grandfather, a Navy veteran and meteorologist who had issued fruit frost warnings on the local radio. After he divorced her and descended to Hemet, she took to the mountains. Much of the addition work on her house came from her own hand. I met her in my late twenties after a long search for my birth family history. Looking back, I remember best of all her intense aliveness, whether she was climbing the roof in her nineties to sweep off the leaves (to the dismay of my aunt), pounding her little fist on the kitchen table to make a point, or daubing on lipstick to flirt with the new mailman truding up the icy road. A lifelong learner forever in self-transformation, she died while reading a pile of books on some topic or other. Several at once, probably, knowing her.

My hotel was in Colton, once hailed by boosters as a healthful abode, as had been nearby Fontana before World War II and Kaiser Steel brought smog-spewing coke ovens, smelters, and rolling mills. On every side lay heaps of sand and gravel awaiting transport. I saw none of this the night I drove in, but I did see an indeterminate figure ghosting down the street in a black hooded robe. In the hotel elevator, an "IF THE SHOE FITS...." ad displayed a woman's feet too small for the severe black shoes she wore.

In the morning I learned that the hotel was just up the street from the Agua Mansa cemetery, all that remained of a town named Peaceful Waters washed away when the Santa Ana River flooded in 1862. The homes were gone, but the river had left the cemetery in place. A cemetery haunted, locals said, by La Llorona.

I paid a visit at twilight, but the gates were locked. Still, with the *assistencia* nearby and the industry all around, I could see why Llorona would be here. Where there was conquest, where nature suffered, there the Weeping Woman wailed her rage and despair into the moonlit night.

Previously I had linked her with Artemis, a goddess of the natural world. A world in steep decline. Now, however, I would see her more as a sister of Sophia. According to Gloria Anzaldua, Llorona and the Virgin of Guadalupe represent two severed halves—one dark, one bright—of an original Aztec whole imaged by Cihuacoatl of the obsidian knife and white dress, Tonantsi, Coatlique, and other lost goddesses. In this connection Anzaldua also mentions Kali.

Mythologically and archetypally, that makes sense. Myths give form to underlying archetypes, and La Virgin, Mary, Sophia, Kali, Durga, Saraswati, Benzaiten, Athena, Minerva, Medusa, Mary Magdalene, Nu Gua, Sekhmet, Kwan Yin, Cailleach, White Buffalo Calf Woman, Brigid, Deborah, and many others express the archetype of Wisdom in feminine form. Her avatars and by-forms descend into darkness and rise again in light. The ocean preoccupies Sophia when she sees her light reflected there.

In most stories Wisdom shows a dual aspect, as with higher and lower Sophia, Athena and Medusa, Guadalupe and Llorona: a hint perhaps that what she offers depends not on light alone, but on its creative relation to the dark. Although quiet at times, Wisdom remains assertive, even warlike, in service to higher goals. When disturbed she protests, loudly, in the voices of the elements, like the Siren, Banshee, Crying Wind, and Weeping Woman. She educates or kills depending on how she is approached. No darkness is as that of deadly as Wisdom fallen.

What did it mean that the Llorona I had tracked up and down El Camino Real and heard about in the Central Valley and now here was a manifestation of Wisdom, like the Sophia who occasionally visited me in dreams? I did not know, but here, I felt, was a piece of the puzzle of my changing relationship to California. For armored Queen Calafia too was a sister of Wisdom, like Minerva on the Great Seal of our state.

Dual aspect: like Lorna and Lenore, my birth mother and her sister. Lorna had lived in Hana, Hawaii, worked as a psychiatric social worker, traveled the world, survived a plane crash, played in the black market, and carried a cloud of bad luck wherever she drifted. Lenore lived in Yucaipa ("Green Valley" in the Serrano language), near Redlands, worked as a forest ranger and paramedic, gave birth to a boy and girl, and looked after her aging mother. Lorna got along with no one, packed a pistol, drank and used, and hated my uncle Truman, who, like me, grew up in the family Hero role. Lenore got along with everyone, including her funny and extraverted brother, carried the sun along with her for company, flew helicopters and gardened, and was mindful of what people needed.

Did they represent the human forms of split halves of a lost original? Lorna was the family outcast, yet stayed in touch with Lenore, the family caretaker. Lenore occasionally asked her older sister for advice and, before Lorna died, kept her updated on my career doings. It was odd, a mother who wouldn't say a word to you interested in where you were headed in life. I wondered if she ever knew what myth was inhabiting her.

Like my adoptive family, my birth mother's had drifted to California from the midwest. The Chalquists, I've often felt, would have found a better cultural fit in the conservative Central Valley, but, "We wanted to leave behind the small-town lack of privacy," my mom once told me, "with everyone watching and judging everyone else." Coastal California offered a welcome anonymity. The Leggs, also politically conservative, came to California to find work and education. Redlands had good red soil back then, space to grow crops, a high school (where Lorna and Lenore were friends with Joan Baez, "Joanie" as my family called her), and a new university.

Although my mother was the identified outsider and drifter, she carried it for all of them, even after the family split.

Back at the hotel, I noted the friendliness of the hotel clerk. Definitely a good place to visit, for a time. The artwork in my room displayed curves, squares, circles, waves, edges, all of different colors and angles, none of which went together--but here they all did, for here, every shape that fits nowhere else belongs. For a time.

Understanding the nature of San Bernardino, the Cahuillas and Serranos had been its first nomadic friends. "Take care of the land," a Cahuilla elder observed, "and it will take care of you."

JURUPA RANCHO ALONGSIDE THE Santa Ana River was granted to Juan Bandini in 1838. In five years Bandini sold a portion of it to Benjamin Wilson, who sold it to Louis Rubidoux in 1847. Part of it, Rancho Cucamonga, became a livestock ranch planted later as a vineyard. Indians provided most of the labor force. Crops included corn, wheat, barley, potatoes, peas, beans, onions, and peppers.

Taking advantage of a subsidy offered by the state of California for fostering silk production, Los Angeles promoters organized a California Silk Center Association and bought part of the Jurupa Ranch. When they failed to make silk, the subsidy was withdrawn, and the promoters sold out to the Southern California Colony Association led by Judge John North of Tennessee. He called for colonists, and they assembled south of San Bernardino in the place now known as Riverside.

To understand the ambition behind these Old West colonies, it's important to keep in mind the religious mythology that drove them --and that continues to drive so much of what goes by the name of "development" in California.

Although around for eons, monotheism took hold in the deserts, especially those of Egypt, Persia, and Palestine. Deserts are what's left after monocrop agriculture dries up some lush Eden to plow one crop, one settlement, one Truth, one God. Instead of sacred landscapes populated by a lively diversity of ever-present spirits, monochromatic wastes are overseen from invisibly far above. The verdancy of one world is made to submit to the aridity of the next.

Perhaps only in the desert would it be possible to
let one sky god take over all creation, to let a single
male deity supplant a pantheon, and for that god to
become super-natural, transcendent of his creation.
— Rebecca Solnit

When Christian colonists set foot in semi-arid California, therefore, they saw a great nothing--"deserted," as the word suggests--
waiting to be hammered and plowed into yet another stage stop on
the way to an otherworldly Paradise. The native people, places, animals, and plants meant nothing to them but hindrances to overcome
with Bible, muscle, and mule teams, or, at best, souls to save or hired
help to deploy. The most tragic consequence of such an anti-ecological worldview was its failure to realize that the people already here
lived in a paradise of living richness inaccessible to Christian belief
until the end of the world. Colonists did not come to California
looking for Eden, as historians sometimes suppose: they came convinced that Eden was lost until after the Final Judgment.

The Edens that kept springing up in the New World badly confused them. Mad Columbus believed he had finally found Paradise
off the coast of Venezuela. Sturdier souls than his denied the lure of
beautiful land altogether, forcing its lure to operate unconsciously,
symptomatically, pathologically, antisocially.

One form this lure took was the nature cure. Colton was hailed
as free from all "malarial influences" and desirable for invalids.
Crafton offered "the most perfect climate on Earth." Riverside
awaited as an "asthmatics paradise."

Paradise. Juan Bautista de Anza had used that very word in
March 1774 while leading an expedition through in quest of a land
route from southern Mexico. In fact, he named the beautiful place
near the river Valle de Paraiso, "Valley of Paradise," for its fragrant
herbs, rich grassland, temperate weather, and abundant river water.

"...We wish to form a colony of intelligent, industrious and
enterprising people, so that each one's industry will help to promote
his neighbor's interests, as well as his own." This was the mandate
of John Wesley North, developer, judge, and surveyor, who arrived
in 1870 to found a religious colony on the banks of the Santa Ana.

But in 1874, the colony was pushed out of Paradise by developers Samuel Cary Evans and William Sawyard, who consolidated fifteen thousand acres under the Riverside Land and Irrigating Company. Soon Alvord was named, after a president of Bank of America, and Christopher Columbus Miller opened his Glenwood Hotel in 1880.

As late as 1893, writer Kate Sanborn saw "flowers enough to overwhelm a Broadway florist, every sort of cereal, every fruit that grows," planted roadsides, well-trimmed hedges, shaded avenues-- and no poor people anywhere. All that was about to change.

I had been in and through Riverside before, but while on this trip of soulseeing I woke up there after dreaming of being watched by a grove of oranges.

Imperial Romans, Bedouin princes, Spanish nobles: all grew and ate the illustrious fruit brought to the New World by Columbus on his second voyage. In 1841 William Wolfskill of Kentucky planted two mediocre acres of Mediterranean Sweets in Los Angeles. But in 1874, cuttings from mutant naval oranges from Bahia, Brazil were planted by spiritualist and suffragist Eliza Tibbets, who, according to legend, gave them dishwater in the absence of irrigation. She and her husband Luther had received the cuttings from the U.S. Department of Agriculture. Given enough water, the large, seedless "Washington" oranges sprouted with such alacrity that the Tibbetses had to raise a fence to keep neighbors from stealing the buds.

After the death of Eliza Tibbets on a visit to the colony of mediums at Summerland, naval orange groves spread throughout Riverside and beyond. By 1900, 5.6 million orange trees and 1.4 million lemon trees shook their shiny green leaves across the county. A Citrus Experiment Station was established in 1907 at the base of Mount Rubidoux. Because Valencias, planted in Southern California since 1876, ripened in the summer, and Washingtons in winter, growing both provided a year-round crop that allowed Californian agriculturalists to transition from wheat to oranges. Lemons and grapefruit grew well too.

Carey McWilliams has noted that between 1883 and 1888, the sudden "recognition" of Southern California's Indian and Spanish (but not Mexican) past coincided with real estate promotion of available land. The resulting golden glow of an idealized Mission past--clever Californios, devoted Padres, blessed Indians, pageants and grapes--sterilized the grit and grime of lived history, at least on the surface.

Yet the presence of the land is never absent from any production, nor can ideologies boosted to dominate territory drown out the myths that naturally grow in certain soils, myth that give form to the character of a place.

Ancient Greek storytellers spun tales of the Garden of the Hesperides, the Sunset Goddesses of the far West who tended golden apples while singing lovely songs. The "apples" came from a bough Gaia offered as a wedding gift to Hera and Zeus. In some versions of the story the Garden sat below a mighty mountain not far from the sea.

To enter Riverside is to enter a fantasyland of houses refitted to look like missions. Others have been decked out in themes left over from childhood: gingerbread homes, for instance. Parking near Main, I began walking near the government center and somehow ended up in an outdoor mall. It was difficult to tell them apart. Gradually I realized that this mall *was* the downtown. Christmas music blasted inescapably wherever I walked, the tunes synchronized over several city blocks. Neatly pruned orange trees stood guard in front of the ornate columns of the county courthouse. The mall included fountains, boutiques, ice skaters, trinket shops, and quotations by Martin Luther King Jr. as well as a statue of him and of Gandhi. I wondered if the sun ever arced just enough for the Inland Empire National Bank towering behind the Mahatma to cover him in shadow.

The eerie entirety of this permanent exhibit / mall / amusement park / arcade had spread from the Mission Inn down the block. Disney's term might be appropriate here: "imagineering."

> In 1902, Frank Miller, owner of the Glenwood Cottage Inn at Riverside, with funds provided by Henry Huntington, began to construct the famous Mission Inn. Designed by Muron Hunt, the Mission Inn was built wing by wing around the old adobe

Glenwood Cottage, until the new structure covered an entire block. Once completed, the inn gave
the initial fillip to Mission architecture, so called,
and soon Missionesque and Moorish structures
began to dot the Southern California landscape. It
was here, in the Mission Inn, that John Steven
McGroarty wrote the Mission Play, for which he
was deservedly decorated by the Pope.
— Carey McWilliams

"The story of Junipero Serra and the Missions for dramatic purposes has been lying around since 1833, at least, for anybody to
grab," wrote McGroarty, a lawyer, miner, and editor, to Charles
Lummis of the *Los Angeles Times*. Lummis played a leading role in
glossing the genocidal mission past into a promotional idyll. "But no
one grabbed it until I did so in 1912. Now it is mine." Thousands
turned out for the campy, self-congratulatory play that made
McGroarty the poet laureate of California.

The Inn (and Spa) contains two hundred and thirty-eight lavish
guest rooms and twenty-seven suites grouped around a restaurant
in the middle by the courtyard. Suites go for up to $1,400 a night.
Amenities include designer linen, a private poolside, steam rooms,
spa treatments ("performed by skilled practitioners in the art of
indulgence"), fitness classes, and a nail salon. Towers, domes, arch-
es, columns, thick draperies, carved beams, and gargoyles fill out the
elaborate decor. A life-sized statue of Frank Miller holds a parrot;
the Inn's caged macaws are named Joseph and Napoleon.
Celebrities, presidents, and citrus industry barons have often
graced this kingdom-in-miniature with their presence in passing.

This domed castle lacked nothing but a moat, I saw as I
approached. Dolls in Christmas dress hung from the ramparts
between palm trees. I wondered in passing whether the bear-
shaped bushes and the puppets perched on balustrades had
inspired Walt Disney or the other way around.

A tour for guests gathered near the front entrance. I merged with
it, remaining in the back but within earshot of the docent. She was
busy discussing the Mission Inn Raincross.

No one is quite sure who invented the design, although it was registered with the U.S. Patent Office in 1908. Frank Miller and architect Arthur Benton usually get the credit for it. The lower part is a framed bell, recalling the bell tower at Mission San Gabriel. The upper, according to the original Handbook of the Mission Inn, recalls a Native American image for a rain deity: a dragonfly perhaps. The tribe of origin is not specified. The reminder of the two-barred cross of the Byzantine Empire is difficult to miss, however.

The tour lecture droned on into facts about how to make lifelike dolls. With "double-cross" and "projection against Indians" echoing in my mind, I left the group and walked around on my own.

The Mission Inn and its quasi-religious symbolism were founded squarely upon the kind of saccharine pageantry that had featured a reenacted Eliza Tibbets planting orange trees, a Riverside Citrus Fair (1883), the Southern California Fair (1925), and a bizarre "Greet 'em with Oranges" campaign started by the Chamber of Commerce to welcome selected trains into town by sending in orange-throwing volunteers dressed in Spanish costumes. Isaac Logan, who lived at the base of Mount Rubidoux (derived from "Robert," which means "bright fame"), acquired the title Keeper of the Bell he rang on the mountaintop at 7:00 a.m. every morning. In 1907 a cross went up there to commemorate Junipero Serra, inquisitor and mission-founder, and an Easter Sunrise service held there swelled into a civic pageant by 1919, the year seven thousand poorly paid Mexicans labored in the citrus groves. For the privileged, life in the fantasy bubble was good. Hesperia lived on not only in myth and in Riverside, but in a town by that name just south of Victorville.

In her book *Savage Dreams*, Rebecca Solnit draws a crucial distinction between nomads and drifters. Nomads like the Cahuilla and Serrano migrate with the seasons, remaining within the boundaries of the territory they call home, and know the lands they live in well. Drifters "blow like tumbleweeds across places they never really knew." The historical record makes clear that the overwhelming majority of conquerors and settlers who invaded California were drifters, whether wealthy, destitute, or somewhere in between: rootless people who got along nowhere, who belonged nowhere, and who cared deeply for no landscape, least of all the one they came to beat into the shape of their insatiable cravings. Outlaws, paranoiacs, missionaries, murderers, gunfighters, prostitutes, pimps, jailbirds, malcontents, tyrants, persecutors, victims, mercenaries, bankers, hustlers, boosters: what they all shared was an urge to run away from some unbearable past into territory they could reshape into sunshiny new beginnings for themselves.

Yet the very newness they sought left them empty and envious, bereft of workable stories and ceremonies enlivening animated, familiar places. Instead, the drifters saw mute, alien, frightening territories in which they rang bells, penned cattle, fought and enslaved Indians, exploited Mexicans, and cobbled together pageantry served up as culture by men rushing here to sell land to get rich. "One can readily believe it all seems too lovely to be true," wrote travel journalist Susie Champney Clark, "like an illusion of some magician's wand." Even as Craftsman bungalows--a stylistic mixture of Japanese, Swiss chalet, and Indian summer home--emerged from Ontario in the early 1900s, Native children from all over the southwest were forced into the Sherman Indian Institute, a boarding school set up to "civilize" them. The train ran through a mission-style depot. The new St. Francis "spring" dispensed bottled water drawn from hidden pipes.

On the corner of Arlington and Magnolia I studied one of the two orange trees that had launched the citrus industry in Riverside. The tree stood surrounded by a cage. The other tree had been transplanted to the courtyard of the Mission Inn, where it died.

The boosting bore fruit. In the 1920s, William Fox founded the theaters named for him and forged into a chain of fifty. The Mission Play showed at the Fox Theater in Riverside. By the thirties, Chinatown had been paved over by a county facility and a parking lot, and the designation "Inland Empire" had come into use thanks to real estate developers. Route 66 brought midwesterners and Chicagoans to town, some to stay. *Gone with the Wind* screened at the Fox for the film's very first showing.

But by 1939, the fabled orange groves were falling before the mechanized might of the war and housing industries. Almost all of Riverside's water flowed from San Bernardino, an unsustainable dependency. The mid-fifties saw the first of massive population influxes that grew ever larger over the coming decades as people tired of the crush and concrete chaos of Los Angeles moved inland.

With completion of Interstate 15 in the late eighties, enormous warehouses sprang up clustered into distribution hubs where ranches, dairies, and citrus orchards had been. In 1987, a year after Eric Drexler introduced the idea of nanotechnology in his book *Engines of Creation*, Alcor, a cryonics outfit, set up shop in Riverside to suspend clients who could afford it in the near-death bubble of perpetual dream.

For the ministers of disembodiment, the future looked bright. In the hands of developers, boosters, and technologists, the Garden of Hesperia could be completely internalized, an introversion so profound that Time itself would seem frozen. Outside the bubble, the character of the land would be conquered at last, a toxic waste walled out by what an Irvine Spectrum slogan preached with such suburban braggadocio: "The Great Indoors."

Just in time, too. If population trends continue, soon more people will occupy the Inland Empire than lived in all of California in 1935.

In the Trickster Shadow of
Mt. San Jacinto

I spent a night in the Mt. San Jacinto State Wilderness because my parents had driven my sister and I here when we were little. The place had awakened my love of the natural world in ways no San Diegan suburb ever could.

On the drive up the mountain I was flagged down by four young people--two girls and two guys--who had pulled over to admire the view and locked their keys in their truck. Their cell phone worked, unlike mine, but they were lost and needed landmarks to relay to the Auto Club rescue driver. I went up the road a bit, located a ranger station, drove down again, and gave them a description and a distance, if not a lift. They were content to wait by their truck until help arrived. I hoped it would arrive soon: the sun was setting and the air already very chilly.

I arrived at the motel after dark. My room key waited in an envelope with my name on it at the front door of the inn. When I returned to my room after driving out for a pizza, the key was gone. Back at the pizza parlor, a patron had seen my key on the floor--it must have slipped out of my pocket--and given it to the cashier, who returned it to me.

Lost keys returned. Was there an echo up here? Did it have anything to do with past and present, North and South Circle, a two-ended town with a two-sided name and two ways in, north and south? Tahquitz ("tah-quish") and Chalquist?

Idyllwild, whose original Cahuilla name meant "Nest of the Chicken Hawk," sits in the Strawberry Valley (called the Hill by locals) a mile up and ten miles from the noise and smog of Southern California. According to Robert Smith, who wrote about the place, children in particular find themselves drawn back here as adults (he was one). George Hannahs and his wife Sarah had opened Camp Idylwilde in 1891, six years before President Cleveland signed into law the San Jacinto Forest Reserve, but too little snow fell to support much skiing. Dr. Walter Lindley opened the Idyllwild Sanatorium in 1901, and a cluster of tourism projects grew around it, but it burned down at midnight three years later just after its debut as the Strawberry Valley Lodge. The Lodge was replaced by the unprofitable hotel The Bungalow, which was sold to Los Angeles developers who renamed it the Idyllwild Inn. Claudius Emerson bought it in 1917 and, Prometheuslike, hoped to make a community. Resorts followed as he subdivided his thousand-acre ranch and built camps and conference grounds and cabins, but he too went broke, chained to the uneven Caucasus of market highs and lows.

Unlike the Klamaths, Cascades, and Sierras, the San Jacintos remained relatively unscathed by logging. Not entirely; in 1896, a mining scam threw up the temporary boomtown of Kenworthy down in Hemet, for example, but by the 1920s, logging camps and machinery lay in ruins. In the late 1940s, Arnold Jorgenson rounded up some of this junk--saws, cauldrons, shovels, wagon wheels, Civil War cannons--into an "Iron Garden" outside his home.

Idyllwild remained tough to reach even by roads, which were windy. When traffic thickened, a "Control Road" restricted them between certain hours to one-way travel up or down the hill. (Another Prometheus, Alex Fulmor, built roads all over Riverside County, even pitching a plan to connect Pine Cove directly with San Jacinto Peak.) Not far from Idyllwild, Percy Walker bought isolated Camp Keen and tried to expand it, but he drowned in Lake Hemet in 1912, and the main lodge burned down three years later.

Renamed Tahquitz Lodge, it was made over into a private club that
failed financially. Nearby Pinewood failed as a town but worked as
a summer retreat.

During the Great Depression, the Civilian Conservation Corps
found its way to Idyllwild to hammer together recreation facilities.
Tents that had not kept visitors warm enough (shades of the
Prometheus tale again) were taken down and replaced by winter
cabins. From the thirties to the fifties, Idyllwild was known as a
workshop for Craftsman furniture, thanks especially to Ellis Griest
and Hal Holcomb. Then as now, tourists arrived to escape from the
city and the suburbs, climbers ascended Folly Peak, Suicide Rock,
and Lily Rock, backpackers camped in the high country, and locals
assembled fences, fireplaces, and entire sides of houses from locally
collected rock. Even Prometheus hadn't thought of using it for that.

Although Idyllwild as image remains embedded in the Riverside
County dream factory mentality, it has successfully resisted resort
overdevelopment. No coherent local government runs the place, just
small groups, councils, and alliances. For the most part the "wild"
has remained in Idyllwild.

In the morning I stopped for a walk around Woodland Park
Manor. The curving roadway, the cabins, the tall pines, and the
trails showed little change from when I had visited as a boy,
although the two mules named Hasbro and Remco were gone, and
the brush seemed higher and thicker, which was good. Simon
Singh's *Code Book* had been left on the trunk of the silver Mustang
parked next to my car; but even as I read the title, a past me played
Simon Says with my mom and sister, fed squirrels, breathed piquant
barbecue smoke, tumbled around the trees, and marveled at the colorful sparks flashing into the night from a toy ray gun I held.

I walked behind the cabins along what I recalled of a trail that
led into the woods, but it was now overgrown to invisibility, so I
stopped. In a way, that's what these last trips were about: ending all
my old California trails to make a fresh start in middle age.

Squirrels and a jay greeted me as I circumambulated the drive
one last time. I loved this place, but I doubted I would pass this way
again. A sudden breeze rustled cold leaves.

LILY ROCK ABOVE IDYLLWILD is also known as Tahquitz Rock. A lot of land features around here bear his name. From here to Mt. San Jacinto to the distant Salton Sea, this is his territory, the playground of the ferocious desert trickster.

The Cahuilla storytellers identified Tahquitz as a shapeshifting troublemaker who could appear as lightning, flooding, wind, the condor, a giant, a hermit, or something else. Mukat the Creator made Tahquitz into the first of all shamans, but the trickster violated the Creator's laws and was banished (like Prometheus, also a fire-stealing trickster) to a cave on Mt. San Jacinto or, some say, into the rock itself. Sometimes he showed up emitting blue sparks; on other occasions trains and cars careened out of control; like the jets that bomb the Mojave he could fly among the mountain peaks; but however he appeared, he brought chaos.

He seems to face northeast rather than west. If you left Idyllwild, headed toward the coast about a hundred and thirty miles away, passing through Hemet (an occasional Trickster fire target) on the way to towns like Sun City, Lake Elsinore, Murrieta, and Temecula, you would feel his influence wane considerably.

Take Temecula, for instance, the ancestral home of the Pechanga Band of Luiseño Indians, who called it *Temeeku*, "Where the Sun Shines through the Mist" where Father Sky meets Mother Earth. For thousands of years the people of the creek-moistened Valley of Temecula knew little of trouble, having adapted well to their surroundings. But after the Battle of San Pasqual in December of 1846, eleven Californio soldiers who entered Pauma Valley were captured and killed by the Luiseños. In retaliation, General Jose Maria Flores ordered Jose del Carmen Lugo of San Bernardino to find the parties responsible. Lugo entered Temecula and massacred at least forty people.

In 1875, the Luiseños who had escaped incarceration at Mission San Luis Rey near what is now Oceanside were evicted because they had no written title to lands they had lived on for millennia, lands coveted by incoming ranchers backed by clever lawyers. By 1882 the exiles were living on the Pechanga ("dripping water") reservation.

In 1903, the Cupas exiled from Warner Ranch were moved to dirt-dry Pala near Temecula after Cupa elder Celsa Apapas said this to Charles Lummis, who had come to give them the news:

> We thank you for coming here and talking to us in
> a way we can understand. It is the first time anyone
> has done so. You ask us to think what place we like
> next best to this place where we always live. You
> see that graveyard out there? There are our fathers
> and grandfathers. You see that Eagle-nest
> Mountain and that Rabbit-hole Mountain? When
> God made them, he gave us this place. We have
> always been here. We do not care for any other
> place. It may be good, but it is not ours. We have
> always lived here. We would rather die here. Our
> fathers did.

Not long after all their belongings were hurled into carts, the Cupa
were told, "Go and see your relatives for the last time now. You're
never going to see them again." The people wept as they departed.

This kind of chaos seems colonial rather than Trickster, as does
the arrival of Louis Wolf, "King of Temecula," who set up a general
store and trading post on the creek. However, the railroad built in
1882 was washed out in two years, and again in 1891. In 1902 the
Ramona Inn acquired slot machines; to the west, Fritz Guenther
bought the Murrieta Hot Springs named after the famous outlaw.
Tricksterish, but not unduly so. In the hills, dynamite blasted granite for paving Riverside, Los Angeles, and San Francisco. Erle
Stanley Gardner bought Rancho Paisano and hired seven secre-
taries. During Prohibition the Ramona Inn served as a blind pig for
roughousers blind with drink.

In the sixties Walter Vail of Nova Scotia added Vail Ranch to his
five-state cattle empire before dying in a streetcar accident. Kaiser
Aetna bought the ranch and laid out a planned community. The
original homestead became an ecological preserve of the Nature
Conservancy. Vintners moved in and grew grapes. A Wal-Mart
opened near the old Wolf store that had served Temecula as an early
commercial center.

Perhaps the local mythic touch is that of a female Trickster: say, Iris, the mist-veiled (Vailed) rainbow goddess and heavenly messenger. THEY PASSED THIS WAY reads a pioneer monument posted at Rainbow Grade.

Be all that as it may, Tahquitz, not the military, owns the deserts north and east of Mt. San Jacinto.

The military presence in the deserts of California is impressive: Edwards Air Force Base between Barstow (also militarized) and Mojave (also militarized, and near California's commercial spaceport), the Muroc Bombing Range, where a replica of a Japanese cruiser was nicknamed the *Muroc Maru*, the Army's Fort Irwin, George Air Force Base near Victorville, Navy weapons testing at dried-up China Lake at the gateway to Death Valley, Phillips Laboratory Propulsion Directorate, NASA Dryden Flight Research Center…. Firmly clinging to pioneer tradition, the U.S. Government figures that desert = empty, so damage inflicted upon it is unimportant. What the public doesn't see--tainted ecosystems, poisoned groundwater, desert-dwelling people pushed off their lands--won't bother anyone. It's a secret until it explodes into cancer clusters, bunker busters, Manhattan at Los Alamos on the Roadway of Death, or radioactive fallout from a hundred atom bombs fired off under Nevada.

Meanwhile, the dark Trickster Tahquitz remains at play, toying with crashed aircraft at Muroc and with F-111 malfunctions at China Lake….

> As if to imbue soldiers with the qualities they may need in battle, there is a certain petroglyph on the base at Fort Irwin, one that is not seen elsewhere in the Mojave. It is not romantic or appealing in the way that certain stone drawings of birds and bighorn sheep are; with its open jaw and exposed teeth it is simply menacing and has to do with a particular state of mind desired by the desert warrior. It's a jackal, and as far as anyone knows, the jackal has not ever lived in the dimension of time and space known as the Mojave and yet here it has

landed, across the eons, homeless and rootless like
those it tracks, sleeping in stone on a military preserve, its spirit waiting to possess the appropriate
vessels, its soul waiting for certain wars to be
waged, certain ill-fated prey to enter its sights and
warm its blood.

— Deanne Stillman

6422 Palo Verde Street, for instance, site of the stabbing of
Rosalie Ortega and Amanda Lee Scott by a soldier stationed at the
Marine Corps Air Ground Combat Center, or "Makax" for short, a
sound almost reminiscent of "Tahquitz." The world's largest Marine
Corps base crouches on nine hundred and thirty-two square miles
just north of Twenty-Nine Palms, the desert town that services it.
The killer, Valentine Underwood, used his knife thirty-three times
on each woman in deference to basketball hero Patrick Ewing,
whose jersey bore that number. Underwood had grown up in a
strict Baptist household where the Bible was read every day.

Trouble here has a long history. The Serrano Indians who lived
here in a palm oasis, and who said that In The Beginning only two
clouds called Vacant and Empty drifted here, were run out by the
cattle-raiding Utes; the remaining survivors succumbed to smallpox
in the 1860s. The Cahuillas came and warned of a desert trickster
who stole things and ate flesh and souls. Here lived Willy Boy, a
Paiute whose girlfriend killed herself and who when caught was
shot with too many bullets to count. Locals still saddle up to reen-
act the chase.

More recent trouble--three grisly ritual murders--found the
basement of Club Max in 1965; and at 6422 Palo Verde Street,
where a tenant had been raped at knifepoint by a Marine, and where
Underwood had done his own knife work, a Marine took a break
from an all-night party to rape a girl with a beer bottle.

People with an otherworldly bent explain such echoes as a
residue of "negative energy" left by some initial tragedy or horror.
But no such imprint has ever been found, nor would it answer the
question: But why here? Perhaps for a more terrapsychologically
tangible reason: the seven known earthquake faults, and others

undetected perhaps, clashing directly below Twentynine Palms.
The fissures here in the Eastern California Shear Zone a hundred
and forty-two miles east of Los Angeles radiate outward like black
lightning for hundreds of miles in every direction--including southward toward Joshua Tree. The Mojave Indians thought the arms of
the "tree" pointed skyward to another world. Today they point at
poor people, drunks, meth addicts, parolees, gangsters, gold
prospectors, card players, bikers, mystics, hookers, and runaways.

> The Marines like to say that no one comes to
> Twentynine Palms on purpose. But history says
> otherwise. Like the Joshua tree, those who plant
> themselves here are also misunderstood, seek and
> require distance, provide shelter for other creatures
> but only because they happen to show up, possess
> an awkward beauty, and will hurt you if they are
> crowded. Although many locals are not natives, in
> this sandy soil they can sink roots and flourish, and
> leave fast and without a trace if required.
> — Deanne Stillman

In her book *Twentynine Palms* Stillman speculates that now and
then the Mojave demands a blood sacrifice because those who rav-
age nature in the name of industry and personal rights have gone too
far. (McVeigh had hung out in the Mojave, as had Charles Manson.)

Could be. On October 16, 1999, a 7.0 earthquake at Lavic Lake on
the Marine base hurled cars, cannons, and soldiers like toys across
the waste. After the land had spoken in a voice louder than any
human artillery, a fault line previously unknown split the earth for
twenty-six jagged miles. On either side of it the desert floor had
moved fifteen feet.

> ....Maybe there needed to be a reassessment some-
> where, maybe something had gone terribly wrong.
> had the live-fire exercises demanded an answer?
> Had they themselves triggered a response? Was the

earthquake a statement that was eons in the making, a distant echo of another catastrophe that had played out on the Mojave's flanks? Of course the suspicion will never be uttered aloud.... Nevertheless, among those who were blown into the night air by earth's buckling crust, among the enlisted trainees who will at some point in the future defend our oil, our water, our personal rights, the message has been received, and classified, to be unearthed at a later date.

Who Else of a mythic nature might live out here besides Trickster? In 1994, a civic beautification project left town-boosting murals painted on the sides of buildings downtown: industrious miners, brave Marines, grinning ranchers, the usual Chamber of Commerce fare. But on the side of 29 Palms Inn, a dark-haired woman in white held below her face a basket filled with the water of her tears.

THE CAHUILLA LIVED ON both sides of the mountain they called *I A Kitch*: "Smooth Cliffs." San Jacinto Peak reaches over ten thousand feet and, still rising, remains the most swiftly ascending of any peak in the United States. J. Seaton Chase, the desert drama queen buried in Palm Springs in the San Jacinto rain shadow, wrote that the mountain "stands isolated and conspicuous," confirming the motif of inward isolation so prevalent in this part of California. On one stony shoulder sits Hidden Lake, a body of water not visible on official maps. "San Jacinto" derives from St. Hyacinth, who set up new monasteries in Eastern Europe. Here they look like health resorts raised over sulfur springs bubbling upward from hot depths.

West of the mountain, in the valley named after it, ancient stones with maze-like patterns recall the Cahuilla term for tribal leader: the Net. But the stones predate the Cahuilla and probably the Luisenos, most of whom died of smallpox brought by incoming settlers. The Soboda Luisenos, who survived, shared pastures with the Cahuillas.

Born in San Diego in 1845, Francisco Estudillo received land grants that included San Jacinto Nuevo y Potrero, a rancho of almost forty-nine thousand acres. He served as mayor of San Jacinto, school board member, and Indian agent overseeing reservations in southern and central California. Losing his house to foreclosure 1901, he moved westward eighty-five miles to Los Angeles.

Henry Hewitt, the founding "merchant prince" of the town of San Jacinto, had more success in the tricksterish loss-gain atmosphere of the valley. Buying eight thousand acres from Estudillo in 1871, he went on to buy the trading post of Russian exile Procco Akimo; the town formed around it. Commerce, a favorite Trickster theme, developed further, particularly cargo, when the first trains arrived in 1888. Rushed through this Santa Fe terminus were fruits, vegetables, grains, lumber from trees on the mountain, and lime from north of San Jacinto. Freight trains still drive through.

In the early 1900s, dairies opened, numbering thirty-one by 1980. In old photographs ostriches raised locally pulled buggies. During Prohibition, bootlegger squatters set up five-hundred-gallon vats along Portero Creek but fled when deputies made themselves at home in the convenient shacks. John Shaver's old Victorian home at the corner of Main and Alessandro appeared in the TV movies *Lassie* and *The Summer of Swans*, but Arbie the ghost did not, although he liked to rock in a chair while watching TV, pulling people's hair, and knocking on wood furnishings. Do ghosts need good luck?

Until enterprising developers arrived, the mineral hot springs along the northern foothills marked sites of ceremonial healing. Tahquitz responded to the building of health resorts--Eden, Gilman, Soboda--by making sure that the tunnel built in 1937 to pipe water from the Colorado River to Southern California dried up the hot springs. On Christmas morning, 1899, an earthquake brought down all the businesses housed in brick buildings, and in 1918, the same buildings fell again. The San Jacinto Oil Company dug for oil but struck water instead; floods roared through in 1917, 1937, and 1980; and in 1951, a fire destroyed most of the block south of Main and east of San Jacinto Avenue. The Soboda Theater (built to resemble a Hopi pueblo) survived until 1968, when it too burned down. In 2007, hurricane-force winds knocked over a hundred-year-old pine and a thousand other trees and left newly developed areas buried in sand drifts.

Trickster themes of flight and acceleration play out consistently here, where balloons went up in 1905. At one time the roof of the Masonic temple displayed the city's longitude and latitude. Pat Sawyer competed in the Powder Puff Derby for women pilots. Women also drove in cross-country car races. In 1937, a Russian ANT-25 flying nonstop from Moscow and over the north pole landed to set a transpolar flight record. The San Jacinto Museum contains a model of the plane. In Druding Veterans Memorial Park visitors can find an anchor from the USS *Cleveland* (a transport ship, of course), a propeller from a Flying Fortress, a replica of a Coast Guard lighthouse, and even a tank.

I was thirty when I finally drove to Hemet to meet my grandfather for the first time.

I had been warned he was a grouch, but I get on well with grouchy old men (perhaps I will become one?), and after eyeing me briefly at the door, he opened it and showed me around. In an hour we were sipping Chianti and listening to Mozart while my wife of the time chatted with my grandfather's.

He was old school: a hunter, a fisher who made his own flies, a weatherman, a gardener, an architect, and ex-Navy. He had saved men's lives when a fire broke out on a battleship, and won awards for being an expert pistol shot with either hand. At first glance he looked cockeyed because of the glass orb he wore in place of a ruined eye. He had been in his shop one day when an awl got away from him. As a result, the Navy turned him down when he enlisted as a sailor to fight in World War II. As another result, he stayed home with my grandmother, resulting in my mother, my aunt and uncle, my cousins, and, ultimately, me. To the glass eye I made a silent toast.

He was moving back to Arkansas, he told me, as he rolled out blueprints for the house he had designed. Yet he had come here to retire.

Hemet was a planned community even before its formal inception. Francisco Estudillo and Henry Hewitt had owned it, and engineer Edward Mayberry (an apt last name for a Hemetite) bought land here to raise Standardbred trotters. Other settlers settled, and soon Mt. San Jacinto sheltered orange groves from frosts of the kind my grandfather used to warn farmers about so they could smudge their orchards in time. Financing from William Whittier of the eponymous town in Los Angeles bought more land laid out for homes and planted with grains, vegetables, olives, fruit trees, vines, and alfalfa. Union Army eterans arrived to recover their health, and to stay to dig ditches and grow things.

Ostriches came too, with Cawston the world's largest ostrich farm by 1909. And horses, at the Hemet Stock Farm, where *Seabiscuit* would be filmed one day. In the twenties, turkeys, a Utility Turkey Show, and Ramona.

Ramona, a novel by Helen Hunt Jackson, told a tragic tale inspired by a real-life Cahuilla named Ramona Lubo. Her husband Juan Diego was shot for taking a white man's horse. When Sam Temple, the shooter, went on trial, Native Americans were not allowed to testify. This outraged Jackson, who began writing up fictional and nonfictional accounts of injustices perpetrated against Native victims.

In 1923, however, citizens of Hemet and nearby San Jacinto stitched fabric to a long frame building to make it look like a ranchero. More than four thousand viewers showed up for this, the first installment of the famously sappy Ramona Pageant. In a year local "troubadors" set it to music; by 1952, the Alessandro character originally inspired by Juan Diego was singing. More mawkish pageantry would follow: a beauty contest, a Farmers Fair and Festival featuring a Farmer's Daughter competition (skills needed: sewing, tractor-driving, milking, fish-cleaning, cooking, and cow-herding), Modern Woodmen of America, Odd Fellows, a Comfortable Rebekahs Auxiliary, the Elks, a Hemet 20-30 Club of young men, a Supreme Emblem Club for women, a Hemet Jeep Club, and a Hemet Jeep Cavalcade that drove boldly into the Anza-Borrego desert in 1948 and got lost.

When fire consumed the top floors of the ritzy Hotel Hemet of Whittier and Mayberry, visiting female apricot pickers stayed two weeks in the relatively undamaged first floor until the hotel was demolished. In 1929, Mayberry opened the Hotel Alessandro on the same site. Its facade suggested a Hopi pueblo. In 1954 it was razed to make way for a Citizens National Bank.

Hemet sits in a valley; perhaps this is why things are stored here so often, like oranges and apricots; like potatoes and sugar beets, crops that keep starch in the ground. Bodies, too: the first Model T in town was driven in by an undertaker from Riverside. Hartford Funeral Home started an ambulance service in 1927 but had to use its hearse for a while; the service closed in 1954, but the funeral home survived. People joked about how the business had run a two-for-one deal.

In the sixties, mobile homes grew in long rows like fruit trees. Art Linkletter advertised the Sierra Dawn Estates, a motor home park converted from a farm, as the "Foothills of Heaven." By 2008, it contained the oddly Columbian number of 1,492 motor homes. Industries to manufacture mobile homes started up too. Which makes sense: "Hemet" might derive from a word for "homeland." The idyllic fantasy glimmered behind local place names like Hesperia, Florida, Idyllwild, Diamond Valley, Pleasant Valley, Harmony.

So I could understand why Edwin Legg was here. What puzzled me was why he wanted to leave. "Better fishing in Arkansas," he said. "More room to build. Fewer code restrictions."

Not long after our visit, I received a call from Lenore. My grandfather, a non-smoker, had been diagnosed unexpectedly with lung cancer. In a flash I knew why he had wanted to move: he left home-like Hemet to die.

In a month Truman, Lenore, my cousins, and I watched my uncle pour Edwin's ashes into the Pacific off Dana Point. No formal service for the sailor who had despised religion. A simple wreath floated slowly away from Truman's sailboat as we watched in silence.

When family members die, families (something within me insisted) are supposed to continue intact. Perhaps cousins David and Brenda would extend and enlarge the family one day. Upon reflection, however, I realized that none of my four families--two birth, two adoptive--had never been fully intact to begin with. As Quentin remembers his mother walking away from his father in Arthur Miller's play *After the Fall*, he asks himself: "Why do I think of things falling apart? Were they ever whole?"

All my families had endured crisis to achieve a workable equilib-
rium. Devastated by battle stress, my birth father lived in Hawaii
with his Australian bride. Presumably my brother, at one time a sea-
faring wanderer, visited them there. Before he died, my grandfather
had married a woman who suited him, which is to say, refused to
put up with any vestige of disrespect. Lenore, also married, had
retired in Yucaipa with her husband while her children, my cousins,
moved confidently into young adulthood. Now in their late seven-
ties, my adoptive parents had rubbed against each other for so many
years that they fit together; as a child I had yearned for them to
divorce, but as an adult I couldn't imagine them apart. My sister,
who had struggled all her life, was as well as she would ever be.

I blamed no one, resented no one; I had gotten along with all of
them; and yet I was close to none of them. They had split into fac-
tions and moved apart, emotionally and geographically, and I was a
faction of one. Why was this, I wondered, when I wanted as much
as anyone to feel like part of a family?

Our current therapeutic paradigms limit family conflict to internal and relational dynamics. At most, a well-designed genogram
looks back at intergenerational turbulence. Look deeper, though,
and the outlines of other traumas emerge from the mists of family
history: displacements, disappearances, class struggles; racism, sex-
ism, warfare, religious judgmentalism, all filtered by the family's
fragile boundaries. "Inner" wounds and "relational" conflicts are,
deeper down, psychosocial and ecological fallout from our collectively pathological relationship to nature and therefore to each
other and to our drifting, rootless selves. When the primary model
for relating to the world is one of thought-based domination, then
oppression, repression, and schism concatenate into all other pathways of relatedness. *I think, therefore I am* gives ground to: *We uproot,
therefore we fragment.*

As I drove northward toward the mountain of Tahquitz I wondered if anyone else in my families would ever feel truly at home on
our still-lovely Earth.

SOUTHWEST OF JOSHUA TREE, the Coachella Valley stretches from Mt. San Jacinto to the Colorado River descending sluggishly along the eastern border of California.

Seventy-five miles long and twenty wide, the valley forms a giant trough between three chains of mountains. At one time the trough contained a forest of palm trees reaching to and around ancient Lake Cahuilla. Before that, the valley lay under the waters of the Gulf of California until the capricious Colorado River laid down a vast sandbar. When the waters receded, they left rich, alluvial topsoil in which the Cahuilla raised corn, barley, and vegetables. As the land dried, they began digging water ditches to moisten their crops.

The valley was never colonized by Spaniard missionaries. Instead, mystically named Professor William Blake rode by in 1853 with a U.S. Army survey party seeking a train route through the southwestern deserts. The party included scientists, geologists, botanists, officers, and an artist who made sketches of the region. However, it would be real estate agents and not Blake's mystical moniker that nicknamed the valley "The Palm of God's Hand."

Bisected by a major earthquake fault named after St. Andrew, said to have achieved martyrdom by being stretched limb from limb, the two-sided valley contained two stories of how it was named. According to one of them, the conchilla seashells found by the Army survey were mispelled "coachella" on a government report. The other story says that in 1901, in a general meeting in Indio, two names were combined: Cahuilla and *concha*, hence Coachella Valley. Either version could be said to affirm the presence of shapeshifting, error-causing Tahquitz.

The Cahuilla say that Tahquitz, who played with fire, soared like an airplane, and named heavily looted Murray Canyon *Eit* ("Thief"), was turned into a fox by Evonganet, Creator and marker of rivers, valleys, mountains, and other natural features comprising a sophisticated place-naming system for precise descriptions of where and when and why. By adulthood, a Cahuilla knew all about the ecology, geology, flora, fauna, and history of places within local sites far across the valley and over the mountain. Some of these sites were centers for lore and sacred ceremony. And for food, 80% of which grew within five miles of the village harvesting it. Respectful walkers left piles of rocks along trails to please the spirits; in another land these offerings were called herms, as in Hermes, god of travel, transport, and elaborately staged tricks.

> Every place is, after all, an impossible land in its own way, until the imagination reaches out to the landforms and transforms them into the stuff of storytelling. Human beings everywhere wish to feel a connection to the earth beneath them, to the land on which they live, against which they survive, and through which they share their lives with each other.
>
> — Phillip Round

Although the Spanish missionaries never set up missions in the valley, they established an *assistencia* in San Bernardino in 1819 to convert the Cahuilla and Serrano. Mission San Gabriel to the west grazed cattle as far as Palm Springs. As converted Indians drifted through, the Cahuilla retreated to the heights of Tahquitz Canyon, to observe what happened below.

Once the Americans had arrived and begun settling, mining, and colonizing, Cahuilla Chief Juan Antonio, known as the Lion because of his powerful shoulders and leonine face--like those of the lion-faced creator-trickster Ialdabaoth--helped the United States capture Antonio Garra, Cupeño head of a revolt throughout Southern California. Juan Antonio lived to regret it: the U.S. Government never ratified the treaty he signed in order to secure land in the San Gorgonio Pass.

The 1863 smallpox epidemic carried off Juan Antonio and decimated both tribes. By 1877, reservations were set up: the Morongo, Agua Caliente, Augustine, Cabazon, Torres-Martinez, Los Coyotes, Santa Rosa, Cahuilla, Ramona, and Mission Creek. Neophytes confined inside continued to sustain meaningful ties to relatives beyond the walls.

The Southern Pacific Railroad had entered the Coachella Valley in 1872. Engineers seeking water for hot steam engines began extensive drilling, unaware of old Cahuilla wells at the bottom of carefully graded access slopes. Equally ignorant of the valley's ancient submersion, railroad crews cooled their temporary wood frame "submarine" housing by trickling water over the burlap covering galvanized iron roofs. Settlements grew up around Palm Springs at one end of the valley (settler Jack Summers lived where the Desert Inn would go up) and Indio at the other: two oases of many left after Lake Cahuilla and its palm forests dried up long ago.

Explorer Anza and soldier Fages missed Palm Springs, although Anza is said to have named Mt. San Jacinto. Brevert Captain Jose Romero marched through in 1823 by order of the Mexican government to find an overland route from Sonora to Alta California. By the time he reached the isolated but now-famous oasis, his men and horses were exhausted from thirst.

Much of Palm Springs occupies the reservation of the casino-operating Agua Caliente band of the Cahuilla. Their original name for the place, *Sec He*, echoes the "boiling water sound" of the 110° hot springs supplied by an aquifer embedded in the Palm Canyon Fault. In 1876, President Grant gave (back) every other section of Palm Springs, which is why the tribe resides in staggered plots of land. Later, the government offered them $22,000 for three of the six nearby canyons, but the Cahuilla naturally refused.

Yet it was medicine man Pedro China who sold the first chunk of land to incoming whites: ten acres of fruit trees to San Bernardino speculators W. E. Van Slyke and M. Byrne for $150. It was 1880, and they had bought three hundred and twenty acres from the Southern Pacific Railroad and wanted more.

John Guthrie McCallum bought from Van Slyke and Byrne, kept on buying, and hired surveyor T. M. Topp to lay out a "Palm City" tract of seventy-six lots. "Earliest Fruit Region in the State," his advertisements blared; "Absolute Cure for all Pulmonary and Kindred Diseases; Perfect Climate; Wonderful Scenery." With three partners from Los Angeles he set up the Palm Valley Land and Water Company in 1887 to develop the desert into Palm Springs and to build a nineteen-mile redwood flume to the Whitewater River. McCallum invited fellow Scot Welwood Murray to town.

"Judge" McCallum was actually an attorney. "Doctor" Murray, actually a Civil War medical assistant, opened the Palm Springs

Hotel in 1887 across the street from the hot springs. Having built his hotel with Cahuilla labor and leased land from the tribe, he proceeded to divert their spring water for his guests as McCallum, an Indian Agent, looked the other way. When both men removed wood from tribal land and bodies from the Cahuilla cemetery, to which they blocked access, the Cahuilla took them to court. The men were acquitted, of course, but in 1893, twenty-one days of rain wiped out newly planted alfalfa, figs, apricots, grapes, melons, corn, oranges, grapefruit, and date palms. The rain was followed by eleven years of drought baking land sitting over an undiscovered aquifer. Most of the settlers left, Murray tried to sell his hotel and was wiped out, and McCallum, having been stopped by the U.S. Government from taking tribal water from the Tahquitz and Andreas Canyons, died of heart failure. His son Harry died of tuberculosis, and his daughter May of typhoid. His daughter Pearl survived and was at hand for the next attempt to settle Palm Springs. Dr. Florilla White and her sister Cornelia bought Murray's hotel.

Reminders of a place's true nature emerge no matter what developers do. When Pearl McCallum and her husband set up Pioneer Properties to establish the Oasis Hotel, the Hacienda Apartments, and the Tahquitz River Estates subdivision, their Tennis Club went up with a clubhouse patterned from a monastery on the cliffs of Amalfi. No Indians dressed up by Murray as parading Arabs, no gated clubs, no spas for the wealthy could erase the underlying presence of a sanctuary of healing shaded by palms, that ancient emblem of resurrection placed by Egyptians on coffins and by Hebrews on decorated pathways to celebrate the autumn harvest. Other nearby settlements failed--the dried-up Garden of Eden by B. B. Barney of Riverside, who set a circle of biblically named streets around the site of a hotel never built; Palmdale, to have been served by a narrow-gauge railroad buried by wind and sand--but Lavinia Crocker's Green Fables Health Resort brought the town back to life.

This was followed in 1909 by Nellie Coffman's Desert Inn, hotel, and sanatorium, a lavish and exclusive spread with walls as impassable to non-members as those of the mountain casting its rain shadow over Palm Springs. In 1915 she excluded guests with communicable diseases, and by 1928 the place went Mission Revival and sported the first swimming pool in the desert. The golf course behind the property was paved over in 1967 to make room for a shopping complex. Once again developers were transmogrifying the sanctuary. P. T. Stevens opened El Mirador ("The Lookout") in 1927 to the delight of visiting celebrities rooming below its bell tower. He also started the Palm Springs Water Company and began more subdivisions, which he toured in a limo with "Palm Springs and Hollywood" painted on the doors; but the Great Depression rolled into the desert and dried up his capital and killed him.

This alternation of health and sickness long preceded American attempts at colonization. They go right back into ancient Cahuilla stories about creator brothers similar to Prometheus and Epimetheus:

> In the beginning, Two Nights gave birth to Mo-Cot and Mo-Cot-Tem-Ma-Ya-Wit. Coyote, whose name means "quick and selfish," helped make the other animals. Because there was no sun, Mo-cot-tem began making people sloppilly and too quickly, whereas Mo-Cot worked accurately by feeling: his people lived. Then Mo-Cot said, "There will be sickness come, they will die, and they will get old, and young ones will come, but when sickness comes we will have those among them to cure sickness."

Many of the sick and their would-be curers made pilgrimage to Palm Springs: McCallum on behalf of his tubercular son Johnny, who died; John Muir, whose daughter Helen was ill; Fanny Stevenson, widow of Robert Louis, dead of tuberculosis; Nellie Coffman, whose husband was an M.D.; Dr. June Robertson, whose husband had tuberculosis (in 1917 she came up with the idea of painting a line down the center of Highway 86 to guide traffic); educator Frances Stephens, for respiratory illness; architect Harold Cody, pneumonia; grocer and postmaster David Blanchard, tuberculosis; high school president Raymond Cree, asthma; Dr. Jacob Kocher, not ill but opener of the Mortar and Pestle, the first local pharmacy; cartoonist James Swinnerton, tuberculosis; photographer W. W. Lockwood, tuberculosis; artist Gordon Coutts, bronchitis; oilman Tom O'Donnell, tubercular designer of Palm Springs's first (highly exclusive) golf course; landscaper "Cactus Slim" Moorten, tuberculosis; Hugh Stephens, M.D., emphysema, father of author Mary Lo Churchwell....In the twenties William Pester, the Hermit of Palm Canyon and the first local nudist, kept mostly to himself, although he posed occasionally for tourist cameras while selling arrowheads and postcards. One day his hut of old palm logs was found to be vacated.

This odd mixture of the tricksterish and the curative (in many mythologies Trickster performs as a healer) would remain a basic Palm Springs dynamism. Doctors and slot machines proliferated. So did tourists:

> Into the village they came, goggles over their eyes, "dusters" over their dresses, waving maps, hankies, and hats. In a convulsion of obscene noises they came, bucking and banging out of the ruts, spewing sand and internal combustion over everyone--and thereby warning that a noisier era was on the way. The dogs, used to sleeping safely at noon in the middle of Main, barked at them furiously. Crowds of suicidal kids chased them through clouds of dust. Meanwhile, with what seemed to be calculated indifference, a few local characters stood by with mules left over from the previous era, hoping to make money off their tomfoolery.
>
> — Mary Jo Churchwell

A flood washed away the entire road that brought them in.

As a Trickster place, Palm Springs has seen its share of fires, of course. Before electric clocks, the "Fire Laddies" on duty would call the phone company next door to the firehouse for the correct time, then synchronize the station clock and blast its horn at noon. Hearing the blast, the phone company would synchronize their time pieces with it: Trickster time.

In 1933, actors Charles Farrell and Ralph Bellamy opened the Palm Springs Racquet Club, but few responded to the invitations they mailed to Hollywood to announce an annual fee of $50 per member. When the actors tried another round of invitations, this time charging $650, so many applications flooded in that the club had to set up a waiting list.

Hollywood followed with it, streaming into the Bamboo Lounge where the Bloody Mary was invented and where a young woman named Norma Jean Baker was spotted sunning herself by the pool. Jack Benny, Bob Hope, and Amos 'n' Andy performed on the radio. In 1936 the Plaza Theater opened to play *Camille*, a performance Greta Garbo attended with a shawl over her head so nobody would recognize her. That year shooting began on the film *Lost Horizon*, with Tahquitz Canyon--its caves filled with hermits and squatters until the Cahuilla kicked them out--standing in for Shangri-La. (The first movie filmed in Palm Springs had been *Lone Star Rush* in 1915.) During filming of *Her Jungle Love*, electric fans making artificial wind in the stage-set jungle fell over as a real wind kicked up to blow away the exotic plants. The film itself is gone because it was shot on cellulose nitrate that burns when improperly stored. On the Cahuilla Reservation in Anza, Ramona Lubo sold baskets and posed for photographs.

Even the streets got in on the act. By the 1930s, some were named after prominent Agua Caliente Indians like Andreas, Arenas, Belardo, Chino, Lugo, Marcus, Patencio, Segundo, and Saturnino. Other streets were named after movie stars. A Walk of Stars rolled out in imitation of Hollywood.

As stars rose underfoot, Trickster reappeared in the air. Howard Hughes, Jack Northrop, and Alan Lockheed all visited at one time or another. Converted into a hospital during wartime, El Mirador reopened, but only to shapeshift into the Desert Regional Medical Center. The sixty-foot tower burned but was rebuilt. Zaddie Bunker, a mechanic who lived with her blacksmith husband (Hephaestus and Athena?) in a metal lean-to on Main Street, became the first woman to break the sound barrier, which she did in old age. The Palm Springs Air Museum accumulated the world's largest collection of flyable World War II aircraft. Windmills more than a hundred feet tall harvested air blown through the gusty San Gregornio Pass.

On Mt. San Jacinto, where an angel, a witch, and other faces and images have been spotted, helicopters flew twenty-three thousand flights to build the Palm Springs Tramway first known as Crocker's Folly. This, of course, is the mountain of Tahquitz and To Quastto Hut, a sky monster that swooped down and flew off with wriggling captives in his talons. A tramway incident report would mention the bobcat that climbed a power pole and was electrocuted, stranding eighty-six people on the mountain; the two tramway employees who used the tram to break into the station vault and make off with $3,000; the Ontario woman who died when a shock absorber bolt snapped, releasing a chunk of metal that crashed through the Plexiglas roof of a tram; a van that overheated and caught fire in the valley station parking lot, with two other vehicles burning and five more damaged; and Linda Richard, Victor Bryan, and Sky (!) Vreeken flinging food and bottles off a cliff while jumping up and down on their dinner plates. During the tram descent, Richard amazed fellow passengers by going down on Bryan. The trip ended with the arrest of all three.

Palm Springs lay cooling around me in blocky low buildings and sandy colors. The inescapable presence of that chain of mountains overlooking the town, immense, majestic, and protective. I watched the sun light wisps of cloud as it dropped behind the range. The shadows it cast over the town were cool and comforting rather than dark and sharp.

Casinos and golf courses, and California's first Holiday Inn (1959). The Washingtonia fan palm was indigenous here. Coyote had gambled here and sometimes lost his life. A place to prompt a scrap of poetry, with due apologies to Coleridge:

> In Coachella did businessmen
> A hundred pleasure domes decree
> Where sacred springs and rivers ran
> Past coves and canyons master-planned
> Down to the Salton Sea.

Meanwhile, the star tours continued.

> The bus swung from curb to curb. Our mass swayed, tilted, and slid. Our heads rolled right, then left, then right. Out the delicately tinted windows we stared at the suggestion of roof lines behind miles of walls that the rich and famous had thrown around themselves to keep us from trespassing visually. What secrets were they hiding? A marijuana patch? A movie great sunbathing in the raw? Oh, occasionally, when someone left a gate open, we got a glimpse of a deep, green courtyard with rare potted palms in the wall niches, a vignette so brief it was only tempting. "Beautiful home," said the man from Seattle, a comment he repeated at five-minute intervals all afternoon.
>
> Beautiful, indeed, but with a self-important showing of seclusion, a seclusion that suggested conflict rather than neighborly love, the iron fences cast in a pattern of spears, the walls postd with warnings of armed response, hidden mikes, and closed circuit cameras. The guard dogs not only warned of intruders but dealt with them.
>
> — Mary Jo Churchwell

Trickster never did like high walls, though. I could feel him all around me. Bullseye Rock, known as "Place of Many Brains" for the Seven Palms Indians whose heads were broken there. VillageFest, Desert Circus, out-of-control rock concerts in Tahquitz Canyon before the Cahuilla closed it off. Biology teacher Edmund Jaeger, who arrived in 1914 and who once dissected a coyote in class, to the horror of parents and the wonder of their children. Skunk Cabbage Meadow misnamed after corn lilies, which are poisonous but which were mistaken for skunk cabbage, which is nutritious. The Devil's Garden stretching west to the Morongo Valley, so named when Angelenos possessed by a trend in the 1920s dug up all the cacti. By 2003, six Indian casinos separated tourists and their money in the

Coachella Valley. The Agua Caliente donated $1.1 million to sixty-four charities and civic organizations....

And a large and growing gay community in Palm Springs, for it was not just Trickster alone out here in the desert among the creosote, brittlebush, ocotillo, and primrose.

Bright Apollo, who was born under a palm, loved the shepherd Hyacinth. All the more painful for Phoebus, then, when he "accidentally" slew him with a thrown discus deflected by jealous Zephyr, the West Wind, who also loved the fair youth. From his spilled blood, the solar god grew the flower that gave its name to the tall mountain behind Palm Springs.

Apollo was also a god of archery of the kind that Mo-Cot, a mythic byform of Tahquitz, taught to his people. With a straight face the trickster told them to shoot each other with the arrows they had made, but with death now abroad in the world, they knew better and held their fire. Still, they suffered other tribulations: not for nothing did the tribe call themselves Moaning in Pain. After they took Palm Springs away from its original inhabitants (Evonganet marked the place for *us*, the invaders argued), the body of a dead woman surfaced in the springs. Only after many sacrifices were the spirits of the waters finally calmed. "This spring," observed Cahuilla elder Francisco Patencio, "always brings everything to the top."

According to his telling, the Creators first fashioned people of many colors. All were happy with this except for one pale group of malcontents:

> Then it was that the white-clay people (white people) were not pleased about being the only ones without color. They cried to be dark, like the rest. They put different clay on themselves, but it was no good. It came right off after a while. So they decided to go away. "Let them go," said Mo-Cot. "They are different. They will always be different."

Even after tanning all day by a walled-off pool glowing in Phoebus' all-revealing light.

That sky-borne tram! This gilded bar!
Those green fairways: planned Paradise!
For we have dined on caviar
And drunk our share of melted ice.

BETWEEN PALM SPRINGS AND Indio, Coachella Valley's first incorporated city (1930), roughly twenty-three miles of Interstate 10 runs
eastward toward Blythe at the state border, pausing first just after
the city of Coachella at the valley's eastern end to drop State Route
111 toward the Salton Sea and the Imperial Valley. Cities and towns
between Palm Springs and Indio sit north or south of I-10:

Desert Hot Springs, home of exclusive spas and resorts. Started
when Cabot Yerxa bought a hundred-and-sixty-acre homestead
for $10. With a burro named Merry Christmas, Yerxa found a
cold water well next to hot springs and called the place Miracle
Hill. On it he assembled a strange pueblo with a Hopi Indian
facade but never finished it.

Cathedral City, former bandit's hideout, gambling den, and site
of 139 Club, a notorious brothel. Nearby Two Bunch Palms had
been owned by Al Capone.

Rancho Mirage, where the Southland Land and Reality
Company bought land in 1928 to recreate the entire Nile Valley,
tents, camels, pyramids, and all, but the stock market tanked a
year later. Mrs. Louis Blankenhorn might have named the place
after seeing a mistry green color along Rio Del Sol and deciding
it was a mirage.

Thousand Palms, oasis and former railroad depot, where date
palms tower in rows visible for miles. Original name: Edmon,
where Esau's descendants settled after displacing the Horites.

Palm Desert, formerly the Old MacDonald Ranch (if not farm),
sprawling site of more than thirty golf courses, countless trinket

shops, Bill Gates, and many resorts. Per capita, by the way, the valley contains more golf courses than any other region in the U.S.

Indian Wells: more resorts as well as plentiful rattlesnakes. One early settler sold the venom to Los Angeles, which needed none.

Sun City: homes, tennis courts, and shopping centers grouped into one big retirement center. A Del Webb production.

La Quinta ("The Inn"), once an old lake bed with rich clay used to make pots; later, a hideaway (container, pot, bowl) for the rich; today, private homes, pools, tennis courts stuffed into a town named after a hotel. Like Indian Wells, Palm Desert, Rancho Mirage, and Cathedral City, built on an alluvial flood plain below the Santa Rosa Mountains. Among the peaks above La Quinta, Charleton Heston received the Ten Commandments.

North of La Quinta, Bermuda Dunes, previously called *Myoma* ("tumor" in English if not in Cahuilla), once home to Clark Gable, now home to the Desert Christian Academy, a private school for ages preschool through twelfth grade. Their mission: "To train students to glorify Jesus Christ," which requires preparing them in "understanding and being personally challenged to receive the gospel of Christ," "developing a personal relationship with God," "being able to defend their faith effectively and intelligently," and "sharing the Gospel message." All aimed straight into the minds of children. The school also covers writing and math.

Continuing eastward: Indio, "City of Festivals" that include the International Tamale Festival, the Southwest Arts Festival, the Riverside County Fair and National Date Festival, the Indio Desert Circuit, the yearly Indio Music and Arts, Stagecoach, and many powwows. Here, the wife of William Cook, a successful date grower, looked out the window at the full moon, heard the sound of coyotes, and said that the place seemed like a fairyland,

although one that had echoed with the blasts of shotguns pointed at rattlesnakes, burros, coyotes, jackrabbits, and wild cattle.
In 1900, the U.S. Department of Agriculture planted Deglet Noor
date cuttings from Algeria, with varieties from Iraq and Egypt
brought the following year and the dominant Medjool by 1927.
As a result, 90% of the nation's dates grow here. With a virility
worthy of Trickster, one King David date palm has fertilized
thousands of female trees. Developers wanted to build a Walled
City of Biskra here--a fake Sahara village around shops and
hotels--but went bust in 1929. In 1938, Fargo Street flooded as
the Desert Theater played *The Rains Came.* The Date Festival of
1947 featured a caliph's palace and market for a stage, a Taj
Mahal to exhibit dates, glittering trays held by young "desert
princesses," and lots of white people sitting on elephants and
wearing turbans and slippers in hopes of seeming Arabian.
Imagine that happening now. Zane Grey's Flying Sphinx Ranch
crouches nearby.

After Indio comes a labor pool named Coachella (98%
Hispanic), followed by aptly named Thermal, a town burned
many times. In the early 1900s, the straw-covered road itself
burned when someone dropped a cigarette on it. At the southernmost end of the Coachella Valley, a few miles north of the
Salton Sea, squats nobly named Mecca, where two-thirds of the
residents live below the federal poverty level and where odors
from a soil treatment plant make school children ill enough to
vomit.

> This was once the Sea of Cortez,
> Now the air is lousy with lost seabirds
> and prayer. Viscous. Thickened
> with the motions of the slowest angels,
> as if they wee swimming in sweet, heavy beer.
>
> How can a farmer, kneeling in his field,
> find himself both worn-out and unborn?
> It's not a new life, or an afterlife,

but the one unlistened to he's farming now....

....We are falling through the air
and we are feathered on the inside.
—from "Farming Below Sea Level" by Mark
Chapman, writing in Mecca

In Ted Hughes' poetic retelling of the Prometheus legend, a lizard who visits the Titan chained to the rugged mountainside by order of Zeus whispers, "Even as the vulture buried its head--/Lucky, you are so lucky to be human!" Some say Zeus had been angered by the theft of fire from the heavens; but others tell that Zeus punished Prometheus for contemptuously mangling the gods' sacred meal. As the Titan lay shivering on the mountain, a vulture (some say an eagle) ate his liver during the day. At night it grew back. Perhaps the lizard speaks the side of Promethus that feels no regret for the sacrifice.

In the Coachella Valley, the fringe-toad lizard--Tahquitz shapeshifted?--became an emblem of ecological redemption in a valley 95% lost to overdevelopment. The lizard lives in the Coachella Valley Preserve ten miles east of Palm Springs and just north of Thousand Palms on seventeen thousand acres set aside for the lizard, its blowsand, and the Thousand Palm Oasis.

The trouble started a few decades back, when a biologist published a description of this remarkable creature. Its head is shaped like the blade of a shovel, a handy feature given the lizard's psychopomp propensity for swimming under sandy surfaces like a desert submersible. Serrated lids shutter the portholes of its eyes. It even has a periscope: a third eye on top of its head for sensing gradations in light intensity. As the submersible breathes, its U-shaped throat traps sand rather like the U-joint of a sink traps fetid air. Its foot scales evolved for the same reason fins do: to provide traction while cutting resistance.

When conservationists began fighting for it, pro-development complaints centered on holding up so much business for "one damned lizard." Ecologists replied that the worry was not about single species so much as about biodiversity loss, the weblike nature of ecosystems, overpopulation, carrying capacities exceeded, systemic damage, soil compaction in and around construction sites, and threats to other local at-risk species like the horned toad, desert cochroach, red velvet mite, Coachella Valley milk vetch, and flat-seeded spurge. Psychologically, of course, it's also about growing a rudimentary sense that other forms of life besides ours have needs worthy of attention and respect. Developmentally, taking without giving back is supposed to stop once children acquire enough object constancy to imagine the psychic insides of others.

Although realtors, developers, and property owners didn't want the lizard listed federally as endangered, something like its ability to live in two worlds evolved into a series of human compromises. In 1984, the Preserve was founded to save habitat for the lizard and other desert beings while resorts went up around them.

Imperial Borders Transgressed

To height belongs depth and vice versa, psychically as well as geo-graphically. The Salton Sea is the natural rundown, runoff, outcome, and sink of the lonely Promethean heights of Mt. San Jacinto.

I pulled off Route 86 at Salton City and photographed three satellite dishes planted in dry ground. They stood over the remains of a wrecked motorboat like preoccupied guardians gazing in the wrong direction. It was hot here. Summers often reached 115 degrees, and annual rainfall seldom amounted to three inches.

West of me stretched the Anza-Borrego Desert State Park, the largest in the state at over a thousand square miles of highland for-est, palm oases, chaparral, and desert drying in the rain shadow of the Peninsular Range along the coast. To the north, that section of the lower Mojave Desert known as Joshua Tree National Park. To the east, very little but desert until the Colorado River on the state border. South lay El Centro and the international border.

Here in the northern sector of the Imperial Valley had once shimmered ancient Lake Cahuilla. In keeping with the Trickster nature of Southeastern California, the lake had shifted its names as well as its shapes over time: Le Conte, Compte, Leconte, Le Count, Lecount, Conte, Count, and others, the French referring to the medieval occupation of actor, especially one who had played a count or nobleman. In 1615, a galleon trading pearls sailed up here from the

Gulf, got stuck, was abandoned, and sank below water and sand.

In its heyday, the Salton Sea, spread over the salt pan of the previous lake, had drawn the fiscal nobility of America to play on its golf courses, float in its yacht clubs, and smoke cigars over brandy in its Desert Modern bars. That was around 1958, but by the 1970s, Modernity ended with a stench of dying tilapia--the fish Christ fed to his Twelve--and birds knocked from the air. The Sea was now deserted but for colonies of eccentrics living in trailers in a stink so powerful one could smell it before glimpsing the water wetting heaps of fish bones along the shoreline.

1871: the year the California Irrigation Company formed to pipe water from the then-plentiful Colorado River into the Salton Sink for farming. The company went bankrupt in the panic of 1893, but one of its engineers, Charles Rockwood, obtained funding through George Chaffey, Canadian emigre, builder of colonial irrigation projects in Australia, and future founder and subdivider of Manzanar in the Owens Valley. Under the new California Development Company and its subsidiary twin in Mexico, the water began to flow in 1901, when the Imperial Land Company rose to draw farmers to divide and conquer the newly named "Imperial Valley." In the place formerly named Valley of the Dead, settlers required to buy water stock and the water itself from the CDC risked loss of home and property for refusing.

Because the Algodones Sand Hills blocked efforts to run water straight in from Pilot Knob near Yuma, the canal had to detour through Mexico and run north across the border. Without studying the behavior and ecology of the river, however, the engineers had no way to learn that it carried thirty-five times more silt than the Mississippi. (The Yellow River in China carries more but is twice as long.) By 1904, the Colorado needed dredging that the CDC had not forseen and could not afford. Nor did the engineers know that water from the shifting Colorado had flooded the Salton Sink five times in the previous century alone.

Rockwell ordered a new intake cut four miles below the international border, but in 1905, two February floods, also unforseen, pushed the entire river through the cut and widened it. Ninety thousand cubic feet of water per second--half the volume of the

Niagara Falls--piled up into a ten-foot wall of water that inundated plots and fields, carried off cattle and crops, and peaked in waterfalls eighty feet high and a thousand feet wide. The Southern Pacific Railroad moved its tracks three times to avoid flooding that washed into the Salton Sink with four times more earth than was excavated to dig the Panama Canal.

By the time the railroad stopped the leak two years later by emptying stones and concrete from more than three thousand cars into the raging river, the new Salton Sea--thirty-five miles long, fifteen wide, fifty-one feet deep, about a third of the size of ancient Lake Cahuilla--had reintroduced the Sink to a marine environment and provided a new stopover for migrating birds as wetlands elsewhere disappeared from the face of California.

A 1906 flood poured through the Imperial Valley, but the monocropping went on.

Sparkling under the distant but potent gaze of Tahquitz, the sea partook of his aerial passion for high-velocity flight. During World War II the Navy set up a secret Salton Sea Test Base (SSTB) on the southwest shores to land seaplanes, drop bombs, and conduct weapons research. The Army Corps of Engineers is still cleaning up the hazardous waste and debris. In 1946, Sandia Corporation took over the site to operated it as a non-explosive range for testing Nike missiles, space capsule parachutes, drones, and atomic bomb payloads. A secret mine west of the sea contained calcite crystals useful for machining Nordem bombsites. (Neanthes, a resident resident pile worm, reproduces by spawning at night and distributing eggs and sperm by exploding.)

Low barometric pressure and high water density sculpted the Salton Sea for racing. In 1948, viewers saw speedboats leap clear of the water for sixty to eighty feet at a time. Speed records for jets were set overhead. Two-thirds of all migratory bird species in the U.S. and Canada combined came in for a landing. The winds themselves blow down into the Sink, here between the Mojave and Sonoran Deserts, as once-cool sea breezes from the Pacific are stipped of moisture by the Coast Ranges and compression-heated from the descent.

The Salton Sea remains the only saline lake in the world to host its own barnacle. Introduced by Navy seaplanes, Balanus amphitrite uses its hairy legs to cling to rocks while straining plankton from the water.

As it happens (and as we might expect by now), the lonesome Sink also collects people dislodged from elsewhere.

Its first eccentric, wanderer, entrepreneur, and fishing captain Charles Davis, returned after the flood and found his land turned into an island. Making the best of this, he built a cabin on it and, in 1908, added a boat landing, cafe, and dance hall. Naming this collection Hell's Kitchen, he sang old sea chanties and mining ballads and served "alfalfa-fed mullet." He also brought in sea lions, which died, and a large fishing barge from San Pedro for use as a showboat, but it sank. Obsessed with the fate of the Donner Party, he painted their faces in oil, retraced their trip, and collected its artifacts, maps, and other memorabilia.

Later, when the Marines left Camp Dunlap, "Slab City" formed atop its cement foundations, here where atomic bombs weighted with depleted uranium had been tested before use in Hiroshima. "Scrappers" living in ramshackle collections of forgotten debris collect and sell spent ordnance.

In the distance my eye caught new houses going up near the north shore. What were they doing here?

Poverty limits options, of course. But plenty of the poor live near lakes not reeking with the stench of massive fish dieoffs. I suspect that the Greeter (a naked old man who waves at traffic) and other colorful outcasts cooking here in the hot waste pile of Coyote suffer from what psychoanalyst Erich Fromm identified as psychic necrophilia: an unconscious but potent love of decay and death. Because outer and inner cleave together, putefaction within finds itself drawn to similar desolation without. No outlet in polluted lake or polluted psyche either.

Possessed of an amazingly dependable capacity for turning anything--transients, real estate, boats, bases, barnacle infestations, name it--into junk, the selenium-laced Sea loses 15% of itself every year to evaporation. The salt stays behind, which is why this water is 25% saltier than the Pacific Ocean. Ninety percent of the Sea's inflow is contaminated by fertilizer that fuels algae blooms that suck oxygen from the water in which the fish actually drown. Above them, hundreds of thousands of birds die of botulism.

In the past, Lake Cahuilla (of which the Salton Sea represents the latest incarnation) uncomplainingly caught whatever entered it, recycled it, and left, leaving dry sand behind until the next watery evolution. In effect, the Salton Sea Authority, by working within a limited budget for bird rehabilitation, shoreline cleanup, hand-operated booms to scoop up dead fish, solar ponds to decrease salinity, and algae ponds to reduce eutrophication, is trying to clean out what the once-mighty Colorado River can no longer flush. Agricultural runoff from surrounding plantations has turned the Sink into an enormous backed-up toilet.

If that toilet dies up, its toxic particulates will blow downwind as far as the heavily populated coast. For the first time in its long history, Lake Cahuilla, the sink, shadow, and unconscious of Imperial Valley, will finally find an outlet.

On the other hand, subsidence from groundwater drawdown could be dropping the Coyote Creek area west of the Salton Sea. Agriculture has spent water heavily from aquifers throughout southeastern and central California. Should subsidence reach fifty feet, the Gulf of California would flush the entire Imperial Valley.

Only by piecing together all the fragments of human experience of an event--the eyewitness account, the letter from a friend, the piece in the Sunday paper--can one begin to formulate a response that is in turn "on-the-ground" and concrete. Only by witnessing a plurality of such utterances can one begin to shake off the mind-numbing abstractions of modern life that allow us to treat a living landscape as board feet and bushel, and the humans who live and work that land as stereotypes--growers, braceros, "non-achievers," cosmopolitans, and locals.

— Phillip Round

WHEN I WAS A boy, my dad used to drive our family out of El Cajon on I-8 very early in the morning through the fire-prone Cleveland National Forest--four hundred and sixty thousand acres set aside in 1908 in San Diego, Orange, and Riverside Counties--and around the southern tip of the Anza-Borrego National Forest to get through as much desert as possible before the sun turned everything blinding-ly hot. We were headed for Arizona, where I put on my ice skates to compete in the Phoenix Open. Afterwards we drove home at night. Through the calming of my jangled post-performance nerves I lay in the back of the station wagon watching the distant red lights of radio towers near El Centro blinking over cooling planted fields I could smell but not see.

The Imperial Valley had long been the place of the Kumeyaay, Quechan, Cahuilla, and Cocopa, all of whom were at home here. But by 1990, nearly half of the valley's twenty-five-year-olds hadn't fin-ished high school, and 40% of its working families spent at least two weeks a year in farm labor outside the valley. Today, almost 30% of families with children are destitute, a third who grow up here will never break the poverty line, and monthly unemployment is the highest in the state. Yet crops of cotton, alfalfa, asparagus, wheat, carrots, onions, and beets bring $1 billion a year to valley growers running their giant engines over half a million acres. More feedlots process beef here--at eighteen hundred gallons of water per pound--than in any other county in the state. Half the county's acreage grows alfalfa shipped to diary farms. What happened?

The masthead of the Imperial Valley's first newspaper offers a clue: "Water is King, Here is its Kingdom."

When the failure of Intake #3 dumped the Colorado River into the Salton Basin, the citizens of the valley banded together in 1911 to form the Imperial Irrigation District, a trusteeship to oversee water use more safely and fairly than imperialist engineers and financiers ever could. The momentum of their outrage might have shifted the levers of power in the valley forever without Harold Bell Wright's recourse to an even mightier force: myth power. In his novel *The Winning of Barbara Worth* (1911), Wright inverted the catastrophe by contrasting a few evil cardboard cutouts of capitalists with Ayn Randian heroes of Progress whose holy mission was to save the desert, even from itself. Never mind that exactly such bombastic and anti-ecological posturing had wreaked the havoc to begin with. Greening the desert, as Wright, a preacher, saw it, must represent a further unfolding of God's plan for mankind.

The capitalists agreed, as did Sam Goldwyn of MGM, who bought the movie rights to the novel in 1925 and picked Gary Cooper to star in a celluloid effort to convert hell into paradise. Even before the film was shot, a Barbara Worth Hotel opened in El Centro. In a large mural on the north wall, heroic characters undertaking "The Conquest of the Desert," although this face of the conquest burned down in 1962. Waitresses and truckers abroad in the valley still believe Barbara Worth to have been a real person.

Hydraulic empire, historian Karl August Wittfogel had named it. Control what people need for their survival and you control them. Dam and divert their water and they will do whatever you demand. Soon entire communities of bronze-skinned helots wandered the plantations of the Imperial Valley picking vegetables for a pittance. What a Civil War had been fought to end had resurfaced in the Golden State where those who owned the gold made the rules. Many of the gold-owners considered themselves Christians and attended church every Sunday to hear sermons about the meek inheriting the earth.

By the time photographer Dorothea Lange arrived in the valley, the labor strikes had erupted. A hundred and eighty of them broke out in thirty-four California counties between January 1933 and the summer of 1939. A full third of agricultural workers risked having their heads broken to demand necessities no cattle of a grower would be without: food, water, a place to sleep at night. The immigrants whose images and stories Lange gathered stood quiet and gaunt against backdrops of unbelievable agricultural abundance regulated by giant machinery. Paul Taylor, co-author with Lange of *American Exodus*, named the Imperial Valley the site of "a large, landless, and mobile proletariat."

All this time the corporation set up by Chaffey and Rockwell had controlled fertile farmland on both sides of the international border. In 1936, in direct response to plans for an All-American Canal that would restrict water from flowing down the Colorado

River into Mexicali, the government of President Cardenas demanded that the land be returned to Mexican nationals. Under a program of socialist reform, his administration set up communal *ejido* farms of laborers who now owned the land and its canals, packing houses, and farming equipment. By 1946, forty-four *ejidos* grew crops in the Mexicali Valley, where their success and that of braceros invited to work in the United States brought an influx of settlers and business owners. (One U.S. grower bragged, "We used to own our slaves, now we rent them from the government.") As novelist Gabriel Trujillo Munoz noted, Mexicali had come a distance some cities needed a thousand years to traverse. Other border cities--Tijuana, for instance, which had enjoyed a vast boost in business thanks to Prohibition--grew rapidly as farmworkers remained near the border.

Calexico, Mexicali's northern mirror image, did not fare so well. In the absence of redistribution policies it withered, ever more dependent on shoppers and tourists from cities south of the border. In the 1990s Calexico revived somewhat as maquila factories moved in, but Mexicali swelled by nearly 75%. Even so, Calexico's prospects brightened, though not for long.

For most of its history, the international border across which California, Arizona, New Mexico, and Texas face Baja, Sonora, Tamaulipas, Nuevo Leon, Chichuaha, and Coahuila was not consistently policed. It came into being in 1848 when the Treaty of Guadalupe Hidalgo ended President Polk's expansionary war for land. The United States came away owning Nevada, Utah, Arizona, New Mexico, Colorado, Texas, and California. Many members of the original border survey team quit to join the Gold Rush. Nobody thought much about the border until Congress suffered a fit of postwar paranoia and passed the 1917 Immigration Act to require a literacy test and an $8 "head tax" for all immigrants. The Act refused entry to "all idiots, imbeciles, feeble-minded persons, epileptics, and insane persons." As paranoia expanded, passports were suddenly required by governments around the world.

Even then, the two-thousand-mile-long border stretching from the Pacific to the Gulf attracted little notice. In fact, the original purpose of the United States Immigration Bureau founded in 1864 was to draw migrant workers to U.S. farms, factories, and railroads. Laborers fleeing northward in 1910 to escape the Mexican Revolution arrived in time to fill U.S. labor shortages brought by World War I. Nevertheless, by the 1920s poor Mexicans were demonized as carriers of tuberculosis and germ infestations and forced at the border to stand in line naked waiting to be hosed off and sprayed with DDT. The newly organized Border Patrol that handled them had started out as the Texas Rangers.

In 1953, the U.S. Government announced Operation Wetback to counter the supposed wage-depressing impact of immigrants and an imaginary infiltration of the U.S. by Communists. This effort was led by Joseph Swing, commissioner of the Immigration and Naturalization Service. Agents stopped thousands of people who looked Mexican to them and asked for identification papers. Children of parents labeled "illegal aliens" were deported despite their status as citizens born in the U.S. Deportation by sea stopped when several prisoners jumped overboard and drowned. Almost half a million Mexicans and Mexican Americans fled the U.S. in fear.

So matters stood along the border until 1992. While campaigning against George Bush, Pat Buchanan claimed an "illegal invasion" of a million Mexicans a year pouring into the United States. Other Republicans, including Pete Wilson, picked up this call to fear, a call amplified in stridency by military base closings, recession, a shriveling post-Cold War defense industry, heavily armed gangs menacing Los Angeles, and the first World Trade Center bombing.

In 1994, the North Atlantic Free Trade Agreement went into effect. One result was to force Mexican farmers off their lands because they could not compete with government-subsidized grains from the United States that flooded Mexican markets at artificially low prices. Furthermore, with the Mexican economy almost totally dependent on U.S. markets, the Mexican government and wealthy growers partnered with multinationals that owned the maquilas. Most of their workers were, and still are, young women forced to leave their children at home. A fourth of Mexico works in maquilas; half the country remains unemployed.

With the onset of Operation Gatekeeper, activated the same year NAFTA bankrupted millions of Mexican farmers, immigrants began avoiding heavily policed checkpoints to cross the dangerous Sonora Desert through Arizona. Operation Hold the Line guarded El Paso, and Operation Rio Grande (1998) Texas. By this time the illicit drug trade brought $30 billion a year into cash-strapped Mexico even as the growth of maquilas and a rise in exports from $40 billion to $200 billion made Mexico's top 10% even wealthier while most of their countrymen lived on a dollar a day.

Presidents Vicente Fox and George W. Bush were shifting toward friendlier border relations when terrorists attacked New York City on September 11, 2001.

As part of the hysterical overreaction (more people die on the roads every year), the INS was placed under Homeland Security. This meant that migrants were now regarded as potential terrorists. The southern border was fortified at a cost of billions with retrofitted walls, fences, cameras, lights, motion detectors, and contingents of newly hired Border Patrol agents driving around in SUVs. Fatalities along the border soon jumped to three hundred a year. Desperate immigrants pushed into the deserts died the horrible death of heat exposure: thirst, seizures, kidneys shutting down, eyeballs drying up, and death throes so extreme that agents found bodies surrounded by sandy semicircles left by thrashing limbs.

Although not a single terrorist entered the U.S. by the border, graves for "John Doe" and "Jane Doe" multiplied in Holtville. Imperial Valley was the deadliest spot along the border because of the desert, the All-American Canal with its lethal undertow, the gunnery range, rattlesnakes, and the New River so packed with factory sewage and pesticide runoff that agents refused to go in after "floaters." Drugs circulated north from here along roads specially paved so they don't melt in the sun.

Organizations like Humane Borders, Samaritans, and Citizens for Border Solutions work hard to provide shelter, clothing, water, food, and medicine for migrant workers, and good-hearted citizens living along the border offer jugs of water, candy bars, packets of peanuts, and old clothes. But the institutionally sanctioned deaths go on. Driven by an utter desperation to find work, more migrants have died along the border since 1994 than were shot by the Volkspolizei during the entire lifetime of the Berlin Wall.

Yet rivers of money flow through this dry no man's land, starting with smugglers and "coyotes" who charge higher and higher prices because of the crackdown and who organize huge crime syndicates that do business with cartels paid well by the "war on drugs." Coyotes equipped with satellite phones, laptops, GPS, and night vision gear earn $7-8 billion a year. In 2006, President Calderon sent his army in after the cartels, but appalled soldiers faced weapons superior to their own. Some of the killers carried assault rifles bought at U.S. gun shows or made available by "Fast and Furious," a Phoenix program set up by the U.S. Bureau of Tobacco, Firearms, and Explosives.

> There was ample irony to be found in the growth and professionalization of the immigrant-smuggling industry, for if there was any primary catalyst for the increased profits and sophistication of the enterprise in recent years, it was the U.S. government's border crackdown. Immigration officials conceded that shifting enforcement had sweetened the smugglers' market.
>
> —Ken Willingwood

Someone has to make all the equipment needed by the Border Patrol, including its computerized fingerprinting system, although after spending $1 billion a year, the agency was still unable to make yearly fingerprint comparisons because of numerous technical glitches. Animals set off motion sensors so often that agents have learned to disregard the warnings.

The federal government spends roughly $85-$135 per immigrant per day for detention. This has proved a windfall to counties struggling with declining budgets. According to a 2009 report by Amnesty International, Santa Clara County built detention facilities just for this purpose. Companies like Halliburton and the Corrections Corporation of America have moved beyond prison construction to build profitable detention and deportation facilities all over America. Halliburton's contract from Homeland Security came to $385 million. CCA, a supporter of racial profiling laws of the kind drafted by Russell Pearce in Arizona, earned revenues above $300 million a year. Each prisoner was worth $50 a day.

Once deported, each costs U.S. taxpayers $12,500. Four hundred thousand were detained and shipped out in 2010, half without being charged with any crime.

> Not entirely unlike the overwhelming of the Great Wall of China by Mongols and other nomads, a supposedly secure wall that was built quite recently is proving so vulnerable that it will soon not count as a border at all--if "border" entails a strict enclosure that is effective in preventing unchecked entry into what lies on the other side of it....It is not just that "something there is that doesn't love a wall, that wants it down." Robert Frost's famous line goes only part of the way toward what we need to realize about security walls of many kinds: in a certain fundamental sense, they are built to be breached... There is something about a wall, we might say, that does not love itself--at least not enough to maintain itself as permanently inviolable.
>
> — Ed Casey

As frustrated Anza tried for two days in 1776 to reach Mount Signal near the border, the mountain seemed to recede before him. Before turning back they named it Cerro del Imposible (Impossible Hill) without learning that only native shamans were invited by the mountain into its interior for initiation into their sacred craft.

Linear vision is uncertain in the Imperial Valley, where two-million-year-old gravel bars lay near the surface of a wash or by rocks thousands of years old just underneath. Earthquake swarms rock the land like waves do the deck of a ship; mirages simulate water or even floating mountains with roots suspended in the air. John C. Van Dyke wrote of "the settler who ever remains unsettled." Audubon called the valley "melancholy." Gloria Anzaldua called its border "una herida abierta": an open wound.

A border is a linearity, whereas life and culture partake of circled nestings of complexity. A border can never stop them. In fact, a border in an age of globalization is a standing absurdity, a monument to ancient strategizing, a Maginot Line waiting for its inevitable circumvention. Of the two hundred and fifty million who cross the border every year, roughly ten million do it illegally by going over, under, around, or through.

In public argument about the border, the fearful emphasize the illegality of crossing (and not the absurdity of enforcing nation-state legalities designed for a different age), the loss of American jobs (although no long lines of Amereicans wait to toil in the fields while breathing carcinogenic pesticides), or the charity burden on local healthcare (on average 2-4% for U.S. hospitals, but 8-10% in El Centro and other border cities because of dehydration, bone fractures, and farmwork injuries). The mirror-image example of Calexico-Mexicali reflects another side of the wound, however: a site of transborder connections of culture and place.

> Along the Mexico-United States border there is now an unprecedented mixing, producing many new cultural and aesthetic forms. For instance, there are more Chinese restaurants in Tijuana than any other city in Mexico, and the desert region outside Mexicali is home to many people of Middle-Eastern origin. Nearby, on the U.S. side of the border (and in Tijuana on the weekends) there are military and surfing cultures. The booming Mexican corrido industry is headquartered in Los Angeles. Tijuanenses and San Diegans can watch television channels that are broadcast from either side of the border in many languages.
> — Michael Dear and Gustavo Leclerc

What feeds this transborder vitality? Networks of informal business, appropriated technology, rapid communication, mobility, family and neighborhood connections, all of it layered across the divided landscape. People living near the border plant gardens next to it, attach clotheslines to it, install phones for border crossers.

> Rather than let the boundary zone continue to be a
> space of liability, a no-man's-land, a zone of insecu-
> rity, potential crime, and international bureaucra-
> cy, local citizens are choosing to humanize the bor-
> der. Monuments to people who died crossing the
> boundary have been erected on the border fence
> itself. The fence is transformed into a public space
> that can be visited by local residents, a sacred place
> that commemorates the regional struggle at certain
> moments in history.
> —Lawrence Herzog

Here cosmopolitan looks plural, particular, localized, and multi-cultural. Not just a mixing, but the emergence of something new enlivened by many languages, centers, and traditions making place (in Ed Casey's terms) out of space.

> *Si el de Berlin cayó, el de Tijuana porqué no?* ("If the one in
> Berlin fell, why not the one in Tijuana?")
> — graffiti on the fence at Tijuana-San Diego

All this has been heralded and carried forward by transborder art of the in-between, an art of rupture and emerging identity, an aesthetic of hybridities growing like hardy flowers in the cracks of conflicting ideologies, performative, transgressive, noncommercial-ized, embodied, politically aware, memorial, ironic, resistant, and culturally convergent. Works that exemplify these kinds of con-sciousness flow from the likes of Daniel Joseph Martinez, Ruben Ortiz Torres, Mark Bradford, Norman Yonemoto, Amalia Mesa-Bains, Joe Lewis, Barbara Jones, Milena Muzquiz, Marcos Ramirez, Rita Gonzalez, Jesse Lerner, Einar and Jamex de la Torre, Mariana Botey, Laura Alvarez, Salvador Torres, Guillermo Gomez-Pena, Richard Lou, and Alfredo Jaar. For decades the Taller de Arte Fronterizo ("Border Arts Workshop") has brought together American and Mexican artists from both sides of the border to launch collaborative projects. In 1997, InSITE-sponsored *Toy an Horse* by Marcos Ramirez: a thirty-foot-tall, two-headed (trojan) horse at the border at San Ysidro. Crossers, we are reminded, go in both directions.

> ninguna
> frontera
> podrá
> separarnos
> (no
> border
> can ever
> separate us)
> — Francisco Alarcón, from "Frontera"

So do films like *The Crying Woman's Inheritance* (1946), *Pito Perez Becomes a "Bracero"* (1947), *The Border Man* (1952), *Northern Border* (1953), *All Friends are Sacred* (1966), *Deportees* (1975), *Cry of the Poor* (1977), *Wetbacks* (1977), *The Night of the Ku Klux Klan* (1978), *Women Braceras* (1981), *Human Contraband* (1981), *The Palms of Cantu* (1983), *Three Thousand Kilometers North* (1984), *Arizona: Bloody Massacre* (1985), *Dying Crossing the River* (1986), *Not from Here nor from There* (1987), *Baja Californians* (1988), *Sacred Fridays* (1991), *Disneyland for Me* (1999), and *Coca-Cola in Our Veins* (2000). Filmmakers exhibiting their transnational passions rely on multimedia and modest resources to work imaginatively, revive abandoned urban spaces, rethink border narratives, and air fresh perspectives that grow from the troubled ground up.

> Living on borders and in margins, keeping intact one's shifting and multiple identity and integrity, is like trying to swim in a new element, an "alien" element. There is an exhiliration in being a participant in the further evollution of humankind, in being "worked" on. I have the sense that certain "faculties"--not just in me but in every border resident,

colored or non-colored--and dormant areas of consciousness are being activated, awakened.

— Gloria Anzaldua

San Diego-Tijuana contains five million people sharing an economy of $6 billion of annual exports and $8 billion in cross-border
trade. With tourism is booming, billions are invested in Baja mari-
nas, resorts, and vacation homes. Workers cross back and forth. So
why not just open the border, like that of Canada or the European
Union? Contradictions would need working out--drugs are allowed
in Mexico but firearms are not, for example--but without the inter-
ference of institutions staffed by profiteers and paranoiacs, they
could be. As always, the walls around the heart interfere.

In El Centro I found a deteriorating downtown along Main
Street, a blocky empty plaza, dying grass in front of the government
center, and no artwork, not even a fantasy of the place about itself
or its image of self-becoming. In a plywood mockup of Bethlehem in
front of a Baptist church the manger stood empty.

However, El Centro is considered by many to be a socioeconom-
ic step up from life in Calexico, where a billboard in front of City
Hall greeted me with the words, "Efficiency is Security." Before 9/11,
grocers lined the streets. Residents left doors unlocked and slept
outside on warm nights. Restriction of border traffic had devastated business here, separated families, withered the downtown.

>   ...I found the downtown opening of the physical
>   abomination that identifies the border, the official
>   crossing point and its huge inspection shed for
>   those driving or walking north, flanked by the
>   harsh barrier that rejects the innucuous label
>   "fence" that so many proponents of the barrier use.
>   But it is a wall, not a fence. And from my perspec-
>   tive of having lived in Berlin when that city was
>   divided, it was impossible not to see it as a variation
>   on the Berlin Wall theme every time I saw it: ugly,

monstrous, insulting, and--ultimately--doomed to failure.

— Ken Ellingwood

Founded and laid out by Rockwood, Calexico ranked lowest in the county for education, employment, and public health even while restaurants, theaters, concerts, and nightclubs jazzed up cosmopolitan Mexicali, home to the Universidad Autonoma de Baja Californa. *Losing It* was filmed in Calexico. But the mostly Latino population hangs together against all adversity. A mural on Imperial Avenue celebrates immigration.

> Calexicos are the grassroots reality of merging cultures, reality-based twenty-first-century hatcheries that have been incubating since the Industrial Revolution. They don't feel bound by treaties or directives from their national capitals. They figure out pragmatic workarounds. Their black-and-gray economies thrive and often dominate. Of course, radical societal change can exhibit problematic and destructive dark sides. But the misery is not caused by the Other coming to America.
>
> — Ken Ellingwood

The border will open one day regardless of outdated opposition. Beyond the rusting fences of Operation Gatekeeper, fences hammered from landing mats left over from the first Gulf War, talks continue toward an international airport that straddles the border. The dualisms that pit us against them, North against South, local against global, and sanctioned against liminal have never been sustainable and cannot stand. As in the psyche, so on the land: no defensive bulwark lasts forever against the forces of vital transformation.

> Here lies the magic of border cities--not only are they defined by distant global processes, but their global character is imprinted in real geographic

space. They literally transcend the physical limits
of nation-states. Border cities are tangible living
spaces that cross national political boundaries. We
can call this new global prototype a "transfrontier
metropolis."

— Lawrence Herzog

In 1848, two regions that belonged together were severed, leaving an open wound at once geographical, cultural, psychological, ecological, and spiritual. Today, after much healing and love, the wound's jagged edges begin to knit together.

In many senses, Southern California and Baja
California—what may be called "Bajalta California,"
consisting of the Los Angeles/San Diego and
Tijuana/Mexicali metropolitan regions—no longer
represent separate growth poles within each
nation. Instead, they have coalesced to become a
single city-region, or regional city, that just happens to be bisected by an international border. This
integrated city-region is as much in tune with
international forces as with anything that happens
on the domestic scene. Bajalta California is by now
one of the planet's most important world cities.

— Michael Dear and Gustavo Leclerc

After decades of enforced separation, Alta and Baja California, and the modes of collective consciousness they hold, are finally, and inevitably, reunifying.

Ultimately, once it has outlived its political or economic or symbolic usefulness, every border is destined to become a boundary and to return to an
abiding state of nature. This is just what happened
in the case of the Great Wall—which, many centuries after its military significance had ceased,

rejoined the open landscape of western China, crumbling into the earth that underlies and surrounds it. Animals and humans move over it at their whim.

— Ed Casey

Across the border in Mexico
   stark silhouette of houses gutted by waves,
     cliffs crumbling into the sea,
      silver waves marbled with spume
       gashing a hole under the border fence.

   But the skin of the earth is seamless.
   The sea cannot be fenced,
el mar does not stop at borders.
To show the white man what she thought of his
   arrogance
Yemayá blew that wire fence down.

— Gloria Anzaldua

ALTHOUGH EL CENTRO, A former barley field made over into the county seat, was intended to serve as center of a desert empire, it also ended up a fixed, dusty point around which odd happenings collected. Like Plaster City to the west along the Evans Hughes Highway: a town dusted white from gypsum emitted by a sheetrock mill. Like Felicity to the east, founded by Jacques-Andre Istel as a New Age shrine containing a chunk of the Eiffel Tower, a copy of the finger of God from Michelangelo's Sistine Chapel work, a pyramid, and certificates for having visited the Center of the World. Like Brawley to the south, a favorite haunt of La Llorona. Like the Imperial Irrigation District in El Centro itself, where nobody uses solar despite plentiful sunshine because the District runs relatively cheap electricity from fossil fuels. Its irrigation pipes and tractors are stolen frequently. It receives 65% of California's allotment of Colorado River water: 2.9 MAF a year injected into the IV.

At the southeasternmost corner of California, the river runs by Quechan Nation, the Imperial Valley's one reservation. The Quechan say they came from the top of Avikame, Spirit Mountain, in what is now Arizona. Put your ear to the sloping ground and you might hear the spirits of the dead as they dance. The Creation began here, they say, not far from the still-visible pathway of the sacred Trail of Dreams. The Quechan are fighting a plan by Glamis Gold, Ltd., to dig open-pit mines near Indian Pass. In a 2002 interview with the New York Times, David Hyatt, Vice President of Investor Relations, stated indifferently, "We've offered to move some of our waste stockpiles to accomodate these trails of dreams and whatnot."

I drove northward across the county toward Joshua Tree.

A National Monument since 1936 and a National Park since 1994 thanks to the California Desert Protection Act, these twelve hundred square miles got their name from their characteristic lily plant whose arms seemed beckoning to incoming Mormons in search of the Promised Land. "Thou shalt follow the way pointed for thee by the trees," as recorded in the Book of Joshua. The Joshua grows on alluvial fans near the mountains and blooms white flowers in spring. Pasadena socialite Minerva Hoyt went to war on behalf of the spiky, armored plant in the early thirties against miners who fought to keep digging for gold in the future park. "Never by day or by night do they loose the armor or drop the spear point," wrote Van Dyke in 1901 about the Joshua Tree. As an example of convergent evolution, a plant like the Joshua grows in the Middle East. Its wood, it is said, made the Crown of Thorns.

The park lives at the intersection of two deserts:

> I like to think of the Colorado as yin (female) to Mojave's yang (male); the Colorado as a beautiful dancer who endlessly swivels and arcs and laments and loves, the Mojave as a goofy, ruggedly handsome killer with a face full of crags that you will never find your way out of, the Colorado that brings the Mojave if not to its knees then at least to a stop, the Colorado that sucks the extreme energy

of the Mojave into its pores and breathes it back,
without the edge.

— Deanne Stillman

Two dominant geologic formations dwell here too: ancient Pinto
Gneiss, dark, rough, more than a billion years old, and risen from the
bottom of the ocean, and monzogranite, lighter, rounder, also from
the sea floor but much younger. Giant granite piles of inselbergs
forged far below the surface have been compared to dinosaur spines.
Malapai Hill is a third type: basalt about 2 or 3 million years old.

Two deserts, two geologies--and a meeting zone of two
mythologies, those of Trickster and Ares, at first a god of agriculture
but later a god of war. The Romans worshiped him as Mars. His
presence emanates from irritating plant hairs, razor-sharp leaves,
oils that burn skin, animals and insects that bite. Even the local lore
reflects him as a plantlike Yucca Man said to attack solitary travelers who get lost under a full moon, as a cholla garden rumored to
jump out to ambush passersby and as park features with names like
Skull Rock and Hall of Horrors. Sculpted by geologic adversity, the
park as a whole has sunk below sea level ten times and resurfaced
through violent upheaval.

Yet Trickster here too: as Hidden Valley, where Jim and Bill
McHaney imitated Hermes by hiding stolen cattle, as coyotes who
roam through the park and howl and as Raven and all his associa-
tions to death and his habit of imitating the calls of other birds.

For me, the intersection of the two deserts is
marked by nothing but a feeling; there is a palpable
energy shift at the very spot where the Mojave and
Colorado merge, where sand from one mixes with
sand from the other and produces the silent song of
Joshua Tree National Park, the one carried on the
desert winds to points east and north and south
and west, the one that tunes the strings of my heart.

— Deanne Stillman

Alfredo Acosta Figueroa, an elder of the Colorado River Indian Tribes in Blythe, believed the Park to be Aztlan, legendary home-land of the Aztecs. He spoke of a prophecy by the last warrior emperor, Chuauhtemoc, who said that the dark cycle of Spanish conquest would end when light returned and the eagle descend-ed. The lingering question, of course, is which eagle he meant.

Below Joshua Tree I found myself staring up the barrel of a 76mm tank gun.

The General Patton Museum shares Interstate 10 with a peni-tentiary. A double sign on the interstate indicates STATE PRISON NEXT EXIT and DO NOT PICK UP HITCHHIKERS. No indeed. At the museum, a desert altar to Mars, tanks and trucks gathered respectfully around a statue of Old Blood and Guts standing next to his dog of war, the bull terrier Willie named after William the Conqueror. A sign posted just beyond thousands of tons of armored equipment parked in palm-shaded sand warned me not to litter.

Patton had trained troops at Camp Young not far from here in 1942. His Desert Training Center would expand to eighteen thou-sand square miles. Patton called the area "desolate and remote." Once in October not far from where musicians would rock Indio one day, men under arms listened quietly to the *War Symphony* of Shostakovich. A soldier himself, he had penned it while fighting fires in Leningrad. "If you can work successfully here, in this coun-try," Patton informed his officers, "it will be no difficulty at all to kill the assorted sons of bitches you meet in any other country."

In Blythe a maze of yellow earthquake tape draped around road construction mayhem surrounded the Blythe Family Counseling Center wedged in next to the Elks Lodge. Seizing my digital camera, I took a picture on the fly for use in later discussions about the rela-tionship between inner turmoil and troubled urban settings.

In archeological circles Blythe is known for its Giant Intaglios. Local tribes engraved these prehistoric figures on a mesa eighteen miles to the north. Oddly, they can only be glimpsed in their entire-ty from the air, which is why it took Army Air Corps pilot George Palmer to rediscover them in a 1931 overflight. The tallest reaches a hundred and sixty-seven feet and could be an image of a hunter. Erich von Daniken claimed they were spacemen before making his

own landing in a Swiss prison for fraud, tax evasion, and embezzelment. After some of the designs were destroyed by Patton's careless
tanks, several of the giants were surrounded by protective fences
that resemble huge coffins. On the Arizona side crouches a rattlesnake with big rocks for eyes.

To drive from Blythe at state's edge to Needles, you take I-95
north and go a hundred and twenty five miles. The Mojave National
Preserve will soon be twenty miles west of you. Route 40 will lead
you westward back through Barstow to Route 395 and northward
into the Owens Valley.

Needles, too, is an edgy place. Lieutenant Amiel Weeks Whipple
named it while conducting a government railroad survey in 1854. He
had seen the needle-shaped peaks at the southern end of the valley.
At the recommendation of Lieutenant Edward Beale, Fort Mohave
was commissioned and staffed in 1859 to protect Gold Rush argonauts from Native raiders. Mojave warriors had purified themselves by negotiating the Mystic Maze ten miles to the south.

The Santa Fe Railroad finally arrived in 1882. The workers who
built it wore sombreros and were known as the Big Hat Brigade in
an unconscious nod to the mythic helmet of Mars. A bridge built a
year later across the Colorado River was washed away. Other
bridges would be too, even after the ferries began to run. Even so,
the town was founded in 1883 on the Arizona side of the river. From
there it crossed the state line into California in yet another regional
border transgression.

With Mars is often found comely Venus. At the Harvey House
hotel, women known as Harvey Girls promised not to marry for the
first year of their contract; if they did anyway they forfeited half
their monthly pay. Across the way, Wyatt Earp stayed at Garces
House, as did Douglas MacArthur and George Patton. It closed in
1949 but is being restored. Charles Schulz attended second grade in
Needles in 1929 while accompanied by a dog named Spike. The film
version of *The Grapes of Wrath* was shot here in 1939. Racing boats
competed in "marathons." By World War II, an army field hospital,
Camp Ibis, and a POW camp squatted nearby.

The frequent floods ended in the early 1950s when the Bureau of
Reclamation dredged and dammed the river to drain soils enough

for crops and housing. An accidental result of this was Topock Marsh, an important wetland and bird stop until the Bureau tried to dredge it and killed it off instead. In the 1960s Desert Strike soldiers showed up to practice desert warfare.

Today, with the fame of Route 66 faded, Needles survives on boat recreation and a trickle of Colorado River water.

"BEST ROOMS IN NEEDLES," blared an otherwise bare billboard busy peeling behind the gas station. I also saw a heap of sand, an open dumpster, a jumble of striped UNDER CONSTRUCTION sawhorses, and a train halted with craggy hills beyond. Speakers above me played the Carpenters: "Darling, can't you hear me? SOS...".

At the hotel I checked into the fountains outside were bone dry and the swimming pool half empty. The coffee maker mustered little more than a dribble, and the waitress at the restaurant down the street from the hotel gave me a glass only half full of water.

"I think I see a pattern," I told Sandra, my trip mate, as I thought about the heavily dammed Colorado River creeping wearily through this neglected place. In my mind's ear three letters repeated over and over: SOS...SOS...SOS....

The Paiutes understood the confictual river. They relate that the love god Shinob warned an arguing couple in his family, "Calm your jealous anger before the waves of hate divide you like a canyon so wide and deep that you cannot speak together." They paid him no heed, only to find themselves separated forever on opposite banks.

Sixty-five million years ago, clashing tectonic plates lifted the Rockies high as Utah sank. An adolescent child of the Continental Divide, the river flowed west until five million years ago, when Utah rose again to compel the flow southward toward the Gulf of California. To this day the Grand Canyon holds the remains of Native American animal figures cunningly worked from split twigs.

> The Colorado River is Calamity, arguing with its split personality, Beauty.
>
> — Jonathan Waterman

In 1776, Fray Silvestre Velez de Escalante led a river expedition upset by the kinds of conflictual mishaps and divisions that would mark so many other attempts: lost pack animals, boats overturned, hunger, thirst, scorpion and rattlesnake bites, unexpected waves. A 1889 railroad survey mission encountered falling chunks of heavy rock, wintry cold in the shadowy canyons even during summer, boiling heat when the sun passed overhead, numerous broken or drowned cameras, travel companions divided, and the drowning of sponsor Frank Brown. A boat named *Colorado* ran aground and sank.

> The Colorado is an outlaw. It belongs only to the ancient, eternal earth. As no other, it is savage and unpredictable of mood, peculiarly American in character.
> — Frank Waters

Since 1919, when Grand Canyon National Park came into being, two hundred and forty people have died in airplane crashes into the river, fifty have committed suicide, fifty have accidentally fallen to their deaths, twenty-three have been murdered, seventy died of natural causes (including heat stroke), thirty from acts of Gaia like lightning and falling rocks, seven in flash floods, and twenty by drowning.

> It is not exactly an earthy red, not the color of shale and clay mixed; but the red of peroxide of iron and copper, the sang-du-boeuf red of oriental ceramics, the deep insistent red of things timeworn beyond memory. And there is more than a veneer about the color. It has a depth that seems luminous and yet is sadly deceptive. You do not see below the surface no matter how long you gaze into it.
> — J.C. Van Dyke

Back in 1893, one-armed Major John Wesley Powell, who had boated the river in 1869, warned river developers that overdoing reclamation would create "a heritage of conflict and litigation." Not long after his warning, the U.S. Government mismeasured the river's volume at 17.5 million acre-feet (maf)--about six trillion gallons a year--during an unusually rainy historical period. The true number is around 15 maf: 2.5 maf less than seven U.S. states and Mexico have divided up between them.

The Colorado drains two hundred and forty three thousand square miles (17% of the continental United States), adjoins two dozen Native tribes, and plummets fourteen thousand feet from source to end, but its vitality has been drained by thirty dams, thirty million customers, and several million acres of agriculture that drink 80% of its total volume. The river runs through fourteen coal or gas plants and a hundred and seven hydroelectric turbines that power a hundred and twenty-seven million homes a year. Boatmen on the river still speak wistfully about the days of the "predambrian."

California is allocated 4.4 maf but draws 5.2, most of it from the Colorado River Aqueduct, a two-hundred-and-forty-mile pipeline of ninety-two miles of tunnels, eighty-four miles of buried siphons and conduits, sixty-three miles of canals, five pumping stations, and three reservoirs. Inspired by how Los Angeles siphoned water from Lake Owens and built during the Great Depression, the aqueduct drove the massive growth and sprawl at its Southern California terminus. Where irrigation runs, population always rises.

> Although hardly the longest river at 1,450 miles--or 1,700 miles from the source of the Green River tributary--it is the most contested, played-upon, silt-laden, diverted, engineered, dammed, stored (four times its volume and one-fifth of its length is held in reservoirs), farmed with, and metro-dependent river in America. Thirty million people rely upon its waters. Seen from different banks of view, it can be a model of supply and demand, or the most imperiled river in the West.
>
> — Jonathan Waterman

Thirty of its forty-two native fish are found only in this river, and many are now endangered. Once a place for jaguars, deer, and beaver, the delta still shelters three hundred and sixty bird species, but, unable to reach the Gulf any longer, its banks are covered with cracked mud overgrown with invasive tamarisk and giant cane. The tamarisk--also known as saltcedar--is especially lethal because it drinks two hundred gallons of water a day and excretes salt. The invasive giant cane (Arundo), first introduced for roofing and flood control, secretes chemicals that kill aquatic life and deter nesting. Arundo grows from Blythe (also home to heavy-drinking alfalfa and cotton fields) down to Mexico. At Palo Verde, the river is loaded with DDT, fecal chloroform, and E. coli.

ExxonMobile, Shell Texaco, Chevron, The Oil Shale Corporation, OXY USA, and Union Oil have bought up land rights along the river. Big Oil now owns most of the four-state Upper Basin yearly allocation of water. They intend to heat the ground at a place named Rifle to produce oil shale. Every cubic yard of shale refined takes twenty-five cubic yards of water. The resulting runoff is heavily toxic.

Additionally, the river runs alongside three hundred and ninety-five uranium claims. Eight hundred new claims have been filed within five miles of the river. Contamination from a single mine could render the entire downstream flow unusable.

So could global warming. The river depends on vanishing snowmelt in the Rockies. In the 1980s, twenty million people needed the river for drinking water, but today thirty million do and the number is rising. Add another ten million and a few of degrees of heat, and the reservoirs--each of which loses annually what Las Vegas pumps from the river every year--will drop so low that dam turbines won't reach enough water to make electricity. Blackouts will strike millions of homes, businesses, neighborhoods, entire regions. If the water is polluted or dries up, much of Southern California and parts of Arizona (including Phoenix, with its hundred and fifty rapid-evaporation golf courses, fountains, and countless swimming pools), Nevada, Utah, Wyoming, Colorado, and New Mexico will have to be evacuated.

> In a hundred years, actually less, God's riverine handiwork in the West has been stood on its head. A number of rivers have been nearly dried up. One now flows backward. Some flow through mountains into other rivers' beds. There are huge reservoirs where there was once desert; there is desert, or cropland, where there were once huge shallow swamps and lakes. It still isn't enough.
>
> — Marc Reisner

What must killing a river do to the souls of people who live near it? Did Needles feel so loveless and impoverish because souls there were drying up, their vitality trickling away, or because the river was? Ultimately, was there any difference between the two?

> It has often struck me how parallel the course of my own life has run with the Colorado. I could no more write an autobiography without the river than I have been able in this to ignore its fellow traveler. We werre both born inthe high Colorado Rockies. Progressively in childhood and youth we made our way back down the peaks and mountains. Meandering back and forth across mesa and plateau our lives assumed their permanent color, our tempers set.
>
> — Frank Waters

"Why do you suppose," I asked Sandra, "this place feels so lonely and depressed?" We looked around at peeling billboards, barren ground, rusting trailers, and, below a roadway bridge, the Colorado River low enough to wade.

She pointed at a wall calendar of a smiling Marilyn Monroe posturing for the month. "That is the only sight of Aphrodite I've caught here."

Yes! In this place of Mars, where was life-giving Venus? Where were love and beauty? What good was anything without Her? The questions squeezed my heart with a sorrow I felt for months afterwards. Did anyone out here on the eastern edge of California love neglected Needles?

We lay down that night to dream about Comstock-era neighborhoods and saloons where men's lives ended in bloody six-shooter battles in the streets. In the morning our faces were pale and lined.

Jonathan Waterman made a canoe trip down the river--and promptly began to relive the death of his mother in his dreams. The river grew more polluted as he proceeded south.

> At regular intervals, incoming canals and pipes spit foaming irrigation water back to its source. The air smells of insecticide. Curious, I paddle into the eddy of a spewing canal, test the water with my right hand, and paddle back into the current. For an hour, my hand feels lit by Bengay.

This dream came to him in the Black Canyon Wilderness Area in Nevada:

> I dream of Mom announcing that she's leaving Dad [an emotionally distant military scientist], as in divorce. But even while sound asleep I reconstruct reality by thinking that she's leaving because she's dying. The dream jumps through time and has me trying to console Mom about her mother dying: She wails, pushing me away.
>
> I bolt upright in my sleeping bag and wake up by unzipping the tent door to make certain the trees remain underwater, that the reservoir is not crowding my camp. I'm safe, but the rotting algae on the shoreline stinks like a septic field.

He assumed he'd been mulling over her recent death in dreamtime, not suspecting that his dreamtime "mom" could be the river personified trying to get his attention.

At the end of the trip: "After being unable to let her go, I've realized that the death of a mother or a river is too much to bear. It is only fitting, if we want meaning in our lives, for us to carry these losses everywhere we go. To remember." His mother's name was Kay, which means "Pure."

> The deeper our United States sinks into industrialism, urbanism, militarism--with the rest of the world doing its best to emulate America--the more poignant, strong, and appealing becomes Thoreau's demand for the right of every man, every woman, every child, every dog, every tree, every snail darter, every lousewort, every living thing, to live its own life in its own way at its own pace in its own square mile of home. Or in its own stretch of river.
> — Edward Abbey, *Down the River*

Remembrance retains its relevancy and sparkle, I was learning from the exhausted river, only to the degree it flows forward into transformative action on behalf of the wellsprings of human and nonhuman vitality.

East of Eden:
Owens Valley and Mono Lake

Wallace Stegner was right, I reflected as I drove westward through the stark, sharp colors of the Mojave Desert Preserve. Natural beauty far surpassed our national fixation on garden, lawn, and greenery.

Mojave is thought to mean "alongside water." The river-cut desert given this name covers a fifth of California to extend eastward to the northwestern boundary of Arizona with Nevada, northward to the latitude of Beatty, Nevada, westward to the eastern edge of the Sierra Nevada, and southward to the outhern side of Joshua Tree and Interstate 10, with its center near Shoshone, CA. The Shoshone tribe are the oldest culture in the Mojave, but the U.S. Government labeled them "squatters" long ago and never gave them parkland. The Halchidmoma and Kohuana lived to the east and the Chemehuevi, Serrano, and Desert Cahuilla to the west. Members of these cultures considered dreaming to be an art.

This desert, which includes Death Valley, Las Vegas, Lake Mead, part of the Grand Canyon, Needles, and Joshua Tree, draws a young (less than ten thousand years old) transition zone between the Great Basin, the Sonoran Desert, coastal California, and the Colorado Plateau. Here in the rain shadow of the Sierra Nevada, Tehachapi, and San Bernardino Mountains, rainfall reaches only four to fifteen inches a year, depending, with most of the spotty storms rolling over the eastern regions. The Mojave's two primary waterways, the Mojave and Amargosa Rivers, descend into the desert floor by the time they reach Soda Lake. The Amargosa used to touch Lake Tecopa, eighty-five square miles and over four hundred feet deep, before it dried up half a million years ago.

> The desert floras shame us with their cheerful adaptations to the seasonal limitations. Their whole duty is to flower and fruit, and they do it hardly, or with tropical luxuriance, as the rain admits. It is recorded in the report of the Death Valley expedition that after a year of abundant rains, on the Colorado desert was found a specimen of Amaranthus ten feet high. A year later the same species in the same place matured in the drought at four inches. One hopes the land may breed like qualities in her human offspring, not tritely to "try," but to do.
>
> — Mary Austin

Because of the dryness of this place of extremes, with itstemperature fluctuations, widely varying evapotranspiration rates, and unforeseen flash floods over sun-baked ground, much of the life here waits for water while conserving energy in anticipation of sudden moisture. Much of the plant life consists of low, open evergreens and drought-deciduous shrubs. Near water dwell mesquites, cottonwoods, non-native tamarisks, ocotillo, arrow weed, desert willow, and seepwillow; elsewhere, near and out from semi-dry playas, grow yucca, paloverde, salt grass, desert rumpet, Mormon tea, creosote, and pickleweed. Water-conserving rodents make up two-thirds of the mammals in the Mojave. Pupfish swim in springs rimmed with green algae, cattails, and ferns; bats roost in abandoned mine shafts; wild burros roam the hillsides; and toads, lizards, squirrels, orioles, iguanas, sidewinders, leopard frogs, and canyon tree frogs wind their way around thick-shelled tortoises dragging themselves forward like the tanks that once maneuvered out here.

Trickster brought death into the world (say the old stories) and, evidently, ghost towns to the Mojave. Oatman, Arizona, was a gold-mining town, and silver was dug at Calico, California. The train stopped at Kelso, and one day stopped forever. Towns more recent sit abandoned and decomposing in the wake of Route 66's death by interstate.

Deaths of native species rode in on the wheels of military and recreational vehicles. Even one drive through terrain compacts its soil, alters its runoff patterns, and introduces non-native species like saltcedar, cheatgrass, flixweed, barley, horsehound, Russian knapweed, Sahara mustard, ravennagrass, Johnsongrass, yellow starthistle, and red brome whose litter feeds raging summer wild-fires. Livestock and water sources like fountains, pools, and irriga-tion also introduce invasives, diminish biodiversity, and disrupt natural fire regimes. Compaction that can outlast a century aids nonnatives that prefer compressed soil. At the end of the 1970s, 9% of Mojave Desert flora was nonnative; by the end of the 1990s, 13%. Most of the invasives are annuals that propagate rapidly.Of the natives, many under threat--phacelia, Mojave aster, prickly poppy, California poppy, Parry saltbush, Mojave sage, yuccas, brittlebush, creosote (some thousands of years old), bursages, and other scrubs--a fourth grow nowhere else in the world.

Nitric acid, ammonia, and ozone drift into Joshua Tree to weak-ening its plant communities, and air pollution from the Los Angeles Basin now hangs ominously over the western Mojave. Some of the pollution emanates from jets and armored cars patrolling Fort Irwin, China Lake, the Marine Corps Combat Center, Nellis Air Force Base, and the Nevada Test Site. Some jets fly over Randsburg, where arsenic levels found in old mine tailings reach nearly half a million times what is deemed safe by the federal government. All told, the U.S. military, the world's largest unregulated polluter, con-trols over 2.59 hectares: more than the Bureau of Land Management or the National Park Service.

South of Death Valley I cut eastward into Searles Valley and, caught between the geographical hammer of China Lake Naval

Weapons Center and the anvil of Fort Irwin, halted briefly at Trona. The dirt was white. Trona is a sodium carbonate used to make washing soda and glass. A mineral extraction foundry filled the air with sour smells and a steady, clanking roar that reminded me of noisy alien fighting machines in *The War of the Worlds*. A market where I stopped to buy a sandwich was tended by a cashier wearing a hook for a hand. Outside, a black plywood lady lounged in a black plywood bathtub.

In 1849, a band of eager Forty-Niners got lost in a wide, dry depression on what is now California's eastern edge. Forced to abandon their wagons and eat their cattle, they were rescued by help organized by Young William Manley and John Rogers. Looking back, the survivors said, "Goodbye, Death Valley," and the name stuck.

Should it have? Other names in the valley seem to suggest so: Coffin Peak, the Funeral Mountains, Deadman Pass, Dry Bone Canyon, Dante's View, Hell's Gate, the Devil's Golf Course, Skull Gulch, Cemetery Mine, Misery Lake.... An old promotional flyer barks,

Would You Enjoy a Trip to Hell?

Probably you would not. At least we will suppose so. Even if you would enjoy it there is no hurry about starting. If you are going you will do so sometime without having to plan ahead of time.

You Might Enjoy a Trip to Death Valley, Now!

It has all the advantages of hell without the inconveniences....

Yet the valley isn't a realm of Pluto like Monterey County, where wealth and depth seem to go together always, where numerous outlaws and David Jacks have liked to live, and where the underwater canyons along the coast yield up mysterious new fishes every year. Roughly a hundred people have died in Death Valley, not a lot compared to the average large city. It's the kinds of deaths that ring the bells thematic in the key of Trickster. Three emigrants traveling from Yuma without adequate planning and hasty for a shorter route reached Yaqui Well parched and hungry. One drank his fill and died; the others drank less and were sick, but lived. The well is said to be haunted like the old Vallecito Station, where a "Lady in White" still waits in bridal dress for her stage to arrive. In the 1930s, miners claimed to have found an immense underground chamber filled with mummies equipped with armbands and golden spears. Frank Norris ended his novel *McTeague* with the protagonist handcuffed to a dead man. In the 1960s, two men who decided to scuba dive at night in The Devil's Hole and never returned left behind only a flashlight. As the sixties closed, the infamous Manson family heard about an abandoned mining claim and staked their own at Spahn Ranch.

The Paiutes named the valley *Tomesha*, "Ground Afire," but *tomesha* derives--possibly by distortion--from Tumbisha, the largest Native village in the valley, there at the mouth of Furnace Creek. In Shoshone *tumbisha* means "rock" and "coyote." Misery Lake owes its name to a mirage, another reminder of how Trickster brought death into the world. Unwary travelers weary with heat see strange things here. J. Ross Browne, 1868: "I have even heard complaint that the thermometer failed to show the true heat because the mercury dried up; everything dries; wagons dry; men dry; chickens dry; there is no juice left in anything, living or dead, by the close of summer." But the Kelso Dunes sing when in motion, dry-adapted life is abundant, and the winters can bring frost.

For seekers attuned to land, Death Valley sends visions and dreams, but for the hubristic it sets a three-million-acre trap into dessicated depths. The first whites here came in 1830 to trade horses and lost them instead. Gold-seekers lost oxen and wagons and even guides, only to see piles of castaway precious metal in the distance, winking but never to be found again. Clothes, jewels, and other accoutrements of persona have been left to rot under the hot sun. In the fall of 1853, John Ebbetts and other surveyors seeking a railroad route across the continent wandered almost dead of thirst through Eureka Valley while missing numerous springs in the Sylvania Mountains. The team was forced to skin some of their mules for footwear. The rest were shot by a Native guide who faded away into the night. A Department of Agriculture expedition led by naturalist Clinton Hart Merriam succeeded, but only after going astray, and only after two men lost their horses and had to walk forty miles in three days.

Little wonder the first to guess, in 1891, that the valley floor might lie below sea level was outlaw and murderer Joel Brooks. A dozen later surveyors came up with a dozen different depth measurements, and the same with maximum summer temperatures. The lowest point in Death Valley is actually Badwater two hundred and eighty-two feet below sea level down in the spreading rift that tore Baja from North America.

Exploration of the valley began in earnest after 1850 when Jim Martin brought forth a small piece of silver-lead ore and had it hammered into a gunsight. This prompted Lieutenant Robert Vailey of Oroville to look for "gunsight silver" and, finding none, to market his own false ore. Charles Breyfogle, whose reputation coined "breyfogling" as a quest for lost mines, showed off small, gold-specked rocks to the tune of vague stories about where he had found them. The Palmetto mining district was named in 1866 after Joshua trees mistaken for palms, while miners over in Lida Valley hacked at a silver vein named the Cinderella. As Eliphalet P. Rains sold fake silver in the Panamints, real silver was found south of Resting Spring on the old Spanish Trail at a site William Brown and his brother Robert named the site The Balance. Lack of water killed their grand scheme. (A Star Trek film shot in the valley in 2002 referred to Nemesis, mythic restorer of balances. An earlier film pitted Captain Picard against a black-garbed enemy who destroyed a star named Amargosa: "Time is the fire in which we burn...") In 1886 Pinney's Richmond Mining and Milling Company's first mill run burned up, and the second was scattered into fragments by a great, unexpected November wind.

Colonel John Jewks claimed to have found hundreds of lost wagons and dead immigrants killed by a deadly but invisible gas wafting through the valley. He escaped it by going in on tall stilts, then lighting a bonfire to ignite all of it at once. The resulting explosion, he claimed, barbequed many buzzards and turned all his hair white just like that.

In the mid-1880s broker and vigilante leader William Tell Coleman found kernite deposits containing borax, a salt used to clean laundry and to fashion glass, insecticide, and pottery. By 1975, waste beside a huge pit dug by Tenneco to mine borax would be visible from Dante's View. On the other hand, Jasper Stanley and two other prospectors from Los Angeles claimed to have found an epsom salt mine and with Thomas Wright turned the "discovery" into a American Magnesium Company that sold shares before subsidizing. To cleansers and laxatives was added white talc, marble, Tecopa ore, niter, potash, and the poison that founded and funded the PDQ Cyanide Company in 1899. A claim about finding an entire mountain made of copper turned out, alas, to be false.

In 1901, burgeoning mining in Nevada depleted the population of Death Valley. Ballarat, a town ringed by hundreds of mines, was hit hard:

> The exodus of 1901 dealt Ballarat a crippling blow, and the elements tried to do the rest. A terrible storm ripped through the town that summer, smashing several houses, killing one woman, and kiting off everything loose. Up in the Panamints it unleashed a cloudburst that sent flash floods down the canyons to the north, destroying the little Gem mill in Jail Canyon and sweeping away many of the abandoned buildings in old Panamint. A year later, just as Ballarat was starting to recover, another cyclone wrought even more havic, tearing the roofs from Calloway's hotel and other adobes and leveling every frame building that was left. Then came a rush of water down Pleasant Canyon, demolishing Anthony's old mill, which he had fortunately just sold to a Boston company, and flooding the tattered town.
>
> — Richard Lingenfelter

In July 1905, Walter Edward Scott refurbished the lost mine story and rode around promoting it from Los Angeles to Chicago on a train he named the Death Valley Coyote. After writing a novel about all this, starring in a film about himself, and landing thirty-nine arrests on various charges related to grifting, Scotty admitted in court to being a fraud and, in 1912, retired to Twentynine Palms with his long-suffering wife Jack. His contrition lasted all of three years, about the length of time taken by former colleague Albert Johnson to talk himself into believing in Scotty again despite all that had happened. After the two reunited for a few Death Valley vacation outings, Johnson bought the Straininger Ranch in Grapevine Canyon so his friend would have a place to stay between trips. But as the solitary Spanish-style structure rose into the dry air, passers-by wondered: Is there a secret mine out here after all? "I am building myself a castle," replied Scotty, "so I can sit back and laugh at the world." In time, however, Trickster's curse on unwanted wayfarers descended again on Scotty as he noted with jealousy that his castle got more attention than he did. He was finally ejected from Death Valley when the federal government declared it a national park.

C. C. Julian liked trains too, and he liked bringing promoters to Death Valley on them in 1926 to ogle Western Lead, his "million-dollar baby" of a mine in Titus Canyon. When the entire operation was exposed as an intricate stage set, he moved on to Oklahoma, where he set up a fake oil venture, and then to Shanghai, where he failed and killed himself. Curtis Howe Springer enjoyed more initial success by staring the Zzyzx Mineral Springs and Health Resort Spa at Soda Springs in 1944. He came up with "Zzyzx," pronounced "zy-sicks," to claim the very last space in the dictionary. Unfortunately, Springer's Boulevard of Dreams led not only to his spa, but to jail time for claiming twelve thousand acres of federal land. The Desert Studies Center and a habitat for chub now occupy the spot. Nevertheless, Springer got at least part of his wish granted because the town named after his resort is listed dead last by the United States Board on Geographical Names. The name also appeared as the title of a 2005 film in which a man was killed by a golf club and a widow walked into the desert bearing cash taken from her dead husband's artificial leg.

Springer also inaugurated the kitschification of the ancient tradition of visionary episodes in the valley where shimmering images lead the way to paradise or perdition (usually perdition). According to George Van Tassel of Giant Rock Airport, spacemen called the Ashtar Command landed near his home to offer him and his followers knowledge published in his *Proceedings of the College of Universal Wisdom*. He channeled it while seated in a hidden cavern beneath Giant Rock. Afterwards the grateful Van Tassel designed a domed building materialized from extraterrestrial blueprints to develop antigravity and time travel for the backward human species. This Integratron now functions as a seminar center.

I got a small taste of Trickster when I called Death Valley to book a hotel room not far from Panamint. I was told there would be wireless available, but when I checked in, I found a sparsely furnished room with no Internet and no phone, which was irritating, and no television, which was fine with me. Isolated, then, like the valley itself. Happy for an excuse to be out of contact with the rest of the world, I drove into Death Valley to admire the astounding colors of blue mountains darkening into purple as the sun set behind them while gently daubing the opposite range in vivid red and orange. Over those crags rose a full blue moon. Unintentionally perfect timing.

Why (I wondered) so much Trickster presence in so much desert?

In a word, transformation, of which Trickster is the master and agent. Transformation of unconsciousness into consciousness, Prime Matter into Philosopher's Stone, higher to lower and back again, decrepit old pantheons into vital new ones. Trickster the psychopomp slips between realms, worlds, eras, states of being. So does desert. Five thousand years ago, Death Valley swam with grass. Aridity from many sources, including massive erosion and deforestation, now dominates 47% of the globe, and it's spreading. If the ecological damage being done continues, one day Earth will look a lot like Frank Herbert's Dune.

Edward Abbey wrote from Ash Meadows, where he composed the final chapters of *Desert Solitaire*, that the desert had altered his senses. He was no mystic, but many, including the Desert Fathers, have come to arid and isolated landscapes for self-purification. "Beatified borax," a cynic might reply, but here I too felt a grounding strength, clarity, alertness, and spaciousness. This place, I sensed, knew exactly what it was. It felt peaceful in spite of everything dug and mined out of it. I looked around and saw everything layered, rocks in particular. I tapped the crusted ground with my knuckles and heard a series hollow knocks.

After camping here in 1984, ecophilosophers Arne Naess and George Sessions worked out a platform for a "deep ecology" able to move below a "shallow" concern with fixes and surface facts to analyze how and why entire societies now devastate the surface of our world as though it were just another resource to consume. How did we come to feel so separated from the rest of nature? To see ourselves as above it, or even as masters of its unfathomable complexities? The platform began with eight principles:

> The well-being and flourishing of human and nonhuman Life on Earth have value in themselves. These values are independent of the usefulness of the nonhuman world for human purposes.
>
> Richness and diversity of life forms contribute to the realizations of these values and are also values in themselves.
>
> Humans have no right to reduce this richness and diversity except to satisfy vital human needs.
>
> The flourishing of human life and cultures is compatible with a substantial decrease of human population. The flourishing of nonhuman life requires such a decrease.
>
> Present human interference with the nonhuman world is excessive, and the situation is rapidly worsening.
>
> Policies must therefore be changed. These policies affect basic economic, technological, and ideological structures. The resulting state of affairs will be deeply different from the present.

The ideological change is mainly that of appreciating life quality (dwelling in situations of inherent value) rather than adhering to an increasingly higher standard of living. There will be a profound awareness of the difference between big and great.

Those who subscribe to the foregoing points have an obligation to directly or indirectly try to implement the necessary changes.

Deep ecology never went mainstream, and it's easy to see why. The notion that the rest of nature has its own value and worth apart from ours insults the industrial/toddler sense of "mine because I want it" entitlement. Achieving full, responsible humanness will require personally *and* collectively outgrowing the primitive impulse to take without giving in return and then mining and whining to force its availability. The alternative to maturity waits in the desert of barren selfishness all around us.

Owens Valley is a land between, a place tucked behind high mountains, arid yet soaked in water history, draped in desert vegetation yet remembered for its verdant farms, sparsely dotted with towns--some no more than dreams on a map. It exists between stories, between vitality and decline, between granite mountains.

— Rebecca Ewan

ROUTE 395 IS A being unto itself, as I found while driving it northward toward the Owens Valley east of the Sierra Nevada. From Interstate 15 near Hesperia the highway runs north to British Columbia. Like an orphan, it never meets its parent, Route 95, connecting only through the third party presence of U.S. 195. It is an orphan prone to many extremes: dry, desert, snow, hot springs, the sheer back wall of the Sierra, ancient Mono Lake, younger Mammoth Lakes, recent avalanches, the oldest trees in the world, Mt. Whitney the highest point in the lower forty-eight states, and tricky Death Valley the lowest.

On my left, to the west, the immense Sierra Nevada ("Great Snowy Mountains") lifted its granitic bulk fourteen thousand feet above the Mojave Desert. With the Central Valley under its west slope and the Great Basin rain shadow under its east, the range covers five degrees of latitude--more than half the length of California--before diving three hundred miles later under layers of volcanic rock near Mount Lassen. Twenty million years ago a shallow inland sea lapped the base of a range only three thousand feet high, but the mountains were already rising and, though long sculpted by glaciers, rise even today. Magma from colliding plate tectonics mixed with and melted the shallower continental rock to produce granites emplaced as early as two hundred and ten million years ago. Westward-washing streams cutting into auriferous veins in the granite pushed gold downhill to be found much later by impetuous men calling themselves Argonauts and Forty-Niners.

Cliffs and steep mountains rose high on my left. The western slope of the Sierra rises gradually over forty to sixty miles of grade, but on this side peaks reach so abruptly for the sky that European settlers could not cross them until 1827. The first wagon train, the Murphy-Stephens party, lumbered through in 1844. Between Donner Summit and Walker Pass, most of the passes crouch higher than some mountain peaks. 395 clings to the cliffs from Mojave to Susanville.

> The whole Sierra along the line of faultage has the contour of a wave about to break. It swings up in long water-shaped lines from the valley of the San Joaquin and rears its jagged crest above the abrupt desert shore. Seen from close under, some of these two- and three-thousand-foot precipices have the pitch of toppling waters.
>
> — Mary Austin

The Numu (Paiute) legends record that Hawk and Fish-eater raised the Sierra to hold back the waters of an immense ocean whose presence lingers in seashells and salt in the floor of the Great Central Valley.

High above me opened Walker Pass. Joseph Walker of the Bonneville Expedition heard about the pass from Native locals and entered after abandoning wagons on the shores of Owens Lake, hiding their equipment, and burning wagon wood for warmth. Walker came through again in 1843 while leading a party of immigrants. His name was bestowed on this slice of terrain by John C. Fremont. The major led a military expedition against Native Californians in 1833 and a mapping party into the Eastern Sierra in 1845. Fremont further blessed the region by losing a cannon near Bridgeport.

Names matter here, where the long, heavy shadows of Adam and Cain lay across the thirsty land. Here stands Mt. Whitney named after geologist Josiah Whitney of the 1860 Geological Survey of California that ran out of funding but finished because he paid for it to. Whitney was famous for his political naivete and for a personality as craggy and abrasive as the chunk of granite named after him. Whitney, incidentally, means "white island," a marker of isolation. Josiah, the monotheist reformer king of Judah after his father was assassinated, fell by murder himself.

Also in Fremont's party were the murderous Kit Carson whose last name, given later to the capital of Nevada, means "son of marsh-dwellers," and Ed Kern ("small dark one"), for whom Kern County was named. Fremont ("free mountain") named Lake Owens after his guide Richard Owings, "a good mountaineer and a good shot." "Owing" and "Owens" both derive from names that mean "well-born" and that could link to the Gaulish god Esus depicted cutting branches from a tree with an axe. Like Cain, Esus seems a shadowy, mythic agriculturalist cast out of collective knowing. In the thirteenth century, Eóghan MacDubhghaill fought for Scottish independence from Norway. In the fourteenth, Owen Glendower fought for Welsh independence from England. In the early 1800s, Richard Owen of Manchester, having lost all faith in religion, promoted socialism and fought for workers' rights. In Irish mythology, Éogan mac Durthacht, king of Fernmag, fought Ulster, changed sides, and treacherously murdered Naoise, the unlucky husband of Dierdre. MacDubhghaill has been compared to the god-king Nuada

Airgetlam whose leadership pitted the Tuatha de Danaan upstarts against the indigenous Fir Bolg and Formorians.

Flanked by the granitic Sierra Nevada and the sedimentary-capped White-Inyo ranges, the valley that became Owens proved a convenient passage between Southern California and Salt Lake City. Nine to twenty miles wide, ninety long, and circled by deserts, it is, like Death Valley, only a few million years old and bounded by faults in perpetual grinding motion. Extremes rise and fall on every side. Mt. Whitney, the Inyo Volcanic Chain, still-active Palisade Glacier, and other heights and peaks soarover ancient depths such as the valley itself, Mono Lake, Long Valley, Bridgeport Valley, and, farther below, magma feeding more than fifty volcanies, many still active enough to mix cold snow with hot springs. "Frost and fire," noted John Muir, "working together in the making of beauty," from asymetrical, sky-filled lakes to the hexagonal basalt columns of the Devil's Postpile. He called this "a country of wonderful contrasts."

Wide variances in temperature and altitude support an unusual range of flora and fauna. Desert scrub marches westward before giving ground before alpine tundra, woodland, forest, and wetland. The wandering eye finds Jeffrey pine, aspen, creosote, foxtail pine, and more than a thousand species of plants, among them colorful wildflowers, Great Basin sagebrush, pinyon, juniper, and hardy perennials with extensive root systems and waxy surfaces on leaves. Sparse greenery and what water there is supports over eighty animal species: mule deer, sage grouse, bighorn sheep, chuckwalla, golden trout, phalaropes, coyote, black-tailed jackrabbit, forty species of reptiles and amphibians, and three hundred bird species, most of them short-distance migrants that stay for the summer and move upslope as the year progresses.

Which makes geomythic sense, for in this graben traveled by semi-nomadic Shoshones and Paiutes long before restless farmers and soldiers and miners came through, Tahquitz the Trickster retreats before the archetypal struggle between Cain and Abel.

> The nature of a land determines in some wise the manner of the life there.
>
> —Mary Austin

Richard Owings crossed the Sierra without ever seeing the lake or valley named for him. Leroy Vining, a gold-seeker who found no fortune in either Mono Basin or Tioga Pass, became the first white settler in the Eastern Sierra after building a sawmill in the canyon named after him to sell lumber and firewood to other other prospectors and Cain-raising drifters. By the 1860s, vast stands of pinyon and Jeffrey pine had already fallen to the busy saw.

The valley had protected the Numu (Paiutes) from mission-building padres but could not guard them from caravans of miners on their way to the Comstock strike in Nevada. As children of Coyote adept at moving with harvest cycles, the Numu had also taken pride, as had Abel, in skillful hunting, but falling trees and clogging streams decimated game even as cattle and heavy-booted settlers trampled food plants. When the Numu fought back, their way of life jolted (as Mary Austin put it) from its foundations and displaced, the California Volunteers, replacements for the army off fighting in the Civil War, arrived to establish Camp Independence on July 4, 1862. Under Lieutenant Colonel George Evans of the Second Cavalry, the Volunteers took up positions to block the Numu from their food stores in the White-Inyo foothills. More than a thousand starving Numu surrendered and were marched off to Fort Tejon, but only eight hundred and fifty arrived. From there they were sent to the San Sebastian Reservation.

When some of those left behind in the Owens Valley killed Mary McGuire and her son in Haiwee Meadow, an armed party retaliated by murdering a Numu camp of forty-one on the shores of Owens Lake. Tales surfaced that the cold, mineral-rich lake crystallized and preserved the bodies fallen into it. Near Mammoth Lakes, Jeffrey pines began to defoliate as Pandora moth larvae once eaten by the Numu now proliferated unchecked.

By the end of the 1800s, ranching and farming supplanted mining. As Numu survivors were forced to work in the fields, pioneers eagerly seized miles of ditches and small earthen dams to irrigate apples, peaches, plums, aprocots, wheat, corn, hay, oats, barley, and potatoes. While greening what seemed to them a barren wilderness they set up towns and ranches. One was *Manzanar*, "apple." *Kearsarge*, from a Native word for "mountain peak," was given to a town by citizens proud that a Union sloop by that name had sunk the Confederate vessel *Alabama*.

In 1872, a massive earthquake destroyed Lone Pine, burying twenty-six in stone and brick, but spared Independence, where where partitions and joists shielded inhabitants from falling walls of timber. Once again the temporary held sway in the valley over the supposedly permanent, settled, and rooted.

> One who builds his house on a water scar or the rubble of a steep slope must take chances. So they did in Overtown who built in the wash of Argus water, and at Kearsarge at the foot of a steep, tree-less swale. After twenty years Argus water rose in the wash against the frail houses, and the piled snows of Kearsarge slid down at a thunder peal over the cabins and the camp, but you could con-ceive that it was the fault of neither the water nor the snow.
>
> — Mary Austin

A strangely prophetic event took shape in 1883 when a tunnel was dug to drain the Golden Trout Creek into the Kern River to bring water to Kern County farmers whose crops were withering with drought. The tunnel collapsed, and when it was turned into a ditch, that collapsed as well. The site where this occurred received the name Tunnel Meadow. An earthly foreshadowing of the water wars to come?

> I like that name the Indians give to the mountain of Lone Pine, and find it pertinent to my subject,-- Oppapago, The Weeper. It sits eastward and soli-tary from the lordliest ranks of the Sierras, and above a range of little, old, blunt hills, and has a bowed, grave aspect as of some woman you might have known, looking out across the grassy barrows of her dead.
>
> — Mary Austin

Austin, who referred to the valley as a "land of lost rivers," moved here in 1900 and, ensconced in a brown house under a willow tree, began work on her book *The Land of Little Rain*. Born at midnight into a family full of depression and death, unconventional Austin wasn't one to stand on any but tribal ceremony. Dream animals had taught the young Artemis who helped raise a little brother a secret Anglo-Saxon language. "A committee of ladies...used to call on me occasionally to ask what I meant by taking part in Indian dances. There was a suspicion that my interest in these things was touched by failure to apprehend the proper social distinctions." Instead, she sought to write "books that you can walk around in." This served her after righteous Methodists barred her from participating in the local theater.

College graduate Mary Hunter came to California from Illinois after her brother Jim moved to Pasadena to buy land. At Fort Tejon she met General Edward Beale, founder of the ranch and of California's reservation system. "It was into Beale's hands the California division of the camel herd, which Jefferson Davis designed to be natural transportation for the Great American Desert, was delivered." He showed her around, and, noting her growing interest in matters Californian, fed her curiosity by providing maps, historical accounts, and scientific survey reports. The camels scattered, but Mary's interest did not.

> There was something else there besides what you find in the books; a lurking, evasive Something, wistful, cruel, ardent; something that rustled and ran, that hung half-remotely, insistent on being noticed, fled from pursuit, and when you turned from it, leaped suddenly and fastened on your vitals.

Watching how shepherds behaved with dogs convinced her that Story is older than humanity and conveyed even between animals.

By 1890, she had lost her teaching position by failing the math section of the credentialing exam and by being found insufficiently attractive by the superintendent of schools. In desperation she became engaged to a wannabe farmer from an old missionary family. Possessed of an old-school disregard for women as intelligent partners, Wallace Austin failed to tell his new wife about his health problems; as a result, her daughter Ruth was born retarded after two full days of labor.

Educated by the University of California, Wallace, trained as a teacher, maintained a mysteriously stubborn refusal to teach. He was better at spending quietly on credit. Mary took a teaching job in Bishop, where she lived near the cellar of the Drake Hotel, and in Lone Pine, where she befriended Numus and miners. By 1897 she found herself in a Los Angeles hospital after a nervous breakdown. Upon her return to the Owens Valley, Wallace informed her that he'd resigned from teaching on the assumption that Mary would finish out his term while he sought work in Independence. The following year she collapsed again and sought treatment in Oakland, where she met William James and heard him lecture about the "transmarginal" borders of consciousness.

> On the surface the story of Mary Austin's life in the Owens Valley is one of hardship and domestic woe, which she later described as "long dull months of living interspersed between the few fruitful occasions when I actually came into contact with the Land." Beneath the stifling frustration, however, the seed of her creativity stored energy from the elements around her. Someday it would burst forth in two powerful channels of expression: a passionate, mystical identification with the land and an outrage against the misuse of women's gifts.
>
> — Augusta Fink

Hardships piled on Mary's head: eviction from her house because of credit debts Wallace had failed to warn her about; an eagle stooping down out of the sky to claw Ruth, marking her; the death of her mother, who'd appeared to Mary dressed in white in a dream; protracted illness and worries about money. In spite of all, she publisedh "The Mother of Felipe," to learn Numu methods of prayer, and to teach a second year in spite of her husband's protests.

While bouncing between the Owens Valley and Los Angeles, two regions so soon to be linked by a vampiric aqueduct, Mary Austin met shadowy notables bent on imposing their visions on California. Two were Charles "Don Carlos" Lummis of the *Los Angeles Times*, a Mission-boosting reporter in sandals, red sash, corduroy suit, and felt cowboy hat; and David Starr Jordan, president of Stanford and a leader in the pseudoscientific movement to sterilize genetic undesirables to improve human breeding. Lummis's lukewarm opinion of Austin's powerful writing proved no better than his taste in clothes, but he did tell her about a seaside place named Carmel. One day she would become one of its American founders.

Part of Lummis's devaluation of her writing might have stemmed from her critical views of campy Ramona pageantry and the campaign to control the future of California by romanticizing its past. The southern half of the state bore the brunt: "....The place of the mystery was eaten up, it was made into building lots, cannery sites; it receded before the preemptions of rock crushers and city dumps."

Time did not sweeten her opinion:

> Sometimes I think the frustration of that incomplete adventure is the source of the deep resentment I feel toward the totality of Southern California. It can't possibly be as inchoate and shallow as on its own showing it appears, all the uses of natural beauty slavered over with the impudicity of a purely material culture. Other times, away from it, I wake in the night convinced that there are still uncorrupted corners from which the Spirit of the Arroyos calls me, wistful with long refusals, and I resolve that next year, or the next at farthest....and I am never able to manage it.

Back in Independence, Wallace built her a house to placate her while directing his attention to local mining and oil projects. In 1903

Mary published *The Land of Little Rain.* In this book she reversed the Adamic anglicization of place names in the Owens Valley by restoring the original Native names taught to her by the Numu.

> The spring winds lift clouds of pollen dust, finer than frankincense, and trail it out over high altars, staining the snow. No doubt they understand this work better than we; in fact they know no other. "Come," say the churches of the valleys, after a season of dry years, "let us pray for rain." They would do better to plant more trees.
>
> — *The Land of Little Rain*

"By God, that woman is the only one who has brains enough to see where this is going," muttered William Mulholland, chief engineer of the Los Angeles Department of Water and Power.

In the summer of 1900, a silver boom in the mines of Tonopah, Nevada led to a feverish demand for Owens Valley fruit, milk, and honey. Finding insufficient water in the Sierra-fed lake and river, farmers of the valley unwisely contacted the Bureau of Reclamation to demand more irrigation. This demand did not go unnoticed in Los Angeles. At the invitation of Mary's brother-in-law Frank Austin, Fred Eaton, founder of Los Angeles Water and Power, scion of the founding family of Pasadena, and boss of Mulholland, showed up in the valley to prepare it, he claimed, for a new Reclamation hydroelectric project. That, he hinted, was why he was investigating, mapping, and buying up property near and around the lake. Meanwhile, engineers quietly spilled the water from reservoirs in Los Angeles to frighten citizens into approving a large bond measure to pay for a new aqueduct laid across the lands bought by Eaton and a small group of Southern California business leaders who knew the city could not sprawl unless it secured enough extra water first.

"Shall the question of domestic water in California be determined by craft and graft and bitterness and long drawn wasteful struggles, or conducted with rightness and dignity to an equal conclusion?" asked Austin. After the aqueduct began draining Lake

Owens, farmers fought back. A few resorted to dynamite. After five Watterson brothers were jailed for embezzelment, their banks in the valley collapsed. As the resulting local depression took hold, the the lake shrank, and croplands dried out, descendants of the generation of settlers who had displaced the Numu and taken over their canals found themselves displaced in turn by the giant aqueduct sucking precious liquid from Payahu Nadu, the valley's original name, drawn from a Numu word for "water." Most residents and farmers departed. So did Mary Austin, leaving behind her husband, who transferred to a Death Valley chemical plant, and her daughter Ruth, placed in a sanitarium in Santa Clara until her death twelve years later. Mary headed for Carmel, from where she would journey far, meeting the Pope, Isadora Duncan, H.G. Wells, Gilbert Chesterton, Joseph Conrad, George Bernard Shaw, Anne Martin, Emmeline Pankhurst, Emma Goldman, Margaret Sanger, Ida Tarbell, and Lincoln Steffens, with whom she had an affair. Fannie Hurst and Willa Cather became her friends. But a persistent pain in her left arm reminded her of deep wounding in the Owens Valley.

Now in firm control of most of the valley, the Los Angeles Department of Water and Power congratulated itself for preserving the valley from suburbanization. To this day most of what remains of a place once called Paradise, Land of Plenty, and Land of Milk and Honey is administered by Water and Power, the Forest Service, and the Bureau of Land Management. By 1941, the Long Valley Dam built on the Owens River Gorge impounded Crowley Lake Reservoir. An arm of the aqueduct reached out for Mono Lake.

The depopulated valley's remaining residents got by on tourism, movie-making (*The Roundup*, *The Lone Ranger*, *Firely*, *Lost Horizon*, *Gunda Din*, and of course *Water, Water Everywhere*), tungsten mining near Bishop, soda ash recovery from the lake, and land management employment. Before dying in a car crash, Father John Crowley helped found the Inyo-Mono Associates to bring tourism and recreation to the Eastern Sierra. Tourism, including trout fishing in Bishop, brought in double the revenue, it turned out, of ranching, mining, and lumbering put together. But as long as the voice of this land went unheard, its rough-cut features the raw, unconscious, unspoken material of mind, habitation, and culture, the legacy of exile and displacement would grind grimly on.

> The slowly shifting human occupation over eight millennia are part of the cultural landscape of the Owens Valley. Since the mid-nineteenth century, human settlement has paralleled more cataclysmic geologic patterns, going along in one direction until some social fault shifts or some human volcano erupts, causing the course of life to meander, to go another way.
>
> — Rebecca Ewan

The year is 1942. Ten thousand one hundred and twenty-one loyal Americans accused by political opportunists of being enemies of the state arrive at the Manzanar War Relocation Center to live in one square mile of thirty-six blocks ringed by barbed wire and, in the distance, the cold peaks of distant mountains. Every two-thou-sand-square-foot block holds an average of twenty people.

Shivering and bewildered, the inmates organize cleaning parties to manage the unmanageable dust. Once moved in they maintain water, storage, and sewage and set up their own repair parties, schools, medical wards, clothing shops, victory gardens, newspapers, and flower gardens. They try to keep out curious snakes. They share their crude dinner tables with hungry Numu construction laborers. They write poetry and wish they could use the toilet unobserved and look past the fences at the valley where Abel is eternally attacked by Cain who finds himself exiled in turn from Eden.

The original plan was to imprison all Japanese-Americans in the Owens Valley, but Water and Power complained about the amount of water they would need.

> It began as truth, as fact,
> That is, at least the numbers, the statistics,
> are there for verification:
> 10 camps, 7 states,
> 120,113 residents....

The F.B.I swooped in early,
taking our elders in the process--

for "subversive" that and this.

People ask: "Why didn't you protest?"
Well, you might say: "They had hostages."
    —Lawson Fusao Inada, from "Legends from
                          Camp"

In three years, enough of the nation came to its senses to allow the closure of Manzanar. By then, four hundred seventy-nine babies had been born in camp and several adults had died there. An entire citizenry no longer felt like Constitutionally protected Americans who need never fear illegal search, seizure, and incarceration without trial. They had been set apart, forcibly, and nothing could guarantee that it would never happen again.

Isolation
is the most profound aspect
of Manzanar.
    — Richard Stewart, from "Pilgrimage"

On April 24, 2004, the Interpretive Center at Manzanar National Historic Site opened in the restored high school auditorium built by the Japanese in 1944. Two thousand and five hundred people attended. The Owens Valley Spirit, a Numu drumming group, performed for the occasion. Former inmate Mary Kageyama Nomura sung, "When I Can." She had sung in camp, too.

I pulled off into the dirt and got out to photograph a stone sentry post. The Sierra wore a white cloak that threw into contrast a wooden guard tower. A Registered Historical Landmark plaque noted the place, Manzanar, and the event, imprisonment:

MAY THE INJURIES AND HUMILIATION
SUFFERED HERE AS A RESULT OF HYSTERIA,

RACISM, AND ECONOMIC EXPLOITATION
NEVER EMERGE AGAIN.

A worthy aim, but here we were in the twenty-first century with
madmen and madwomen posing as patriots while calling for the
racial profiling, federal investigation, and polical isolation of
Mexicans, Muslims, and Arabs. Imagine everyone presuming to run
for high office being required to come here and learn what has happened, remember from the heart, and reflect on it here.

> The valley's slim profile and steep relief seem to
> force contrary things together--Manzanar and
> Independence, cattle and backpackers, alpine fell-
> fields and desert sand, banal conversations and
> majestic views from Whitney Peak, meadow wild-
> flowers and twisted pines, Numu subjugation and
> settlers' loss of land, abundant water and aridity,
> the City of Los Angeless and wilderness recreation.
> — Rebecca Ewan

....And to think about the state of the land.

Here, where Numu, farmers, and Japanese Americans were
placed in exile, where John Wayne starred in his first and last west-
erns, where *Star Trek V* shot a desert Paradise City where the
galaxy's outlaws mingled while confined in a dusty bar, the former
Lake Owens has been reduced to a salt flat with a shimmer of briny
pond. Half a million tons of trona are mined from this lakebed to
make glass and detergent. Four million tons of alkali a year--6% of
America's dust--blow from it into the skies above. Rising and coil-
ing, the dust reaches out for, ironically, Los Angeles, the sprawling
destination of so much valley water.

And yet the valley was drying and desertifying even before the
Los Angeles water grab: Abel's Eden gradually erased by Cain's cold
desert. In most of California, aridity, not greenery, has always been
the primary ecological reality. As Marc Reisner wrote in *Cadillac
Desert*,

Desert, semidesert, call it what you will. The point
is that despite heroic efforts and many billions of
dollars, all we have managed to do in the arid West
is turn a Missouri-size section green—and that
conversion has been wrought mainly with nonre-
newable groundwater.

California's immense water projects, and the aqueducts that feed
them, move 81% of the state's water into agricultural empires subsidized by a federal government and politically and fiscally inter-
locked with the chemical industry, Reclamation, construction
firms, the Army Corps of Engineers, and the likes of Chevron, Shell,
Prudential, Tenneco, Mitsubishi, and the Southern Pacific Railroad
(which also owns a sizable chunk of downtown San Francisco).
None of this land would be in production without cheap water
moved around a dry state. As a result, drawdown on aquifers attain-
able by the invention of the centrifugal pump out of mining technology, has accelerated, as have unprecedented overdevelopment,
subdivision, and urbanization. Sprawl, pasture for cows, alfalfa, and
cotton are the true winners of the California water wars. The
depleted land and its inhabitants are the losers.

As with civilizations everywhere, control of water--hydraulic
despotism--erected the interlinked maze of metropolises, freeways,
cities, and factory farms of California. Engineers, architects, attor-
neys, salesmen, growers, railroads, auto plants, power grids, security forces, entire industries, whole bureaucracies occupied brown
lands greened by artificial irrigation. But with irrigation comes
salinization of soil, depletion of groundwater, subsidence,
inevitable siltation of reservoirs, air and water pollution, sacrifice of
fertile fields for subdivided tracts, dying fisheries, drying wetlands.
Irrigation seems a muscular, heroic miracle--until the bill comes
due.

As we discover afresh each day, those forces can
only be held at bay, never vanquished, and that is
where the real vandalism--the financial vandalism

of the future--comes in. Who is going to pay to rescue the salt-poisoned land? To dredge trillions of
tons of silt out of the expiring reservoirs? To bring
more water to whole regions, whole states, dependent on aquifers that have been recklessly mined? To
restore wetlands and wild rivers and other natural
features of the landscape that have been obliterat-
ed, now that more and more people are discovering
that life is impoverished without them?

— Marc Reisner

With the depletion of aquifers, rivers like the once-abundant
Colorado, and the Sierra snowpack, where 65% of the state's water
supply will fall drastically because of global warming, the deserts,
held at bay by decades of irrigation, will reassert themselves in the
Central Valley and in Southern and Eastern California. How will we
adapt? *And Cain went out from the presence of the Lord, and dwelt in the land
of Nod, on the east of Eden....*

An ancient Numu story relates that angry bears made a hole
under Owens Lake one day and set a fire there to dry up the waters.
With nothing more for the people to live on, they were forced to go
away. But eventually they returned, and, wiser now, made do with
the pinyon nuts grown by the wisdom of Nature.

NEAR BIG PINE, UPSTREAM of where the Owens River finds itself
sucked toward Los Angeles, something about the valley undergoes
a subtle shift: of flow, of terrain, of psychic intensity here in a geographic bottleneck between mountain ranges separated by only a
dozen miles or so.

Twenty-five miles east of Big Pine grow the oldest living things
on earth. Some of the bristlecone pines clinging to the White
Mountains have reached the age of four thousand five hundred.
They were seedlings when Pyramids were being built in Egypt and
writing taught in Sumer. The oldest sequoias in the western Sierra
are at least a thousand years younger. Bristlecones achieve longevi-
ty in harsh soil and weather by clinging patiently to dead wood.

They stay in steady touch, as it were, with their ancestry. Greener, faster growers soon perish of heart rot.

The headquarters of the Paiute Shoshone Band resides in Big Pine. In 1924, fifteen-year-old Alice Piper was denied entrance to a Big Pine school for being Native American. Setting a precedent against segregation, the State Supreme Court settled the resulting lawsuit by declaring separate schools for Indians and Asians to be unconstitutional. The real lesson was not for Alice, but for a historically young educational district schooled by a much older Native culture about the nature of inclusivity, fairness, and justice.

Numu elder Hoavadunuki (Anglo name Jack Stewart) attributed his stature in Big Pine's Native community to the power and wisdom of nearby Birch Mountain:

> When I was still a young man, I saw Birch Mountain in a dream. It said to me: 'You will always be well and strong. Nothing can hurt you and you will live to an old age.' After this Birch Mountain came and spoke to me whenever I was in trouble and told me that I would be all right.

After he lived in San Francisco for a few years,

> I saw my mountain in a dream. It rose up in the east and looked for me. It looked first to the south and then to the west, and when it saw me near San Francisco it said: "You must come back soon to your own country and your own people."

> Everything that I sense about mountains--high, vertical, beautiful--echoes with archetypal imagery. Conversely, when I consider the mountain archetype, my mind's eye spontaneously envisions a snow-crested peak piercing through a crown of clouds. Such an image fills me with reverence and fear. My very real self is affected by the image.
>
> — Betsy Perluss

Big Pine also hosts the School of Lost Borders founded by Meredith Little and Steven Foster to conduct vision fasts and quests, rites of passage for adolescents and, later, end-of-life rites for adults. Where else to do such transitional work but in a valley passage by a river?

In the late 1960s, Dr. Steven Foster, an instructor in the Department of Humanities, was fired by San Francisco State University for supporting students during a strike on campus. This opened an opportunity to spend time in the deserts of Nevada, to dialogue with ecopsychology founder Robert Greenway, and to lead wilderness rites of passage ceremonies whose indigenous and cross-cultural roots eventually wound into the performative core of the School of Lost Borders named after a Mary Austin poem praising the land and the Numu name for it.

In an interview with Ann O'Shaughnessy published in Heron Dance (#47), Meredith Smith recalls a solo fast in the desert:

> ....As often happens on a fast, I was questioning things in my life and experiencing a certain despair. I was wondering what it was that carries me on, what is was that could lead me to say YES to life. And the answer came as the word "Beauty." Perhaps there might be a moment of beauty just around the next corner. In some ways I see these "moments of beauty" as authenticity — moments so often found amidst suffering. They can be found in the midst of war. They can be found in a hospital where a mother is losing a child. They are often the places in life where everything is stripped away and all that is left is that moment.

Trust an elder to see the value in beauty. Even at a pragmatic ecological level, people will not protect from destruction what they do not love or appreciate.

> What I've learned through the rites of passage work we've done at Lost Borders is very similar to

what a hospice worker would learn over years of working with the dying. It is the learning that comes from holding a container for the passage, either from one phase of life to the next or from one life to the next. This form of midwifing is about how to listen, how to set aside our own judgments or values, how to empower and honor another human being. And the lessons do not come from book learning, but rather from literally being with people who are dying in all the different ways people die, and are ultimately renewed.

All this echoes the specific characteristics of Owens Valley, place of transition, replacement, mourning, renewal--and marking, the signal of exile and, on its far side, initiation.

Every marking lasts in this dry land. The entire landscape bears scars and wrinkles from endless seasons of human activity and the molten unrest that left volcanic bumps and folds all along the long thin valley.
—Rebecca Ewan

I passed Bishop, where I had learned to fish long ago without suspecting my dad and I of immersion in a myth out of Genesis, frozen Lake Crowley, where I photographed an information stand featuring a man holding a fish ("Enjoyment for Anglers"), and Mammoth Lakes, where my ex-wife and I had stayed for a wintry honeymoon. Perhaps it amused some local god or other to see a man whose name means "crag" consummate his marriage on the flank of a volcano.

Seven hundred and sixty thousand years ago, in Long Valley just southeast of here, an eruption blasted a hundred and fifty cubic miles of debris--more than the volume of Mount Shasta--skyward. This left the seething Long Valley Caldera, and several states blanketed in ash. More eruptions at the caldera's western edge raised pumice-covered domes that merged two hundred thousand years ago into the dacite and rhyolite of Mammoth Mountain. Still active, the hot mountain is often covered in snow that blows through the Mammoth Pass in the Sierra. Although the name "Mammoth" derives from General George Dodge's Mammoth Mining Company, the word itself means, appropriately enough, "earth horn." Of northern Russian origin, the word entered American English in 1802 when a "mammoth" chunk of cheese four feet in diameter and bearing the motto *Rebellion to Tyrants is Obedience to God* found its way to President Jefferson courtesy of a Baptist church in Cheshire, Massachusetts.

The mining camp and settlement did not survive, but the first resort was founded by a man with the improbable name of Charles Wildasinn. Plumes of carbon dioxide emitted by the mountain kill trees and sicken people near Horseshoe Lake on the mountain's south flank. Earthquakes frequently roll through. Although the last blast was two centuries ago, another could arrive at any time.

> Although archetypal motifs are found in myths, fairy tales, legends, and dreams, most of these motifs can be traced to the shapes and patterns found in the natural landscape. Thus, in addition to being a mass of rock, the archetypal mountain is also the cosmic mountain, linking heaven and earth and fastening the four cardinal directions. Similarly, in addition to being an eroded crevice in the earth's surface, the archetypal valley is the valley of shadow and death or, in other cases, a paradisiacal recess flowing with milk and honey. The archetypal motifs that emerge from the natural landscape are as diverse as the landscape itself, and throughout all cultures and locations we find a vast range of archetypes that take on the appearance of mountains, rivers, trees, oceans, caves, and canyons. Archetypes symbolize the union of soul and earth, and from this union is the birth of a world that is living and sensual, full of character and meaning.
>
> — Betsy Perluss

Onward to June Lake, where I stayed one terrible spring as my parents fought so violently and continuously that I ran out of the cabin and sat on a rock on the shore wondering if I should keep running and never return. I was on the point of executing this desperate plan when a vast, and cool sensation seeped into my feet, legs, and rear as they rested on the rocky sand. *No*, said something invisible and autochthonous; and for a moment I would have sworn that the lake had spoken wordlessly to me like an elder giving wisdom with a gesture both powerful and quiet. I took its advice and did not run.

A few miles north of Mono Lake, William "Waterman" Bodey found gold near a bluff. In 1861 a mill and mining town sat there. By 1880 the town was already notorious for its prostitution, gunfights, saloons (sixty-five of them), gambling, and assorted mayhem. Murder was so frequent, especially at night, that residents would joke in the mornings, "Have a man for breakfast?" A little girl whose family moved from San Francisco to Bodie wrote, "Good, by God, I'm going to Bodie"--or, "Goodbye God, I'm going to Bodie," nobody knows for sure. When ill-named businessman Jim Cain (note the name) was caught in bed with his Chinese maid, he killed himself, and, so the story goes, has haunted his former home ever since. A park ranger's wife sleeping overnight in the Cain House felt someone lying on top of her. Ghostly children have been heard playing near the Mendocini House. To this day visitors who take keepsake items from Bodie send them back to the park rangers after hearing about the "Bodie Curse" of bad luck.

Mono Lake is no less antisocial. Even its name sounds as though uttered with unbreakable singularity.

Three million years ago, the Sierra's eastern escarpent fractured and warped, and Mono Basin found itself enclosed by rock, its outlet shut, and its growing bed of sediment overseen by extinct volcanoes to the north, east, and southeast. Like a solitary artist scrounging for materials, the basin gathered glacial, volcanic, and erosional deposits as well as silt, gravel, and pumice washed from adjacent mountains against the day a lake would form to shape these materials into twisting, elaborate designs.

There, with no avenue through the terrain to continue their seaward journey, the waters of Mono
have always gathered and--like a handmirror held
to earth's creation--silently, solemnly reflected
ongoing changes in the land.

— Mark Schlenz

At seven hundred and thirty thousand years of age, Mono Lake
is the oldest living lake in North America. At its most voluminous,
which was thirteen thousand years ago, the lake stretched twenty-
eight miles long, eighteen wide, and nine hundred feet deep. No one
has ever successfully developed, colonized, or cultivated the Mono
Basin. Lieutenant Tredwell Moore returned from warring on the
Yosemite Miwoks with samples of gold ore from the basin in 1852,
prompting prospectors like Lee Vining to invade, but without
enough water to work the claims, mining ceased. An 1860 strike in
Aurora brought roads, settlers, and loggers, but the town closed
again five years later. The same occurred with the 1877 silver rush at
Bodie despite a narrow gauge railroad laid from there around the
east end of Mono Lake.

Swimmers, skiiers, and the ailing showed up to what Mark
Twain described in *Roughing It* as a "solemn, silent, sailless sea" to get
fit, have fun, and recover, but by 1941, when Los Angeles sucked the
lake surface down to forty feet below normal, halving volume and
doubling salinity, Twain's "loneliest tenant of the loneliest spot on
earth" found itself lonelier still, and in jeopardy. A second pipe
arrived in 1970.

The University of California and the Point Reyes Bird
Observatory studied the basin in 1976. They found brine shrimp
endemic to the lake, alkali flies, seventy species of migratory and
nesting birds, and the largest California Gull rookery in the state all
suffering as their supportive ecosystems collapsed. In response,
ornithologist David Gaines and others formed the Mono Lake
research team and environmentalists the Mono Lake Committee.
The Committee, the National Audubon Society, and Friends of the
Earth filed suit to stop the drainage of Mono water. Although
Congress established the Mono Basin National Forest Scenic Area

in 1984, dust storms rising in 1993 prompted the EPA to list the Mono Basin in violation of the Clean Air Act. In a year the State Water Resources Control Board decided that the lake level must be increased.

Gaines, who was killed in a car accident, had written in his *Mono Lake Newsletter*, "If Nature can heal an injured land, it can heal our blighted souls as well. That's why saving Mono Lake is a matter of saving and healing ourselves."

> Sometimes I like to think of us all as part of the exotic landscape, like the salt lake and the tufa that draw the tourists to this town.
> — Martha Cummings

Visiting the ancient sites of my homeland always makes me wonder who lived here long before the Cross and Sword marched into Alta California. The survivors of that campaign had a tough time hanging on, but many of their descendants remain and abide:

> I cannot ignore that this first seasonal snowfall that marks the beginning of winter in our culture occurs on the day I began writing the final draft of Walking Where We Lived. My heart says this isn't a coincidence. My grandparents said stories were to be told only on the snowy days of winter so as not to disturb Rattlesnake, snug in his winter home, because he, in turn, disturbs all other living creatures.
> — Gaylen Lee, Nim (North Fork Mono)

The Nim made seasonal forays to reap their harvests, cooking food in watertight willow baskets, and returned to their permanent homes to settle in for the long winters. The anthropologist Alfred Kroeber believed the word *mona* came from the "flies" around the lake, but their edible, high-protein pupae were called *kutsavi*. In the Nim language *mona* means "top of the hill to to the other side"--of the Sierra threshold separating Mono Basin from the Central Valley and the rest of California. Paoha Island gets its name from the *paoha*, wraths that hover around hot springs.

As elsewhere in California, missionaries who arrived--American here rather than Spanish--tried to forbid the native tongue. They taught that one separate, mighty God oversaw a world without sentience. The Nim of this part of Owens Valley perceived otherwise:

> After Grandma had attended the Presbyterian service for several years, one Sunday she told the preacher she wouldn't be back. He asked why. She replied that for years she'd heard about a person called God who could do so many things, a God she was to worship and ask for help. "I've never seen God or been aware of him," she added. "Every day I go outside and see the trees and flowers, hear the wind, feel the sunshine or the rain or the snow. They talk to me and answer my questions. They are strength when I need them." We never returned.
>
> — Gaylen Lee

The usual Western bias, of course, is to regard this sort of knowledge as superstition. Another, and increasingly common, Western bias among those sophisticated enough to be interested in indigenous lore and spirituality is to idealize such knowledge as Edenically, exotically superior to anything ever attained by non-Natives. The first bias sees only childlike primitives, the second Noble Mystics "in harmony with nature." Both biases ignore three important facts: indigenous tribes composed of fallible human beings have occasionally fallen out of balance with nature and hunted species to extinction; animism as a worldview is found at the roots of every enduring culture; and all long-standing cultural bodies of knowledge evolve whether sanctioned by the West as "scientific" or not.

Knowledge of nature's aliveness might be expressed by Native people in the old terminology, especially as a reaction against colonization and objectification, but the insights and deepenings have never stood still. They are not prehistoric or prerational, but updated continually through time.

> Sometimes, when I'm out-of-doors, I sense some-
> one. Peering skyward, I see Kwi'na (the golden
> eagle) soaring on wind currents, gliding easily,
> thrusting himself with great strength to unbeliev-
> able heights. My heart soars with him. Kwi'na, the
> mighty hunter and provider, "is over all of us," my
> grandparents said. They never described him as
> God or gods, the Great Spirit or any other spirit, to
> be worshipped or honored. Rather, they said, he is
> the finest example of the type of person we are
> taught to be. He is also our messenger, carrying our
> thoughts to the six directions: north, south, east,
> west, up and down.
>
> — Gaylen Lee

Mono Lake has earned the English sense of its name, I thought as I trudged out to it through six inches of snow piled on mud. Hardy brownish-green scrub poked up through the snow. The stench was more bitter and acrid than even the Salton Sea: *Stay away!* Even the brine flies avoided people. In the lake's still surface hovered blue mountains turned upside down until I tossed in a penny for watery thoughts. My boots sinking into the mud beneath the snow forced me to halt a dozen feet from the water of the lake that hoards every-thing flowing in. Abrupt realization that the unclosed distance was the point.

> Non-Indians ask so many questions! If only they'd
> be still for a while, they'd learn: from the wind and
> fog, from the heat of the day, from the darkness of
> the night; by watching the insects, birds, animals,
> and reptiles. They all have knowledge to share with
> us....
>
> — Gaylen Lee

I stood listening from the heart, the imaginal ear in the chest, and seemed to hear a voice from outside echoing within:

All I want is solitude, and to feed birds and dream up my sculptures.

I saw them then: eerie tufa towers breaking the surface of the water like vertical outcroppings on some alien planet. Below, the alkaline currents provides carbonates that mix with calcium brought by freshwater upwellings. Tufa are congealed springs crafted and frozen underwater by the old hermit of a lake for inhumanly mysterious purposes entirely his own.

YOSEMITE. IT DOESN'T MEAN "bears" or "grizzly." It means "those who kill." In Miwok, *yos*: "to kill," *c*: "one who," made plural by *meti*.

"Those" would be Miwoks married to Mono Paiutes and other tribal renegades (from the Miwok point of view) organized under Chief Tenaya as the *Ahwahnechee*, "dwellers in Deep Mouth," referring to the gaping valley in which they lived until the Mariposa Battalion under Major James Savage went to war in 1851 to push them out of it. Seeing Tenaya pluck grass while indicating "depth" with his hands, Savage, a kind of psychopathic Yosemite Sam with blond hair instead of red, misread "deep mouth" as "deep grassy valley." L. H. Bunnell was along; it was he who, mistaking "those who kill" for "grizzly bear," named the valley Yosemite:

> As I did not take a fancy to any of the names proposed, I remarked that "an American name would be the most appropriate"; that "I could not see any necessity for going to a foreign country for a name for American scenery—the grandest that had ever yet been looked upon. That it would be better to give it an Indian name than to import a strange and inexpressive one; that the name of the tribe who had occupied it, would be more appropriate than any I had heard suggested." I then proposed "that we give the valley the name of Yo-sem-i-ty, as it was suggestive, euphonious, and certainly American; that by so doing, the name of the tribe of Indians

which we met leaving their homes in this valley,
perhaps never to return, would be perpetuated."

So the valley, he hoped, would receive its name from the people
they drove out of it.

The stony temple that is Yosemite perches on the western side
of the Sierra wall separating the Central Valley from the Owens
Valley and from Route 395 as it runs north past Lake Tahoe toward
Carson City after leaving California for Nevada at Topaz Lake. That
wall extends south to Isabella Lake, where 178 departs 14 just below
Indian Wells to snake westward on the way to Bakersfield. East of
the wall, from north to south along the route I had covered, were
Indian Wells, Lake Owens, Lone Pine, Independence, Big Pine,
Bishop, Mammoth Lakes, and Mono Lake. West of the wall, the
Sequoia National Forest began just north of Isabella Lake, followed
by Mountain Home State Forest, Sequoia National Park, Inyo
National Forest (west of Lone Pine), Kings Canyon National Park,
Sierra National Forest (west of Bishop), and Yosemite National
Park connected to Mono Basin National Forest and Lee Vining by
Route 120. I was headed this time for Yosemite through the Sierran
thicket of national parks.

> We simply need that wild country available to us,
> even if we never do more than drive to its edge and
> look in. For it can be a means of reassuring our-
> selves of our sanity as creatures, a part of the geog-
> raphy of hope.
>
> — Wallace Stegner

Mythopoetically speaking, the national parks movement started
at the altar not of fertile Demeter, evocative Aphrodite, or lovely
Flora, but of dark Hades and his aide Thanatos.

Lewis Mumford called unchecked urbanization Necropolis. By
1831, when Boston opened a cemetery just outside the city, so many
bodies lay in urban churchyards that the threat of toxins and diseases forced a change of attention outward. Mount Auburn proved
so popular for strolls and picnics and taking refuge from the clamor

of city life that rural cemeteries appeared soon in Philadelphia and Brooklyn. A year later, Congress got involved by setting aside oak preserves in Florida and Hot Springs, Arkansas, and in the 1840s, horticulturalist Andrew Jackson Downing and *New York Evening Post* editor William Cullen Bryant called for a centrally located reserve in the heart of New York City. Frederick Law Olmsted and Calvert Vauz designed one.

Around this time Niagara Falls' obscurance by fences, shops, mills, stables, and crowds of tourists convinced disappointed visitors that the time had come to protect scenery from further encroachment. Much of that scenery survived in the (as yet) sparsely colonized west. West, Thoreau wrote, was "but another name for the Wild, and what I have been preparing to say is this, that in Wildness is the preservation of the World." Hearing about Yosemite, and seeing it promoted by Horace Greeley, painted by artists like Albert Bierstadt (his *Domes of the Yosemite* sold for $25,000), and photographed by Carleton Watkins and John James Audubon confirmed for many the need to preserve the wild for future generations. Of humans, primarily: not until the Everglades received protection in 1934 did wildness seem publicly worthy of preservation for its own sake apart from human needs.

On June 30, 1864, Abraham Lincoln signed the Yosemite Park Act into law.

However, "Nothing dollarable is safe, however guarded," observed John Muir. Land was set aside for its fiscal worthlessness. If it could be mined or logged or otherwise made use of, it was....except for the watersheds guarded by the long-legged, Scotland-born, thirty-year-old naturalist and writer who first saw Yosemite in the spring of 1868, five years after Whitney, Brewer, and Hoffman spent eight days mapping the valley: "No temple made with hands can compare with Yosemite..."

Taking his cue from Muir, *Visalia Delta* editor George W. Stewart went to Congress to fight for the giant sequoias. Farmers got behind him because eroded mountain forests would damage good cropland. The railroads liked the idea of more tourism. "Even the soulless Southern Pacific R.R. Co.," admitted Muir, "never counted on for anything good, helped nobly in pushing the bill for this park through Congress."

With Yosemite, Sequoia, Yellowstone, and General Grant in place by the 1890s, the United States enjoyed a bold start on a national system of parks. By 1909, President Theodore Roosevelt had more than tripled forest reserves alone. But the argument from use and uselessness lingered to torment of later naturalists, environmentalists, and deep ecologists critical of seeing everything, including the natural world, through a lens engraved with dollar signs. Under Roosevelt, Gifford Pinochet's U.S. Forest Service claimed jurisdiction over the parks and oversaw logging, damming, and mining within their borders. After the San Francisco earthquake of 1906, a catastrophe that incinerated a city of broken water mains, incoming Interior Secretary James Garfield, a fan of Pinochet, gave San Francisco permission to dam Hetch Hetchy.

Pinochet and his allies fought the national parks movement, but the tide of public opinion prevailed. Once the Panama Canal opened, the World Exposition in San Francisco (1915) displayed a Union Pacific-sponsored copy of Yellowstone on four and a half acres and a Santa Fe Railroad-sponsored Grand Canyon on six acres. In 1916, President Woodrow Wilson signed the National Park Service Act.

The first automobile to enter Yosemite ("Those Who Kill") had been a military vehicle. That was 1915. Ten thousand more arrived four years later as ninety-eight thousand cars drove through the nation's parks. The rising popularity of "sagebrushing" (automobile camping) presented environmentalists and preservationists with a dilemma. Cars allowed the middle class to view the parks, and that meant tourism dollars and widening appreciation for the natural world. But that much driving also brought pollution, crowding, and destructive road-building. Olmsted had warned about the ecological consequences in 1865, but, ignored, he resigned from the Yosemite Park Commission the following year. Soon the valley filled up with dance halls, golf courses, bear pit shows, movie theaters, swimming pools, and other "improvements" to entertain visitors. Bears and other creatures fed by human hands began to sicken and grow aggressive. A proposal floated to tunnel into Lassen Peak so tourists could see what a volcano looked like from inside.

Ecologists were aware, of course, that politically drawn boundaries could not protect an ecosystem adequately. Rachel Carson's *Silent Spring* came out in 1962, the year of the First World Conference on National Parks. "Nature does not respect political boundaries," noted participants. As park visitation rose toward forty-six million by the mid-1970s, coal-fired smoke and smog from cars and factories hung over the entire Southwest.

> Preservationists still confronted the paradox of their own beginning. For 100 years, the success of the national parks movement lay in its concentration on natural wonders. Now that preservationists understood ecology, they first had to undo the prevailing image of their founders. Not until the substitution of environmentalism for romanticism would that kind of park system have a chance.
> — Alfred Runte

A scientific Leopold Committee report issued in 1963 by UC Berkeley had made a case for "greater respect for the importance of natural forces." Scientists and environmentalists (as preservationists began calling themselves) found themselves increasingly appreciative of how the natural world maintained itself as a system of interlocking resiliencies. How to convey such knowledge to the public?

The environmental movement faced another paradox made increasingly visible by the Civil Rights Movement: that of prioritizing resources, in this case natural ones, ahead of people. What about the rights of Native Americans shoved off their lands? Of people of color forced by economic hardship to live in polluted neighborhoods? People without the means to visit a national park? To them, "nature" did not mean Yosemite or Yellowstone, it meant a backyard full of toxic runoff emitted by an unregulated factory. Industrialists "redlined" entire regions to place dumps and mines and refineries away from the affluent (who complain by hiring lawyers) by targeting decaying neighborhoods too sick or poor to fight back. In 1979, however, attorney Linda McKeever Bullard represented Margaret Bean and her African American neighbors to stop a landfill from being dug near their homes in Houston. *Bean v. Southwestern Waste Management, Inc.* and the research and advocacy of Bullard's scholar husband Robert brought forth an Environmental Justice Movement to clean up Cancer Alleys around the nation and confront white environmentalists with the needs of people deprived of rights and health.

In 1978, Congressional Representative Phillip Burton of San Francisco, chair of the House Subcommittee on National Parks and Insular Affairs, had pushed through the enormously influential National Park and Recreation Act to designate nearly two million acres as wilderness. The bill included plans for new parks and historic sites, increased funding for existing parks, trail development, and $725 million to renovate urban recreational areas for use by city-dwellers. Twenty-five rivers were singled out for futher study and protection.

Things seemed to be looking hopeful for the parks. A *State of the Parks Report* drew further attention to the impact of air pollution and other threats faced by parks in 1980. In 1983, James Watt, namesake of the steam engine's inventor, was forced to resign after an ecologically disastrous run as Secretary of the Interior for a racist Chamber of Commerce speech in which he made fun of Affirmative Action. Later, he was found guilty on one count of influence-peddling. Unfortunately, his replacement, William Clark, was no more critical of mining, coal, or oil interests. As the "Conservative Revolution" picked up steam under the Reagan Administration, attacks on the park system intensified. Forests fell to insects and invasives amplified by global warming, visitation fell off dramatically, a result (some studies suggested) of TV and video game obsession, and Arnold Schwarzennegar and other emboldened conservatives routinely threatened to cut state and federal funding for park services.

By 2010, when traces of pesticides pooled in even the highest of the High Sierra lakes, the fantasy that slices of "wild" nature could be fenced off was effectively dead. In place of it former park ranger William Tweed suggested strengthenening ecosystem resilience and resistance to threats while allowing what changes were needed:

for example, supporting sequoias already headed upslope in response to an altered climate. "The National Park System Comprehensive Survey of the American Public" conducted by the University of Wyoming in 2011 showed that only 22% of park visitors were Hispanic or people of color. According to "Made in America: Investing in National Parks for Our Heritage and Our Economy," a report by the National Parks Conservation Assocation, funding for parks was not only declining steadily over the past decade, including $140 million cut this year, but even deeper cuts, as much as 10% of budget, might be expected from a Congress dominated by Republicans determined to wipe out social and ecological services in the name of "debt reduction"--presumably the debt left after the last Bush administration threw a national surplus into a fiscal void deepened by exhorbitant petroleum subsidization, bank bailouts, and ongoing warfare around the world.

I entered the southern forests with this legacy of mistreatment very much on my mind. The first ten years of the Gold Rush reduced the Sierra Indian populations by two-thirds, especially in the western foothills: Nisenan and Miwok near the rivers first, then Maidu, Konkow, Yokuts, Mono, Tubatulabl, Kawaiisu, Washoe at Lake Tahoe...90% of them gone by 1900, with most of the survivors forcibly relocated.

As this genocide gathered momentum, loggers and miners went to work. After 1860, as mercury and acid runoff ran all the way down to the Central Valley, a third of the Sierra's timber was gone. The predictable consequences began with erosion, runoff, and destroyed habitats and built as fish and game were poisoned and hunted out, especially deer, mountain sheep, wolverines, martens, antelope, and trout. The California Grizzly vanished forever thanks to the invention and overuse of the repeater rifle. Congress authorized forest reserves in 1891 and an Organic Act of 1897 to manage them, but the damage was extensive and the infliction of it ongoing: air pollution, insect damage, fire-suppression policies, invasive plants, salvage cutting. "Sierra in Peril," a *Sacramento Bee* article published in June 1991, presented images of frail trees and erosion gullies. Last Chance Creek wobbled on its last legs. In fact, by the

1990s, a full quarter of the state's plants and animals faced the threat of extinction.

> When I first entered this region as a teenager, I perceived a tough and enduring remnant of an earlier, preindustrialized time. Now, four decades later, I see instead a fragile and damaged landscape headed toward inescapable change. Aldo Leopold, the prescient, mid-twentieth-century ecologist who anticipated so much of our modern world, understood this too. "One of the penalties of an ecological education," he wrote, "is that one lives alone in a world of wounds." This morning, as I descend from the Bighorn Plateau, I sense wounds everywhere.
> — William Tweed

What remains (I reminded myself) remains resilient. On a granite core lifted skyward and tilted west--on mud brought from below by Duck, the Yokuts creation account tells us--stand the eight national forests of Plumas, Tahoe, Eldorado, Stanislaus, Sierra, Toiyabe, Inyo, and Sequoia. Fourteen rivers water them; three--the Sacramento, San Joaquin, and Tulare--capture all the stream flow of the western Sierra and store much of it in thousands of lakes (four hundred and twenty-nine lakes in Yosemite alone). The rest feeds Jeffrey, lodgepole, nut, sugar, and Ponderosa pines, cypresses, sycamores, bays, oaks, giant sequoias, incense cedars, mountain hemlocks, Douglas firs, Pacific dogwoods, quaking aspen, water birch, whitebark, juniper, and piñon.

The conifers that dominate California's forests and woodlands and the western edges of the mostly alpine Sierra go back three hundred million years, earlier even than flowering plants. Here are found redwoods, sequoias, and bristlecone pines: the tallest, largest, and oldest trees anywhere.

With its high peaks, double crests, deep canyons, and spacious uplands, the southern Sierra contains Sequoia National Park established in 1980 on four hundred and four thousand acres. The park reaches northward to join with Kings Canyon National Park. Two-million-acre Inyo National Forest stretches between the two on the eastern side of the range. Wildflowers bloom on these slopes from January until October, but snow glitters on the highest ridges all year. Names like Valhalla and Giant Forest echo the mythography of Norse lore, with the former bridge at Hamilton Gorge standing in for Bifrost.

The sequoia tree is named after Sequoya, the silversmith who gave the Cherokee the written word. Giant sequoias grow naturally only in the central and southern Sierra. The largest on earth, General Sherman, stands two hundred and seventy-five feet high within the Giant Forest and bulges thirty-six feet in diameter at the base. General Grant, the national Christmas tree since 1926, also serves as a memorial to fallen soldiers. The sequoias don't grow in pure stands, but with sugar pines, white firs, and incense cedars. Though too brittle for lumber, a mature sequoia can carry forty thousand cones that bear tiny seeds only an eighth of an inch long. Fires open the cones to release the seeds. At higher elevations grow foxtail pines that live more than two thousand years and reach into the ground with bulbous roots that resemble huge feet.

The Sequoia National Park hosts the largest trees in the world, but also the highest ozone levels of any national park in the U.S. Pesticides and runoff from Central Valley factory farms contaminate the western flank of the park; the eastern falls within the R-2508 Military Operations Area overflown by aircraft from Edwards Air Force Base, Lemoore Naval Air Station, Nellis Air Force Base, the California Air National Guard, and the Marine Corps. A pack trip sponsored by the National Park Service to show officers what remained to preserve was buzzed by a jet.

It isn't easy to manage thousands of alpine acres surrounded by a world economy run by consumption and pollution, both of which have degenerated into an entrenched collective psychology of irresponsible expansionism and waste. Installation of bear-proof food lockers at Sequoia and Kings Canyon National Parks brought a higher concentration of hikers and heavier human impact. Some of the campers used the lockers as waste bins. On the other hand, a 2006 restoration project on two hundred and thirty-one acres of the Giant Forest removed two hundred and eighty-two buildings, twenty-four acres of asphalt, a sewage treatment plant, dozens of manholes, aerial phone and electrical lines, exposed sewer and water pipes, and propane tanks.

Much of seven-hundred-square-mile Kings Canyon National Park named after the Kings River remains inaccessible by road as though shrouded in a magisterial aloofness that protects not only sequoias, but gray foxes, gray squirrels, red-tailed hawks, Pacific tree frogs, owls, bobcats, and mule deer. Although alien grasses that pushed out the perennial bunchgrasses are also supplanting the oak woodlands, horsetails and willows share streams with alders and sycamores, wild oats, and chamise.

Probably the first whites to glimpse Kings Canyon were the company of Captain John Kuykendall of the Mariposa Battalion marching in pursuit of Ahwahneechees and Chowchillas in 1851. The Shoshone resided here, the Western Mono in the lower canyon country, and the Tubatulabal near the Kern River. Old native camp-sites dot the park. In 1856, Hale Tharp departed the Placerville gold fields to bring cattle through, establish a summer horse ranch at Log Meadow, and bury Native victims of scarlet fever and smallpox. Later, French and Spanish Basques herded sheep in the canyons until driven out by soldiers. In 1890 the Kings River Lumber Company floated timber down a flume to Sanger fifty miles away; in a few more years this company would leave the Converse Basin empty of giant trees.

> Lodgepole
> cone/seed waits for fire
> And then thin forests of silver-gray.
> in the void
> a pine cone falls
> Pursued by squirrels...
>
> listen.
>
> This living flowing land
> is all there is, forever

We are it
it sings through us....

— Gary Snyder

Muir arrived in 1875, stood in awe below the sequoias, named the Giant Forest, and published accounts of his trip in San Francisco newspapers. An 1891 article he wrote for *Century Magazine* called for the protection of Kings Canyon. Protection arrived eventually but was delayed for five decades by industrial interests seeking, like the Forest Service, to dam the river. National park status for Kings Canyon was fought by the Forest Service, the California Chamber of Commerce, the Farm Bureau, the Kings River Water Association, and Congressman Alfred Elliott of Visalia until a curious incident made him retreat. When Elliott received a letter from a park advocate with $100 enclosed by error for Congressman Bertrand Gearhart, who supported the park, Elliott alerted the FBI and sent the envelope to Gearhart as if nothing had happened. The scheme to entrap backfired when Gearhart returned the check to the donor with a suggestion to send it to the Sierra Club. Kings Canyon National park was signed into law by FDR in 1940. Captain Charles Young, the first commissioned African American officer in the U.S. army, proposed that private lands be bought up to add to the park. It took time, but this too was accomplished.

As the Sphinx rock formation looks on beyond Road's End, the park's ascension toward Muir Pass begins in Evolution Valley. Theodore Solomons, a young San Francisco mountaineer, named named six peaks here after famous evolutionary biologists Darwin, Fiske, Haeckel, Huxley, Spencer, and Wallace. Solomons wanted to mark a trail that would guide visitors (including those of the new Sierra Club of eager mountaineers) from Yosemite along a route now known as the John Muir Trail. The naming precedent of Solomon continued with Evolution Meadow, Valley, Creek, and Basin. Below the heights run hundreds of multicolored caves carved in marble by carbonic acid leached from soil and snow melt. Many of the caves--Lilburn, for example--bear "rooms" given dreamlike names such as Curl Passage, Anastomoses Room, Great White Pillar, Malachite Room, Schreiber Complex, Impossible Dream, Hog

Heaven, Southern Comfort, Mousetrack, Junction, Hex, Mud Heaven, Echo River, Clay Palace...

> Moses forced his society to accept a unifying law; Jesus forced his to accept the unity of all humanity; Darwin forced his to accept the unity of all life. I doubt whether any of the three would have been able to influence his society so strongly if he had not been fortified by a season in the wilderness.
> — David Wallace

In this park whose name points to the Magi, evolution also runs backwards as species move upwards to cope with a warming planet. The park suffers air pollution, blister rust that attacks the pines, bark beetle infestations, pesticides from Tulare County (whose growers spray more than fifteen million pounds of them a year), and ozone levels so high that rangers now warn summer visitors that hiking among the sequoias can cause lung damage. Two-thirds of the park's Jeffrey pines show ozone damage. In fifty years, most of the alpine tundra of the Kern River headwaters will end up as lost over history's horizon as the wise kings themselves.

Below Yosemite, the Sierra National Forest contains 1.3 million acres placed under federal protection as a forest reserve in 1893. It was the second such forest set aside in California and the largest until other reserves like Yosemite were brought forth from it. The oak-dotted foothills and higher alpine slopes display granitic Arch Rock sculpted by rain and wind, the redwood Dinkey Creek Historic Bridge, McKinely Grove, Nelder Grove, Mile High Vista, Fresno Dome, Angel Falls, the Devil's Slide, and a Bass Lake loop trail with a commentary about how the early Mono people lived. Will an interpretive trail ever describe how we lived?

> Thousands of tired, nerve-shaken, over-civilized people are beginning to find out that going to the mountains is going home; that wildness is a necessity; and that mountain parks and reservations are

> useful not only as fountains of timber and irrigating
> rivers, but as fountains of life.
>
> — John Muir

Muir would have appreciated a distinction made by Sierra poet and naturalist Gary Snyder. In *The Practice of the Wild*, "nature" refers to the physical world, human artifacts included, but "wild" means the state in which plants and nonhuman animals live as free agents unmanaged by us. By capturing the bear cub "Ben Franklin" in 1854 near Yosemite and collecting his menagerie of formerly wild animals, James "Grizzly" Adams was involving himself in nature even while working to diminish its sphere of effective wildness. By injuring Adams lethally, an angered female grizzly, the seasick bear "Old Fremont," and the monkey that bit him to protest circus training pushed their sector of the wild back out again.

> Arriving by the Panama steamer, I stopped one day
> in San Francisco and then inquired for the nearest
> way out of town. "But where do you want to go?"
> asked the man to whom I had applied for this
> important information. "To any place that is wild,"
> I said.
>
> — John Muir

MUIR MIGHT HAVE HEARD of Yosemite while recovering his sight after an accident in an Indianapolis carriage firm. A file went into his right eye, causing his left to close temporarily in sympathy. (Sight: a quintessential organ of perception in Yosemite.) This mishap effectively ended any remaining affection for industrial technology but opened in Muir a new vision of the beauty of the natural world. In October 1872, while suspended perilously from Mt. Ritter, he felt a new peaking of the senses that helped him get safely off the isolated mountain.

All this combined with a childhood spent immersed in Christianity, a religion of the archetypal Allfather, to prepare Muir to take up the mantle of high priest to the soaring verticality of

Yosemite. Muir baptized the glacier-sculpted Olympus of the Sierra Nevada the "Range of Light."

> Down through the middle of the Valley flows the crystal Merced, River of Mercy, peacefully quiet, reflecting lilies and trees and the onlooking rocks; things frail and fleeting and types of endurance meeting here and blending in countless forms, as if into this one mountain mansion Nature had gathered her choicest treasures, to draw her lovers into close and confiding communion with her.
>
> — John Muir

Effective priests harbor a dash of worldly strategist, and Muir was no exception. In 1889, he persuaded Robert Johnson, editor at *Century*, to camp in Tuolumne Meadows. The obvious damage from erosion, tramping, and overgrazing enlisted Johnson in the campaign to protect Yosemite. The resulting bill went through Congress on the last day of the session and passed within hours to authorize a new national park.

Josiah Whitney and Muir had argued about what sculpted the valleys, canyons, and domes of the valley: glaciation, as Muir maintained, or faulting, as Whitney insisted? Both were right. When the Sierra rose twenty-five million years ago, streams cut into the Cretaceous rock of quartz, potassium feldspar, plagioclase feldspar, biotite, and hornblende. Glacial erosion then carved into uplifted joint and fracture systems--ice on stone--to make Muir's "incomparable valley" four thousand feet above sea level while pushing along debris that weathered into Central Valley topsoil. Most of the falls, cliffs, spirals, and domes are visible from Mt. Hoffman (named for a member of the geologic survey) standing in the valley's center. The oldest plutonic rocks in the valley compose the walls of Merced Gorge and the Rockslides, Arch Rock, and Gateway in the west end of the valley. A 1980 survey found almost five hundred small glaciers in the valley, but all are melting now.

Giant "stairways" of rock like those at Vernal and Nevada Falls formed by the downcutting and runoff of jointed granite. Domes stay mostly free of vegetation because their fine-grained granite lacks vertical joints. El Capitan's outstanding brightness reflects from very light blends of quartz, plagioclase, orthoclase, and biotite mixed with less dark hornblende than that found in other Yosemite mountains. What black there is in this grand temple of stone comes from shiny, hexagonal biotite.

It would be difficult to find a more eye-minded valley anywhere. Although the valley takes up only 1% of the park, nearly all the 3.5 million park visitors a year come here. The valley's east-west orientation lets in enough sunlight to afford a god's eye view. That of Zeus, perhaps. The crafty deity who avoided being devoured by the deep mouth of Cronus when Rhea gave her husband a stone to swallow instead grew hidden away in mountain heights. The Kouretes of Rhea, armed dancers ("those who kill") who stood guard over Zeus, clashed their shields to drown the baby's cries so Titanic enemies could not find him until he was ready for them. The U.S. Army managed Yosemite for long enough to guard it against encroaching herders of "hoofed locusts," Muir's term for sheep. James Dwight Dana, Lyell, Brewer, Hoffman, Watkins, and other names of pioneers graced peaks in Yosemite like those of heroes elevated into the sky god's constellations. El Capitan, Eagle Rock, Bridalveil, Cathedral Rocks, Three Brothers, Tenaya ("our father"), the dangling climbers, the great unsheathed blade of Tis-sa-ack (Half Dome), named from a woman who had argued with her husband and had been turned to stone, Tioga Pass Road from a Miwok word for "where it forks" like lightning, and the valley itself named a Deep Mouth full of rocks presented a geomythic landscape of what in European lore would announce themselves as Cronus, Hera, and far-sighted Zeus.

If Yosemite signifies an earthly temple for a presence like that of the Allfather, it makes sense that pious men would adore its soaring beauty. "Yosemite burst upon us and it was glorious," wrote Ansel ("God's Helmet") Adams. Like Muir, he had been stricken by an illness that forced him to lay for weeks in the darkness. "There was light everywhere, and seeing it, a new era opened for me." He also referred to the valley as "a great natural shrine." Before him, Galen Clark came to the Sierra to heal from tuberculosis and found the giant trees in the Mariposa Grove: "I was awed and felt as never before the greatness of God's power." Geologist Joseph LeConte: "Was there ever so venerable, majestic, and eloquent a minister of natural religion as the grand old Half Dome?" Lafayette Bunnell: "I have here seen the power and glory of a Supreme being; the majesty of his Handywork is in that 'Testimony of the Rocks.'" Bunnell named after Chief Tenaya a lake already named *Pyweack*, "Shining Rocks." Tenaya was tied to Bunnell with a rope, but Adamanthea had prevented Zeus's capture by suspending him from a rope. Muir himself, who worshipped "King Sequoia" and called the Sierra "God's mountain mansion," hiked to Yosemite looking for avalanches to watch, got caught in one, and rode it down a mountain: "Elija's flight in a chariot of fire could hardly have been more gloriously exciting."

In 1903, the father of the Sierra Club repeated a successful tactic and invited President Roosevelt, the father of a nation, to camp with him in Yosemite. I got out of my car and, hugging a down jacket against the cold, read a marker planted to commemorate the spot.

Of this excursion Roosevelt wrote,

> The first night was clear, and we lay down in the darkening aisles of the great Sequoia grove. The majestic trunks, beautiful in color and in symmetry, rose round us like the pillars of a mightier cathedral than ever was conceived even by the fervor of the Middle Ages.

By the time Roosevelt left office in 1909, he had authorized sixteen national monuments, established five national parks, and protected six hundred thousand acres circling Mount Olympus in Washington. One of the parks was Yosemite, of course, "the grandest"—Muir again—"of all nature's temples."

It makes sense, then, that the valley is one of the most photographed in the world. Bunnel was a photographer. Adams started his career at fifteen, when he brought a box camera to Yosemite and shot El Capitan to take pictures of things in lieu of naming them. C.L. Weed had gotten there first in 1851. Carleton Watkins, Edward

Weston, painter Albert Bierstadt, Eadweard Muybridge....so many photographers and artists stood separated by entire decades, yet with twelve hundred square miles of park to choose from, somehow selected vantages clustered next to each other. Muybridge included the dimension of depth by taking stereo photographs. "In a Muybridge panorama," writes Rebecca Solnit, "several moments of a day seem to exist as one superhuman glance...." Elsewhere she describes Yosemite as "an infinity of potential views" that makes the onlooker feel like "a midget among a crowd of giants."

As though in recognition of a transhuman presence at Yosemite, whose stairways and battlements surpass mortal proportions, Muir, Adams, Muybridge, and Bierstadt gathered images that excluded people. Ignoring the Ahwahnechee, Muir felt inspired by the valley and its peaks to write, "When we try to pick out anything by itself, we find it hitched to everything else in the universe." But there is more than otherworldly height to this mythology, especially when lived unconsciously in the shadows cast where places, myths, and dwellers clash.

Yosemite's exemplar of unconsciously and therefore destructively lived mythology arrived once reports had circulated of gold found along the Tuolumne, Merced, Mariposa, Chowchilla, and Fresno Rivers. Originally from Springfield, the illiterate, insomniac, lethal Savage worked for a time with ill-fated John Marshall at Sutter's famous lumber mill. Trading goods for gold dust, he achieved enough wealth to pose as a modern El Dorado and self-proclaimed "Tulare King" to Native Californians he bullied into bringing him gold dust for pieces of cloth.

William Penn Abrams might have been the first non-Native to enter Yosemite. On October 18, 1849, Abrams made this diary entry:

> Returned to S.F. after visit to Savages property on Merced River, prospects none too good for a mill. Savage is a blasphemous fellow who has five squaws for wives for which he takes authority from the Scriptures. While at Savage's Reamer and I saw grizzly bear tracks and went out to hunt him down, getting lost in the mountains...found our way to

camp over an Indian trail that led past a valley
enclosed by stupendous cliffs rising perhaps 3,000
feet from their base and which gave us cause for
wonder. Not far off a waterfall dropped from a cliff
below three jagged peaks into the valley, while farther beyond a rounded mountain stood, the valley
side of which looked as though it had been sliced
with a knife as one would slice a loaf of bread and
which Reamer and I called the Rock of Ages.

Savage wired up a grizzly pelt to a battery and even shocked his
audience with electricity to show off his Zeus-parodying danger-
ousness. Loading a pistol with blanks, he ordered a Yokuts man to
fire it at him while making catching motions in the air before opening his hand to reveal the six bullets.

"Major Savage, he say, 'I big medicine man with big
father at Washington. You haf do what I say. I hurt
you if I want to. I make all your people die. I make
all fish go out of river. I make all antelope, all elk go
'way. I make dark.'"

When Savage returned from San Francisco to find his Fresno
River outpost raided, he retaliated by convincing government officials and fellow miners that the Indians with whom negotiations
proceeded were actually planning to eject all whites from
California. By the fall of 1850, the miners wanted to kill the Indians
and the Indians were ready to fight back against the miners. Having
lost his crown by his own miscalculations, Savage lost his Native
wives too.

The "Battalion" was named "Mariposa" (Butterfly) for the estate
of John Fremont that flew away later on the wings of debt. One of
the band was Leroy Vining. Firmly in the grip of his Zeus complex,
Savage burned everything his enemies owned as he marched toward
Yosemite. Once there he replied to Bunnell's description of the valley as a Paradise for the Indians by comparing himself to Satan.
Rebecca Solnit compares Savage to Conrad's Kurtz.

"My intended, my ivory, my station, my river, my--"
everything belonged to him. It made me hold my
breath in expectation of making the wilderness
burst into a prodigious peal of laughter that would
shake the fixed stars in their places. Everything
belonged to him--but that was a trifle. The thing
was to know what he belonged to, how many powers of darkness claimed him for their own.
> — Joseph Conrad, *Heart of Darkness*

Tenaya was captured on the shores of the lake named for him after his son was shot in the back by one of Savage's captains. "Exterminate all the brutes!"

After the Mariposa War, Savage got a contract (along with Fremont and an associate named Vinsonhaler) to supply beef to tribes on reservations. The three used this opportunity to swindle everyone concerned. By 1852, Savage and one Dr. Leach were at the Fresno River giving medicine to Indians dying of an unknown dis-ease. Belatedly, Savage seems to have acquired at least a rudimenta-ry conscience because he denounced Judge Walter Harvey's mas-sacre of several Indians at the Kings River. Savage also called for an inquiry, but on the way to it he ran into Harvey, punched him in the face, dropped his pistol repeatedly (he was drunk), and was shot by Harvey four times. These bullets he could not dodge. Harvey was arrested but acquitted.

As for Chief Tenaya, he left the reservation where he'd been imprisoned, but he never returned safely to his Olympus. During a violent argument with his Mono Paiute hosts he was stoned to death.

Americans have often liked to believe that atroci-
ties and extremes of injustice are themselves for-
eign, prefer to save the rainforests of Brazil to those
of their own Pacific Coast, to worry about tragedies
that don't implicate them. Heart of Darkness sets
the task of the colonialist as local rather than exot-

ic--not as understanding the natives, but understanding one's own origins: "Is not our own interi-
or white on the chart? black though it may prove,
like the coast when discovered"--and it has seemed
to me that there is something in Savage himself--his
lack of restraint, of doubt, and of introspection--
and in the fools, liars, cannibals, and opportunists
that surrounded him--that brings this lesson home
again.

— Rebecca Solnit

That something the ancient Greeks would have identified as
hybris: "wanton violence, insolence, outrage; presumption toward
the gods," Who responded by arranging a deflationary fall from the
heights. *Hybris* derives, after all, from *ud-*, an Indo-European root
that means "up." In Yosemite the fall can look like suicide, drowning in rivers, getting caught in avalanches, or simply disappearing--
but with a twist. In June 1909, San Francisco jeweler F. P. Shepherd
left the Glacier Point Hotel to walk toward Sentinel Dome but
dropped out of sight, loupe and all. Frank Koenman, an amateur
photographer from San Francisco, failed to develop his presence in
May 1925. Most of the disappearances involve lone spectators going
out to see something. Many of those lost bear thematically interest-
ing names. Tourist Godfrey Wondrosek never returned from a hike
to Half Dome in April 1933. In 1954, Walter Gordon (Walter: "army
commander"; Gordon: "hill fort") was searched for by helicopter but
never found. Tim ("God's honor") Barnes exited July 1988. A few
months later, Donald (Don: "great chief" and king of the Irish under-
world) Buchanan abdicated near Half Dome. Another Walter,
Reinhart, went AWOL in September 2002 in spite of being a
Marine with wilderness survival training. In June 2005, Michal (like
God's archangel) Ficery entered the backcountry...

Yosemite has witnessed the Stoneman Meadow Riot and rock
fight, BASE jumper deaths, accidental falls, seventeen waterfall
plunges during the 1970s, more after--usually visitors climbing over
the guard railings--and, in 1976, an airplane dropping when the
Lodestar Lightning, a refitted bomber piloted by cannabis smugglers

Jon Glisky and Jeffrey Nelson, lost an engine over Yosemite and went down. The rangers failed to guard it, so people hiked in to make off with the pot. In 2004, a Japanese couple was found dangling arm in arm from a rope at El Capitan. Many who have fallen off cliffs or down waterfalls went over still clutching their cameras.

Native stories describe troubled spirits inhabiting Po-ho´-no Lake, the headwaters of Bridal Veil Creek running down through the Yosemite Valley in which an evil wind had been said to cause accidents. In July 1985, five hikers were scaling Half Dome when a storm raged in. Lightning striking the dome killed two and singed the survivors. In August 1990, sheets of lightning ignited a huge fire at Foresta.

> I'm interested in the intangibles and subtleties that appear slowly, that can't be controlled, and that don't appear on demand. Certain qualities of experience, of recognition, of consciousness seem to appear only gradually--or appear like a bolt of lightning, but only if you have found the place that will be struck and have settled there.
>
> — Rebecca Solnit

The first time Solnit visited Lake Tenaya she fished from the water a pamphlet about missionaries ministering to violent natives. "Like wolves stalking their prey," read this epistle, "savage men were closing in on the small Christian community...." The chapter of this highly projective fantasy bore the title, "A Child Shall Lead Them." Ten years later she returned with Byron Wolfe and Mark Klett to rephotograph sites where Muybridge had positioned himself to make his shots of the valley ("....we decided that Adams was no longer the Great Oedipal Father of landscape photography"). In the same place near the lake they saw pine cones washed up in the shallows to be gilded by mica flakes. Nearby, they met a old, white-haired, straight-backed widower who had camped there on his honeymoon. His wife had died recently of cancer, and he had come to spread some of her ashes here, a Zeus in mourning for his Hera. He was a photographer, it turned out, and asked to be photographed himself while standing on a rock with tall trees as a backdrop.

> Truth is like rock. But meaning is like the pines.
> — Rebecca Solnit

Solnit's account intuitively reflects the aura of Olympian timelessness at play in the park. As the team's panoramic photo work in the present echoed that of the past, "Time was a fan to fold, an accordion to squeeze, a collapsible ladder, a hand of cards." Mark Klett found a toy caldelabra discarded at the Wawona Tunnel overlook. During an attempt to rephotograph Agassiz Rock a camera lens dropped down an avalanche chute. "Landscape's most crucial condition is considered to be space, but its deepest theme is time." No wonder the Park Service tries to make Yosemite resemble its images in old photographs. The Temple of Zeus has been confused with the Garden of Eden in an implied nature/culture split like that made by Muir, for whom civilization was Bad and nature Divine. Visitors are instructed not to touch any plant life except the apple trees.

The history books say the Ahwehneechee perished long ago, but Solnit found one direct descendant born in Yosemite working there as a forester while fighting for the rights of his tribe. When he was retired and evicted from the Park Service in 1996, floods arrived the very next day to sweep through the valley removing some of the development: "...pretty much what his father said would happen when their people had all left the valley."

When Zeus had tired of men's evil ways and decided to consume the world in a flood, Deucalion, a son of Prometheus, and Pyrrha, his companion and a daughter of Gaia, were warned to construct a chest that would bear them to the shoulder of a mountain. After the deluge, the couple covered their heads and threw stones over their shoulders. The stones grew into people. In earlier versions of this tale, those who were saved from inundation and death lived because they were warned to scale Mt. Gerania ("Crane Mountain") by the cries of cranes soaring and circling like those that raised their young at the summit of Crane Mountain, the older name of El Capitan.

A Miwok legend tells us that one day a giant named Uwulin appeared in the valley and began to eat people. He was ravenously hungry, and eventually he ate almost everyone on earth. He had no brain, and his tiny heart was in his heel. Fly bit him all over until finding his heel, which made his leg kicked; Fly then told the remaining bird and animal people, who laid out large stakes for the giant to walk on. After he died, peace was restored to the valley.

— Frank La Pena, Craig Bates, and Steven Medley

The stony heights of Yosemite depend, however, on what is low, soft, and moist, just as the life and majesty of Zeus depended on the foresight of his mother Rhea, daughter of Sky and Earth, wife of Cronus, mother of all the Olympians: Rhea whose Roman name Ops connects to *opus*, "work," in this case seven flowing miles of the Merced River that carved the entire valley. The inescapable truth of our world's increasing thirst finds expression from the vantage of Yosemite, where the fate of all depends, not on the deeds or misdeeds of solitary men or even gods, but on the liquid abundance that supports all life and tinges our planet blue.

The Eye and Echo of Tahoe

Between Yosemite and Lake Tahoe rise the Stanislaus and Eldorado National Forests. Because roads through them tend to reach east-west rather than north-south, the indirect drive up to Tahoe pleases an eye appreciative of trees, streams, and lakes brimming with plant and animal life. The bald eagle flies here, and the peregrine falcon. On average, fifty-six inches of rain and snow fall from October until April. The Tahoe National Forest lies adjacent just east.

At year's end I drove into a forest sparkling with brilliant sunshine that deepened the shadows into pools and folds of ink.

"Introverted exteriority" is how I would describe Yosemite; while there, walking on wet roads snapping photographs of snowy peaks on every side, I had lost almost all sense of myself. Beingness shone outside, eclipsing interiority even while ringing it in stony stairways of granite. Here, however, lurked an extraverted interiority, a bright, loud turning inward amplified by my dismay at seeing light bouncing from the shiny surfaces of casinos, multi-story resorts, and sides, tops, and windshields of cars backed up on Route 28 into South Tahoe.

Once I had parked after deciding against my first choice of hotel, I found myself surrounded by endless small bands of teens and twenty-year-olds chatting about skiing into the New Year. Many yelled their enthusiasm; some hooted at young pseudo-blondes with artificially mahogany-colored faces and hands. Mothers in their forties dressed and acted like their daughters. It wasn't even having fun. It was acting out, as when three leering young men shouting at passing girls were asked by Marriott security to move on down the sidewalk. Near a ski lift I saw carved bears on tall pillars, garish fast food joints crammed with skiers in heavy coats, and a sign hung in a gallery: MEET THE ARTIST - MOST WEEKENDS. Above, around, and behind this frenetic crowding, pushing, and howling, casinos and hotels rose up to blot out the snowy, tree-clad hills. I withdrew to my accommodations and waited for nightfall.

Was I cursed to repeat everything here? Two hotels, then two hotel rooms when the first turned out to be a dingy little cave next to a noisy party, two walks to the market because I'd forgotten to buy tea the first time. When I slipped on the same patch of ice that had almost downed me before and sprawled heavily on the sidewalk, the driver and passenger of a truck waiting to turn onto 28 glanced incuriously at me without so much as rolling down the window to ask if I were hurt. The first hotel room had been shabby, with a falling-down wall heater and a broken bathroom mirror, but the second was luxuriant, with a large sauna, redwood paneling, heavy red drapes, a better fake plant, and no fewer than three half-size mirrors on the walls. A tree symbol repeated itself over the spa. In the bathroom, the place of flowing waters, I counted two towels, two wash cloths, two soaps, two lotions, and two shampoos. A roll of toilet paper sitting on the lid of the stool bore the brand label ECO. I pulled out my portable eye of Zeus and photographed it.

VANITIES AND ECHOES.....

The mountain nymph loved the beautiful hunter, but Narcissus did not care.

Having been born in troubled circumstances, he was of concern from the start. When his mother Leirope asked wise Teiresias how the boy would do, the prophet said he would live to old age so long as he never knew himself.

Narcissus loved to hunt, and on one expedition in the forest he was seen by Echo. Her voice had been all but silenced by angry Hera for distracting her whenever Zeus's wandering eye fell elsewhere. Echo could still speak, but only a repetition of what she had already heard.

Narcissus craved mirroring, but even Echo's echo proved insufficient to draw his interest from himself. Seeing his own image in a clear pool of water, he wanted utterly to possess it but could not. Cursed by Nemesis, he lay there until he died--some say by his own dagger-wielding hand, others by pining away, still others by drowning as he bent to embrace his lovely reflection. Where his body had crouched in self-desire budded a purple and white flower named after him.

Freud was not the first psychological theorist to use the word "narcissism," but in his hands this clinical coinage gained psychiatric currency. For him it was a neutral word for self-love. At birth the baby swims in a sea of *primary narcissism:* the diffuse but magical sense that parents, objects, surroundings exude a pre-individualistic me-ness. Out of this inclusiveness grow I, you, and world as different but interrelated psychic realities, each with its own needs, limitations, and inner laws, unless the emotional matrix in which these differentiations are supposed to take root does not hold and instead leaves the child a wounded adult who self-soothes by turning his portion of narcissism back toward himself (*secondary narcissism*) instead of investing it in other people. "Mirror-hungry" is the term with which clinicians describe the narcissistically injured. As the old joke puts it, "Enough about me. What do you think about me?"

To be narcissistic is to be caught in the painful, mind-splitting paradox of needing to be Echoed--made to feel special, visible, adorable, grand--while racked with envy of and contempt for anyone able to induce these pleasant states of mind. The oversized ego perpetually threatened with quick collapse strives to be totally self-reliant but cannot even stay inflated without emotional infusions of specialness from beyond itself.

Whether a lake can be narcissistic is the wrong question. The right one is, What might be the ecological echoes that sound the earthly structures of our narcissism?

Fed by more than seventy creeks, streams, and rivers, the largest of which is the Upper Truckee River at the southern end, Lake

Tahoe fills a fork between the Sierras and the Carsons where they split at Hope Valley. Self-enclosed in a valley sealed by volcanic action, the largest mountain lake in North American holds thirty-nine trillion gallons of water to a depth of sixteen hundred forty-five feet. Washoes visiting there during the summer might have woven the legend that gave Squaw Valley its name for the wife who pined for her husband after he had been killed by the Paiutes. Settlers entering the valley in 1849 saw only women and children because the men were away hunting.

Fremont and cartographer Charles Preuss glimpsed the lake on Valentine's Day, 1844, from a nearby summit. Fremont's name for it --Lake Bonpland after a notable explorer--gave way to Mountain Lake and then Tahoe from the Washoe word *daow* (big waters). After Fremont marched away, the cannon he left behind so he wouldn't have to drag it over snowy mountains moved around like a lost dream image, receded from view, reappeared, and receded again. Because his map (complete with an imaginary river linking Tahoe with the sea) placed the lake too far to the west, newly drawn state lines split Tahoe again. Its division between Nevada and California piled up enough bureaucracy to prevent the lake from being dammed and diverted.

Of course famous people visited. Muir saw the results of logging, erosion, overfishing, and unplanned wildfire--by 1860, sawmills at South Lake Tahoe supplied Comstock demands for lumber--and got his activism fired up. (Ironic that Nevada should be deflowered of its silver at a place called Virginia City.) Samuel Clemens stayed by the lake and said camping there for three months would restore an Egyptian mummy to life. The notes he jotted while watching Hannah Clapp's Carson Valley schoolroom in 1862 found new life in chapter twenty-one of *Tom Sawyer*. Enclosed by a cabin, Bertrand Russell removed his clothes and wrote the ambitiously titled *Inquiry into Meaning and Truth*. C.S. Forester, who lived at Lake Tahoe, compared his creative upwellings to submerged tree logs breaking a watery surface. While working at the state fish hatchery in Tahoe City, John Steinbeck bragged in letters about the homemade fish-gut condoms he used on pretty tourists, one of whom was his future wife Carol Henning. He lost the job when his boss found him drunk in bed with a pistol in his hands casually firing holes in the ceiling. George Sessions attended Sierra College and cited Russell as an inspiration for the Deep Ecology movement. Furthermore, Twain, Muir, Russell, Steinbeck, and Sessions all launched a new life phase after introspecting at Tahoe.

At Yosemite egoic disregard of limitations brings descent, but at Tahoe, submersion. Steinbeck was by no means the only Tahoe resident fond of regressing his consciousness in the bottled narcissism of potent drink: accounts of alcohol-related drownings go all the way back to the 1800s. In 1866, some young women and their male companion visited Dead Man's Island so called after the drowning of Captain Dick Barter. A note found inside an empty champagne bottle left after the visit described the place thus: "The island appears to be in the center of a brilliant circle of admirers who, attracted by her beauty, still know she has a stony heart." It was renamed Fannette Island as a corruption of Coquette. That year in September a six-foot cone of water rose just offshore of Saxton's Mill, and where it sank, a whirlpool spun for two days.

Narcissists fear death and try to preserve their youth against it; losses do not change when submerged in the unconscious; and bodies, say the legends, do not rise in Lake Tahoe because the cold water stops them from filling with buoyant gas. Be that as it may, most of those who drown in the lake are never found. In 1908, Robert Watson, his son, and others unearthed caskets from an old cemetery to move them to another graveyard destined to lie behind the Tahoe City golf course. Many of the bodies were "metalized and fossilized" by snow water seeping into the graves. Watson tapped a baby on the forehead and heard a metallic ring. Except for being dead the bodies looked quite fit. Perhaps they had drunk the mineral water of Rubicon Springs, a "Fountain of Youth." A fossilized Indian woman surfaced at Cascade Lake. According to an old Laker custom, attendance is unnecessary at the funeral of anyone deceased in such pristine surroundings before the age of eighty. At the bottom of Glenbrook Bay rests the old SS *Tahoe*. Locals still murmur about Tahoe Tessie, the Lady of the Lake, and Water Babies who drown incautious men.

History books about Tahoe echo with the boyish nicknames of

early pioneers and settlers: "Billy" Morgan, "Yank" Clement, "Billy" Lapgham, "Lucky" Baldwin, "Sis" Knisley, "Cock-Eye" Johnson, "Snowshoe" Thompson, "Hank" Monk, "Curly Bill" Gerhart, "Big John" Littlefield, Charles "Coon Hollow" Saddle, "Newt" Spencer, Jacob "Big Jake" Putman, "Baldy" Green, "Al" Sprague, "Doc" Benton, and "Pop" Church, a Truckee stage driver who loved to bestow on the land names like Devil's Slide, Bluff, and Rockpile. Disruption of self-image extended to local namings and renamings of the lake itself (Maheon Lake, Bigler, Big Truckee, finally Tahoe), Colwell's changed to Casnells Mill by accident, Hunter's Retreat left off the map, Meeks Bay changed to Micks Bay by accident (also known as Meigs, Meegs, and Buttermilk Bay), *Tahoma* perhaps meaning "high mountain" in Washoe but no high mountain stands nearby, Waterniche changed to Frost's Homestead to Rubicon Park, its waters deepest of any near a shoreline anywhere; rough climbing of surrounding mountains has been compared to egomaniac Caesar's crossing of the Rubicon, Emerald Isle has been known not only as as Coquette and Fannette but as Baranoff, Dead Man's, and Hermit's. Copeland's Grove changed to Ziegler's Grove to Camp Richardson, and of course Carnelian from Cornelian by accident.

Acting out has been as narcissistically boyish as drinking and gambling in floating palaces, smuggling, shooting, and stabbing, each incident of emotional regression echoing in the presence of the lake-unconscious. Between 1960 and 1963, bad boy Frank Sinatra owned the resort Cal-Neva (even its name self-divided). Other celebrities often visited, among them Dean Martin, Ava Gardner, Howard Hughes, and Marilyn Monroe. Former Cal-Neva employee Jack Ruby killed Kennedy's assassin before he could be interrogated. Evidently JFK and his father and brother stayed at Cal-Neva too. According to released FBI files, so did several Mafia kingpins, including Sam Giancana of Chicago. Nancy Sinatra and others have claimed that her father was a liaison between the Mafia and the Kennedy clan. Illegal liquor and prostitutes crossed the state line through hidden tunnels. One ran conveniently to Sinatra's bungalow. The Nevada Gaming Commission, after years of looking the other way, closed down Cal-Neva after a corpse was found near the front door. And so the echoing "Curse of Cal-Neva" as seen in

Sinatra's self-destructive behavior, Monroe's suicide a few weeks after staying there, the Kennedy assassination, Sinatra's teen son kidnapped and ransomed from a South Lake Tahoe casino, Sam Giancana shot in the head shortly before testifying to the Senate about CIA-Mafia connections...

At Lake Tahoe Echo finally joins Narcissus. Rancher Ramsdale Buoy named the lake in May, 1866, when he called out, "It's just like advertising for a wife—pop the question once and you get more answers than you can attend to in a month." Narcissus flowers are often spotted growing around South Tahoe and Echo Lake. In 1876 a dam raised the waters enough to connect Echo with Lower Echo.

Visitors often see life-sized faces, animals, and other shapes mirrored forth in the granite mountains. A mermaid stands at the end of Drum's pier, Sleeping Lady below the Gladiator, above him Old King Cole (also known as the Turk in Turban, Grinning Negro, and Old Squaw) facing the Stone Seal. Many of these apparitions cluster near Rubicon Point like frozen memories climgimg to an unresolved complex. While sketching scenery in the summer of 1862, the wife of Reverend J.A. Benton of Massachusetts found Shakespeare Cliff, now Shakespeare Rock, site of various tourist fatalities. The first such tragedy involved Carrie Rice and William Cramer while they explored the cavern within the rock. Halfway across the cliff Rice slipped and pulled at Cramer, who grabbed a ledge but lost his grip on her hand. As she fell to her death she said, "We must go, Will. There is no hope for us." An Indian head stares out of a nearby rock.

Around Lake Tahoe surface replicas of what has been lost to time. Captain Dick Barter built an accurate seven-foot model of a steam frigate with a clock mechanism to turn the propeller and two hundred and twenty-five tiny crew to man the model. He too was a drinker: "Why, 'Tahoe' is Injuyn for lager beer." Emerald Bay's likeness to a Scandinavian fjord prompted Lora Knight to pay architect Lennart Palme to design a Viking's Castle (finished 1929) with furniture meticulously copied to resemble the Norse originals. Vertical scars from abandoned flues run up steep Incline Mountain. Near Incline, San Francisco millionaire George Whittell built the Thunderbird Lodge of granite blocks, leaded windows, and stone, all of it ornamented by iron thunderbirds. Millennia before he or anyone else arrived at the lake, subterranean lava flows shaped the Sunken Cliffs into an underwater amphitheater. When the water is clear, they look so much closer than forty feet below the surface that the viewer momentarily feels pitched forward into the depths.

It's as though the images, motifs, and faces that assemble here echo like dream images emanating from the spacious psyche of the lake. In Native origin tales an old Indian fleeing an evil presence received a leafy branch offered by a helpful spirit who told him to pluck its leaves and drop them. Each would turn into enough water to offer a barrier against what followed. First the Indian created Lake Tahoe, then Fallen Leaf Lake in the shape of a human foot--an echo of Tahoe three miles long and a mile wide--before crossing Desolation Valley to find refuge in a flood plain that Spaniards would name Sacramento after seeing Native fishers soaked in running blood.

ON THE MORNING OF September 26, 1998, an enormous waterspout rose on the lake not far from Cave Rock. Spinning clockwise, which is rare, it swelled to two hundred and fifty feet in diameter. According to Washoe myth, Cave Rock is the home of the Water Babies. Squirrel saw one sitting on the rock and reflected that his brother Weasel might enjoy having beautiful hair like hers. "If you try to take my hair," the Water Baby warned him, "the lake will swallow you." Each time he plucked a hair the waters rose until, finally, he and Weasel found themselves up to their necks in trouble. Persuaded by his brother's pleadings, Squirrel gave back the hair, and the lake retreated to leave many small lakes around it.

Since 1957, when the League to Save Lake Tahoe formed ("Keep Tahoe Blue"), the lake has lost a foot of clarity per year. Eutrophication from runoff accelerates algae growth. Stormwater, auto and boat exhaust, road dust, erosion, and fire danger from dying white fir forests eaten by bark beetles contribute to the fact that Tahoe's visibility--its capacity for reflection--has dimmed by half over the past forty years. A 2011 study found an alarming decline in native fish outcompeted by introduced stocks of Mackinaw, rainbow, brown, and brook trout, bluegill, and largemouth bass. The native Lahontan cutthroat trout died off back in 1939, and the red-side shiner and speckled dace are disappearing from the Lake of the Sky. Thanks to environmentalist pressure, however, 80% of the terrain around Tahoe has been returned to public control so the waters can heal.

> So singularly clear was the water, that where it was only twenty or thirty feet deep the bottom was so perfectly distinct that the boat seemed floating in the air!
>
> — *Roughing It*

On New Year's Day I woke early as, possibly, the only sober man in Lake Tahoe. I had not timed it on purpose, but above me shone a blue moon as a perennial symbol of romantic aloneness. On a last walk to the market I nearly collided with a self-preoccupied teen fiddling with his phone. It's not *that* a theme happens, I reflected, but where and in how persistent its pattern.

> Perhaps, I wake up dreaming, there is a spirit lake somewhere deep inside us as reflective as Tahoe itself--a place where all our deeds, good and bad, flow and collect and merge together; a place that mirrors our own being back to the sky.
>
> — Scott Lankford

I walked down a side street to be closer to the lake. The beach was locked, though, and the sign said you had to have a membership card to get inside. Fortunately, a man came up and held the door open. I walked out onto a snow-covered shore where a stiff, chilly breeze sent small waves to clear a few brown feet of shoreline. Winds across the lake blow in different directions, and the lake never entirely freezes over. Dead calm, chop, and storm waves can coexist like psychic compartmentalizations in different parts of the twenty-two-miles-by-twelve length and width of cold water cupped between mountain ranges. One of the winds is named the Zephyr.

What does Tahoe dream? I wondered as the sun set behind a line of oncoming clouds. Ducks huddled on the sand. An eagle flew up the shore, paused directly overhead, regarding me, and flew off. I saluted it.

What had the original mythic spring or lake done with Narcissus? The water tried to take Narcissus under, introduce the hunter unable to see past his vanity to his own depths and, beyond them, the world's. In dreams demarcated bodies of water can indicate a need to reflect on or deepen the life of the conscious mind.

As is evident on a map, Tahoe is the interior counterpart to extraverted Point Conception spiking outward into the Pacific. *Fail to reflect* says Tahoe to all California from within its eastern joint, border, turning, medial epicondyle, *fail to reflect through the haze of your own images to the world around you,* fail to connect Narcissus and Echo, self and other, height and depth, inner Nevada and outer California, *and you will lose your balance, suffer self-intoxication, and go under.* Mirroring can awaken or kill, after all. Narcissism can bulge the ego bubble or interiorize attention in service to self-reflection pointing beyond itself to what awaits notice outside. Cold, elevated, and brilliantly refractive, Tahoe reflects back our American narcissism even while opening a view by which to see ourselves as clearly as an image in a mountain lake.

What did I see in the lake? As the grown child of a musical mother, my perceptions sometimes tend more toward the auditory than the visual. I came out here to hear here, to listen to and write the unspoken and ignored voice of place. To recognize the lake (and every other place) as the only real boss, owner, and landlord to which we must all report. And to leave behind, at last, my lingering identity as a Southern Californian. From the edge of the state, the edge of my state, I belonged, I saw clearly, to the northern tribe now.

The wind brushed the unruly hair of nodding pines. An oddly straight bank of clouds stretched like a celestial roadway pointing due north. Goodbye for now, Tahoe, crystalline lake in which Narcissus and our narcissism drown.

Northeastern Workshop of Vulcan

I wouldn't have thought that getting lost crossing the Sierra and then resorting to cannibalism to live would have been worthy of a memorial, yet here it was on a base twenty-two feet high to match the height of the snow that winter. The plaque on the Pioneer Statue announced:

VIRILE TO RISK AND FIND; KINDLY WITHAL
AND A READY HELP. FACING THE BRUNT OF
FATE; INDOMITABLE,—UNAFRAID.

In May 1846, a loose affiliation of wagon train pioneers suffered through a swarm of self-inflicted setbacks, among them an ill-advised shortcut across the Great Salt Lake Desert and two murders, before they had even arrived in the Sierra. They were nourished along the way by pine nuts collected for them by the Miwok. Blizzards pinned down the party for five months before rescuers from Sutter's fort led them into Sacrmento. Afterwards, two of Sutter's slaves and guides, Luis and Salvator, were found shot in the back and partially eaten.

Tragedy and Truckee have endured a long relationship. Situated within the Tahoe National Forest a few miles north of the lake, Truckee took its name fom a Paiute leader saddened by a vision of a great emigration and a sound of many people weeping. Before this (1863) Truckee had been a stage stop called Coburn's Station. "Truckee has since survived fires, racial purges, and carousing," boasted a sign in the historical museum, "that would have wiped a town three times its size off the map." Perhaps unmitigated violence was something to be proud of here.

The "racial purges" referred to the Chinese who, fleeing their country because of warfare and famine, and driven from the gold fields by white miners, hacked through solid granite a transcontinental railroad. The tracks run by the Donner memorial. Thousands of workers died or were maimed for life from avalanches, accidents, and explosions. Some dangled from cliffs while loaded with dynamite as others down below hit a spike with eighteen-pound sledgehammers to make a hole for the charge. A mining tax levied specifically against the Chinese provided two-thirds of the state's revenue for ten years but caused such hardship that laborers were forced to become "Crocker's pets." When they struck for an eight-hour day, clean food, and an end to whippings, Crocker--"They built the Great Wall of China, didn't they?"--cut off their food until they went back to work. The day after Leland Stanford hammered the Golden Spike to ceremonialize completion of the railroad, eleven thousand Chinese laborers lost their jobs.

Some wound up in Truckee looking for work wherever they could find it: as cooks, laundrymen, servants, lumberjacks, ice-sawers, anything that paid even a little. After the Panic of 1873, "601" vigilantes assaulted the Chinese and repeatedly burned Chinatown. "601" stood for "six feet under, zero trial, and one bullet." Running for governor, Charles McGlashan, editor and publisher of the *Truckee Republican*, relentlessly attacked the Chinese and called for a boycott against anyone who hired or supported them. As this "Truckee Method" of deliberate starvation spread to other states, the Chinese and their employers were surreptitiously threatened with death, arson, rape, and other expressions of domestic terror. Even Crocker was afraid to set them to work sawing timber in Tahoe. Meanwhile, McGlashan branded the Chinese "sons of Cain" and enlisted other Christian imagery for his cause. Some of the Chinese defended themselves, some tried to live quietly, others left, but on June 17, 1886, the inflammatory rhetoric materialized as a fire that wiped out Truckee's Chinatown. Sounding eerily like Glenn Beck would one day, McGlashan gloated, "The present struggle is a final one."

Truckee was not "cleaned up" after the Chinese left. In fact murder became commonplace with bodies simply dumped off at the cemetery. Speakeasies proliferated in the back streets, as did displays of public drunkenness.

Today, along the main street through town, I saw brick buildings and rustic chalets inhabited by Wells Fargo and other big box stores inserted inside them like viruses into host cells. Three churches along Church Street at the south/east end of town were punctuated by a mortuary.

> I suppose all this talk about ancient history is just another way of saying that the collective unconscious was put together at a series of truck stop meetings on a long highway through time. I'd like to know what went down at each truck stop. Trucks from the past are still delivering.
>
> — Craig San Roque

The emphasis placed on flesh here was disconcerting. Built into a red railroad car, Jerkey Junction advertised "Fresh Elk, Buffalo, Salmon, Jerky." A rack of white antlers sprouted from the rooftop. Up the road a red brick building housed the Truckee Tannery.

Catching I-395 again as it swung back into California, I passed Honey Lake, having dipped briefly into the greenery of the Plumas National Forest, and caught Route 36 west to Lake Almanor. Somewhere around here African American pioneer Jim Beckworth had opened a wagon train route across the Sierra. Too bad the Donners hadn't heard of it. A pass was named in his honor. I changed to Route 70 and saw oceans of dry, yellow grass between gargantuan cattle ranches. Small towns occupied highway junctions next to collapsing barns, faded wood sidings, and a boarded-up church at Loyalton. A marker at Vinton Cemetery informed me that Swiss-Italian dairymen had settled in the mid-1800s. A sign

prohibited alcohol use and unauthorized "internment"--not "inter-
ment"--of remains. "Any person visiting the cemetery does so at
their own risk." I shook my head. What was the worst that could
happen? In Adin, someone had celebrated September 11 by sticking
small American flags into door and window jams, mailboxes, even
fence posts and the crotches of trees.

Pines, oaks, and fields full of stones; reddish soils, a gradual
grade. The white crown of Mount Shasta rose from the western
horizon. When I entered the Lassen National Forest my body
relaxed for some reason. I expected to see Duke Senior around every
bend in this lovely Forest of Arden. *Sweet are the uses of adversity*...As I
closed on Chester, however, the trees shortened and grew dry tan
splotches. Fallen branches lay around many stumps. A billboard
shouted, "Save Lake Almanor! Stop the Thermal Curtains"--refer-
ring to PG&E's plan to prevent the North Fork of the Feather River
from overheating its trout by funneling cold water from Lake
Almanor. They plan to do the same at Butt Valley Reservoir (named
after miner Horace Butts). This minor improvement in downstream
habitat is expected to cost PG&E subscribers $53 million and to
block pond smelt at Lake Almanor from reaching the trout at Butt
Valley Reservoir, in effect robbing Peter and Andrew to pay a little
to Paul. Perhaps Modernity should be redefined as a knack for using
solutions to compound problems.

At Chester and Lake Almador, the increasingly familiar regional
blend of Subway-style chain stores in log cabins as well as retailers
with folksy names like Busy Bee Real Estate, Knot Bumper
Restaurant, Antlers Motel, Serendipidy, the Giggling Crow, and
quotation marks around "Quality" Car Wash hinting an inadvertent
double message. The blue lake was wide and full of birds. A breeze
ruffled placid waters just enough to wash a small, rocky shore.
Silences lengthened between passing cars. Near town squatted a
helicopter base where copters and jets perched atop pedestals like
the busts of generals in a military museum. A structure had burned
to the ground at Fire Mountain Trailer Park.

In the mid-1800s, rancher, miner, blacksmith, and sawmill oper-
ator Peter Lassen brought William Nobles to the Honey Lake
Valley. Soon after, Isaac Roop of Shasta City heard Nobles talking

up the valley, so Roop arrived too and bought a land claim of one square mile. His log cabin served as a trading post for wagon trains until squabbles with the federal government over land boundaries prompted Roop, Lassen, and thirty other men to declare the independent Territory of Natauqua (thought to be a Paiute word for "woman"). This was in 1857. In a year the "Sagebrush Rebellion" petered out, immigrants arrived from Germany and Switzerland, miners sought gold in the hills, ranchers bred horses, mills sawed down trees, and two Chinatowns grew in Susanville. Named after a settler's daughter, this town gathered around Roop's Fort and reached its adulthood as a small city. (Incidentally, *Lassen* means "son of Lars," a name similar to Lawrence. *Lars* and *Lawrence* mean "crowned with laurel.")

Some places require extensive analysis to figure out Who, mythically speaking, lives there. Not this place. As soon as I drove into town I got lost looking for Diane Drive (where was it hiding?), saw two deer on a front lawn on Ash Street, and several other of Diana's sacred animals elsewhere. I on Main, where I looked back at six shooter signs and a gun store, and stared up at a mural starting (left to right) with a Native woman holding a basket and ending with one logger sawing down a tree while another logger looked upward at a white goose. Another mural depicted women weaving fabric together as a crowd of happy onlookers grouped behind them by a river. Diana (called Artemis by the Greeks) having been a goddess of childbirth as well as a hunter ranging into undomesticated wildness, it made sense to see an archery store on Main and a foster and adoption agency next to City Hall. *Susan*, by the way, means "lily." In the Book of Tobit, Susannah stoutly defended herself against accusations made against her. The Acteons locked in the prison outside the city enjoyed less success.

Women ran the hotel and restaurant. Diana and Artemis are leaders, if introverted ones. Susan Roop had fed the poor and been quite active in community affairs. The city gained Gladys Spencer Burroughs, its first woman mayor, back in 1924. She was also a Superior Court judge for Lassen County and Assistant Attorney General of California. Miriam Colcord was the city's first librarian. Midwife Ruth Potter opened a maternity home despite the initial skepticism of male doctors. "Old Lucy," Native American Sallie Norman, practiced a nomadic lifestyle and lived to over a hundred. Stories still circulate about red-haired Grace Lucero and the pink Cadillac she drove so unpredictably that drivers and pedestrians took pains to avoid the car. Perhaps as a joke, her daughter claimed after her mother had died that Lucero had been buried in the car.

I sat down to dinner with a hunter's appetite and ate an unusually large quantity of red meat. Cookies and milk waited at the hotel under nature scenes and flowery decor. As I lay down in bed, images of forests and the elf Galadriel bubbled forth in my mind's eye accompanied by waves of maternal, unconditional welcomeness so tangible and intense that sleep eluded me until very late.

I rose early still glowing with it. *Thank you, Susanville.* The showerhead emitted a thin banshee wail. In the restaurant a glass jar sat ready to accept contributions for the family of someone named Diana.

As THE GREAT GRANITIC plutons of the Sierra congealed and rose, Lassen County still lay close to sea level. But thirty million years ago the land began to lift as the climate turned subtropical. As the Juan de Fuca plate crunched northward under the North American plate, eruptions intensified too, of basalt and basaltic andesite that slowly raised the Cascade Range from Lassen to southernmost British Columbia while burying older volcanic rock below younger. The oldest still exposed, at five to ten million years of age, juts from the Burney Falls-Lake Britton area just north of Highway 299. Lava poured steadily from several volcanoes and from huge fissures in the earth. Had colonizers immigrated to northeastern California back then, the Paradise they expected to find in the Golden State would more closely have resembled Hell.

A quarter of a million years ago Mt. Tehama's dacite domes exploded, but already the eruptions were gradually dying down. Glaciers doing their patient pruning at the higher altitudes left hills and ridges and six hundred lakes. Laboring through opposition, eruptions raised landscapes and glaciers ground them down again. A prominent feature of today's landscape was missing, however, until eleven thousand years ago, when a dome of dacite rose, pouring lava as it grew, for about a year. Glaciers moved in, but because the Ice Age had ended, they took a little off the top of Lassen Peak and retreated. Meadows filled with deposited debris bloomed with wildflowers tended by buzzing insects.

The Yahi people called Lassen Peak *Waganupa*, "Center of the World." The county occupies a widening depression between the Sierra and the Klamaths that once opened onto a vast inland sea in the heart of the state. The Cascades, the Sierras, the Central Valley, and the Great Basin overlap at Lassen Volcanic National Park within the most volcanically active region in the state. Bumpass Hell sits directly over a magma plume. At sites with names like Chaos Crags, Sulfur Works, and Devil's Kitchen cook mud pots, boiling springs, cinder cones, dacite domes, and steam vents smelling like sulfur.

So much restlessness rumbled in my lower chest and upper stomach that I could scarcely stay in the park Visitor Center long enough to learn anything. Going outside did not tamp down the restlessness, but it did allow me to note sulfurous smells and dark, rocky soils. After hundreds of miles, the Sierra had given its granitic way before volcanic rock. A rotten stench arose from sulfur pits emitting plumes of white steam. *This is what the planet Vulcan must be like*, I thought, and with that, a laugh because I realized then Who was here. Was not the formation on Lassen Peak named the Eye of Vulcan after the lonely god of the forge? The Greeks had called him Hephaestus. The mountain he lived in rang with his solitary labors. His mighty hammer had knocked the head off Camel Rock.

I pivoted for another look around. Spikey roadside vegetation armored in translucent membranes shone green, gray, and gold as though transplanted here from another world. Grasshoppers flying invisibly by emitted strangely mechanical clicking sounds like automatic sprinklers or typewriter keys. Immense piles of boulders that covered hillsides and filled valleys were blocks knocked from an unfinished terrain sculpture still under construction. The dacite lava forming Vulcan's Castle near Lassen Peak had been poured geologically recently. Edward Abbey had worked here as a fire lookout. The park had assembled a perfectly Vulcan motto for itself: "Land of Many Uses."

Peter Skene Ogden, possible namer of Mount Shasta and trapper for England's Hudson Bay Company, entered the land of the Maidu, Atsugewi ("Pine Tree People"), Yana, Yahi, and Washoe in the 1820s as (probably) the first man of European descent to arrive. When trapper Jedediah Smith wandered through, he saw Lassen Peak and named it Mt. Joseph after the carpenter father of Jesus. Peter Lassen arrived in 1843 and bought land near the mouth of Deer Creek on the Sacramento River to set up Rancho Bosquejo ("sketch, draft") as the town of Benton City. When this did not work out, Lassen tried prospecting, looked for a rumored golden lake, and settled in Indian Valley near Greenville while promoting Susanville to the east. Killers never identified murdered him while he prospected with a partner. After his death, William Nobles found a more direct route over the mountains to the Central Valley than Lassen had uncovered. William Brewer reached Lassen Peak in 1863.

Lassen County's remoteness has discouraged colonization, but what towns and cities grew there clanked with a Vulcan thematic. Lyonsville, named after Darwin Lyn, superintendent of the Sierra Lumber Company in Red Bluff, was settled in 1862 between two forks of Antelope Creek near an old Yahi trail. The elaborate flumes constructed by Lyn remained after he departed in 1918. Railroad work and Champion Mill infused new life into the sparsely settled town whose later flumes carried boats for rapid transportation. Big Wheels serviced at the Champion machine shop hauled logs to waiting trains pulled by one of the first all-iron locomotives running anywhere. Giant logs were hauled by steam engine. At Beale's Camp, a logging truck normally drawn by horses was attached instead to a crawler manufactured by a train company. Thousands of old nails, bolts, and railroad spikes rest in the ground near the old Champion Mill. Native tribesmen mortared shut the Cave of the Spirits between Deer and Mill Creeks to protect its sacred creek-etched stones and bones of fallen warriors. Native watchers stood atop the hundred-foot-high Pinnacle posts to see for great distances.

Is this only a feeling of familiarity or am I in the company of my ancestors? Am I seeing again

through their eyes that with which they were familiar?

Is my life a dream of my father's who is imagining he
has a son? Did my grandfather stand upon this spot
and dream three generations ahead while conjuring
up my being? Do I dream or am I the dream?
　...I was here before when I wore my father's
shoes and dreamed his father's dreams.
　　　　　　—Ray Munjar at the Susan River

The name of Papoose Meadows recalls a massacre of Paiutes by
U.S. troops in June 1866. Survivors heard a baby crying in the trees.

My grandfather was the only survivor and the reason he survived was he ran down Papoose Creek, he
hid in the creek, and crawled and ran. He was shot
in the back and the soldiers left him and were
shooting at him when he dove into the lake, but he
grabbed one of the reeds and he broke it off with
both hands and he put it into his mouth and he
swum under water out to a little island there.
　　　　　　— Harold Dixon, Wadatkut Paiute

On Memorial Day, 1914, the southernmost Cascade volcano
woke up again in the first of two hundred and ninety-eight eruptions that put a quick but definite end to plans to develop the area
around Lassen Peak. Muddy lava flowing for miles blackened the
Devastated Area. Lance Graham went to the summit with two other
men and was knocked cold by a flying rock that also broke his col-
larbone. He had to be dug out of the ash. Mud loosed in May 1915
formed Hat Lake by damming Hat Creek.
　I parked near Lassen Peak and walked toward the summit. The
Eye of Vulcan stared down into the valley. What work was being
done here besides restructuring the landscape?
　An amazing profusion of plants grows here where so many soil
types gather. Not only grasslands, shrubs, sages, and junipers, but

mountain mahogany phlox, mariposa lily, yellow rabbitbrush, Ponderosa pine, reenleaf manzanita, red fir, and seven hundred species of vascular plants (ferns, herbs, shrugs, trees) in seventy-five plant families. Fern mosses, frogs, pack rats, and brown bats inhabit seven hundred caves in the Lava Beds. On the ground cluster Sierra onion, white brodiaea, dogbane, borage, King's sandwort, catchflies, long-stalked starwort, goosefoot, thistle, daisies, funflowers, and mountain mule ears. Kangaroo rats dart to and fro with jackrabbits, gopher snakes, badgers, bobcats, raptors, Western fence lizards, scrub jays, purple martins, lazuli buntings, Western tanagers, ducks, snow geese, tundra swans, barn owls, prairie falcons, great-horned owls, Brewer's blackbird, water scorpions, trout, garter snakes, blue herons, pied-billed grebes, Canada goose, golden eagles, bald eagles, mountain quail, spotted sandpipers, great horned owls, rock wrens, mountain bluebird,s various shrews and moles, foxes, martens, coyotes, bobcats, mountain lions, bats, and bears. Like shy Vulcan, most of the mammals come out at night.

On my drive out of the park I halted to wait while crews in orange vests repaved the road. Heaps of gravel lay around stacks of logs and cinderblocks. I fingered the pocket knife I had bought and wondered what was taking so long. Come to think of it, long intervals characterized this visit. A quarter of a mile separated the park's fee box and the ranger station. Visitor centers stood well apart. The pilot truck to guide traffic through the construction zone took nearly half an hour to arrive. Of course: the long intervals between ventings.....

Residents of this county often feel isolated from the rest of California. In part this is geography, but Vulcan is, after all, a god whose self-isolating conservatism echoes the sort hold-out lifestyle found here at the northeastern edge of the state.

When the god was kicked out of Olympus for being lame, the resulting crash turned his feet around to point permanently backwards. According to Jordan Clary, travelers like to hang shoes on a gnarled old cottonwood next to a Lassen County highway fifty miles from Susanville. Donators leave cowboy boots, construction boots, satin high heels, birckenstocks, sandals, dress shoes, and tennis shoes (some of them a startling pink: a wink from Venus, sexy wife of Vulcan?). The highway department cleared them away, but they reappeared.

Someone cut down the Shoe Tree one Friday 13th, but afterwards other Shoe Trees were seen all over the county. At Thompson Peak Jeanie French spotted a lone white fir wearing a cotton bra with cones placed in the cups and a golden belt spray-painted around its waist along with a poignant plea: "Don't cut."

I SPENT A NIGHT in Burney. Twisting fish had been painted on store windows to make visiting sportsmen feel at home. At Chatty Cathy's restaurant a sign suggested, "Bring a Buck, Save a Buck—10% Off for Hunters." As dusk darkened into night, truckers parked their rigs behind the motels lined up along Highway 299.

In the morning I left just before daybreak. The truckers were already gone, of course. I headed east as the land and I woke up together. Autumn mists hung over dew-moistened meadows whose mysteries I would never have time to discover.

Before entering the Modoc National Forest I needed Route 395 one more time to have a look at Goose Lake. I would pass through Alturas, seat of Modoc County, to reach the northeasternmost part of California, double back to Route 139 to Lava Beds National Monument, where the Modocs had made a last stand against the U.S. Army, and drive to Tule Lake and Tulelake just under our border with Oregon. From there I would drop into Weed and Mt. Shasta before heading west for a long descent down the coast.

Online maps revealed a large blue orb I took for Goose Lake, but after driving down a long levee past road signs pocked with bullet holes, yellow grass on the west side and cracked gray earth trampled by cattle on the east, I halted in a cloud of dust and realized that Goose Lake no longer existed. The water had gone to agriculture. Only a shallow wetland remained for the birds and other forms of life that had once clustered here so thickly. Now the region was a moonscape relieved only by tules and clumps of weeds. I turned around and crossed westward over the rugged Modoc Plateau.

That three-million-acre volcanic plateau spread and hardened a million years ago. Today it supports high desert ecocommunities

containing perennial grasslands, sagebrush, scrub, antelope bitter-
brush, mountain mahogany, juniper, aspen, and, high up on the
Warner Mountains, conifer forests, although erosion, hunting, overgrazing, agriculture, housing development, and altered fire regimens
have threatened impacted ecosystems heavily.

A quarter of a million years ago, an eruption from the depths
piled and hardened lava until it breached the surface of Lake
Modoc, an ancient body of water that covered much of what are
now the northern and eastern borders of California. As Petroglyph
Point rose above the lake, birds nested in the plateau's cracks and
crevices. Swallows, owls, hawks, and falcons still do. Petroglyphs
no one now understands line the cliffs. Designs left by Modoc sculp-
tors floating up in tule boats look like arrows, sun symbols, or tri-
angular lines like this: /Λ\ /Λ\ /Λ\ /Λ\ /Λ\ /Λ\ /Λ\. Many were carved in
the soft sandstone more than four thousand years ago.

Lava Beds National Monument emerged as a hot belching of lava
from Medicine Lake Volcano forty thousand years ago. The last
blast a thousand years ago left the cinder cones, spatter cones,
fumaroles, craters, hornitos, tube caves, darkened fields, and jagged
rocks so characteristic of Vulcan's fiery smithing. Twenty-five caves
are open to visit.

Before entering them I walked into the lava maze where fifty-
three Modocs had held off three hundred and thirty U.S. troops.

In fifteenth-century England, the gentry had the idea of reducing
rural peasants to rootless laborers by forcing them to cede portions
of land plus grazing rights. These portions were then enclosed and
reorganized as monocrop operations in a far-off foreshadowing of
California's "factories in the fields." The Enclosure policy aided the
Industrial Revolution by converting land-holding peasants into
landless wage slaves desperate for work. A similar policy in
California forced Native people to cede four hundred and fifty million acres of land to the U.S. by the late 1800s.

Most of the American settlers of Modoc County lived in the
Langell and Poe Valleys at first. These Lost River farmers and ranchers grew grain and raised livestock, but lack of water limited crop
production until Tule Lake was drained. The Modocs responded to
this invasion of their homeland by stealing cattle. In 1873 Judge

Steele got them to agree to live on a reservation near the lake in exchange for halting their raids, but the settlers enroached onto the reservation. Then these settlers petitioned the U.S. Government to remove the Modocs altogether.

> From the 1820s until after the Civil War, the con-
> tacts between white men and the Modocs were
> intermittent, but they produced a crisis in Modoc
> society that had to be resolved. White miners
> crossed the Indian hunting range. White miners
> disturbed the streams. White traders changed their
> economic way of life. White settlers fenced the
> meadows along the lakes. White religious teachers
> upset the traditional Modoc system of ethical
> behavior. By the time the different white groups
> had become well established, such a tight noose had
> been drawn around the Modocs that the Indians
> had to struggle for their cultural life.
> — Keith Murray

Struggle was rooted in the Modoc heritage. Having split long ago with their relatives the Klamaths, they had moved south (*modoc* means "southern people" in Klamath) across a fault line and into the badlands with nothing to trade with their neighbors. They took to raiding and occasionally captured Shasta, Paiute, and Pit River people to sell as slaves in what is now Oregon.

The first Europeans they saw were armed Hudson Bay Company traders from Fort Vancouver. Soon a northern branch of the Oregon Trail established by Lindsay and Jesse Applegate ran through Modoc country.

It was harsh country, volcanic, rugged, and sparse, but for the Modoc it was home. Their name for Lost River, an underground flow connecting the Lower Klamath with Tule Lake, was "Smiles of God."

> We cannot estimate the love an Indian has for his
> country. His holy places are not in far-off Palestine;

they are before his eyes in his own birthplace,
where every river, hill and mountain has a story
connected with it, an account of its origin. No people could be more religious than were the Indians
before the advent of the white man; they had no
observance, rite, or custom which they did not
believe to be God-given.

— M.A. Curtin

Their eviction, wrote Reverend Alfred Meacham, who had been
shot by a Modoc and recovered, was completed "under the sanction
of law, and in the shade of Church-steeples, and with the sanctimo-
nious semblance of honesty and justice."

In 1852, settler Ben Wright, who had lost a young girl he loved
to a Native (but not Modoc) attack, invited the Modocs to peace
negotiations at Tule Lake. Although he offered them a truce, the
feast he laid out for them was laced with strychnine. They were
alert enough not to eat any of it, but Wright and his men pulled concealed weapons--as the Modocs would later to attack U.S. peace
commissioners they suspected of treachery--and killed all but five of
the forty-six Modoc negotiators. A few years after the massacre a
drunken Wright stripped an Indian interpreter who had angered
him and drove her with a whip through the streets of a mining
town. She responded by having him killed and eating his heart.

In 1848 the non-Native population of California barely touched
fourteen thousand; by 1860, it had passed three hundred and eighty
thousand. Settlement in the West exploded with astounding rapid-
ity not because settlers wanted a fresh start, although some did, but
because settlement was heavily subsidized by the U.S. Government
after gold showed up in California. ("....The hills have been cut and
scalped and every gorge and gulch and broad valley have been fairly
torn to pieces and disembowled," wrote Muir about the gold mining, "expressing a fierce and desperate energy hard to understand.")
The Homestead Act (1862), the Pacific Railway Act that year, the
Mineral Resources Act (1866), the General Mining Law (1872), the
Timber and Stone Act (1878), and the Desert Lands Act (1877)
placed gigantic, resource-rich tracts of formerly public land into the

sleighting hands of industrial entrepreneurs. The land was supposed to go to small farmers, but loopholes in the Homestead Act
allowed it to be bought up by speculators, railroads, cattlemen, lum-
bermen, and miners. Of five hundred million acres dispersed by the
General Land Office between 1862 and 1904, only eighty million
went to homesteaders. By that time plantations controlling over a
thousand acres each owned 62% of farmland in California.

Surveying of Modoc County started in 1866 and finished by 1872.
By 1874, as ranching and planting diverted water and disrupted
indigenous cycles of fishing, gathering, and hunting, only four thousand of the original inhabitants remained. Aware they were being
exterminated, the Modocs strengthened their resistance.

During an initial round of negotiations, with Meacham trying to
get the Modocs onto the reservation set aside for them, U.S. negotiators secretly sent to Linkville, Oregon for military assistance. The
squad rode up during a break in the talks, and, drunk with whiskey,
rounded up the Modocs without having received any orders to do
so. As Captain Jack (the tribal leader) and Curly-Headed Doctor
(the priest) slipped away, the rest were marched to Fort Klamath to
be incarcerated. The newcomers were taunted by Klamaths who
lived there and who considered them ungrateful guests. Some
Modocs escaped.

When settlers continued their complaints about Modoc raids,
and about the Modoc habit of requiring token payments of hay or
food in exchange for grazing rights, the stodgy, bureaucratic
General Canby arrived to take charge.

Captain Jack's Modoc name was *Keintpoos*, possibly "Heartburn,"
although one historian translates it as "Man of Few Words." As a
tribal leader he knew how to make them count. During the next
round of negotiations (Canby was not present), Captain Jack said:

> We are good people, and will not kill or frighten
> anybody. We want peace and friendship... I do not
> want to live upon the reservation, for the Indians
> there are poorly clothed, suffer from hunger, and
> even have to leave the reservation sometimes to
> make a living. We are willing to have whites in our

country, but do not want them to locate on the west side and near the mouth of Lost River, where we have our winter camps.

This more-than-reasonable request was ignored. T. B. Odeneal, who received it, recommended to Washington that the Modoc leaders be seized. A military force was dispatched to bombard and storm the lava beds on the south shore of Tule Lake.

On this spot a wooden stand dispensed a pamphlet--"Captain Jack's Stronghold Historic Trail"--that laid out the genocidal war scene by scene: "Modoc Outpost"; "Main Defense Line"; "Firing Position." "Imagine yourself in command of about half of the 60-man force defending the Stronghold." "This outpost is typical of the hidden vantage points which enabled the Modocs to defend the Stronghold so well." The Romans must have had literature like this to describe their conquests to their own citizens. "In this diagram, the Gauls stand on one side and Caesar's legions on the other...." "The Woads fought bravely, but for a lost cause...."

This was rugged terrain. The jagged rocks sliced at fingers, palms, pants, and boots. The Modocs, who knew this terrain well, called it His Grimace and "the land of burned-out fires." One soldier remarked that the lava beds were "one hell of a place." Another wrote that they were

> black ocean tumbled into a thousand fantastic
> shapes, a wild chaos of ruin, desolation and barren-
> ness--a wilderness if billowy upheavals, of furious
> whirlpools, of miniature mountains rent asunder, of
> gnarled and knotted, wrinkled and twisted masses
> of blackness, and all of this far-stretching waste of
> blackness with its thrilling suggestiveness of life, of
> action, of boiling, surging, furious motion was pet-
> rified--all stricken dead, and cold in the instant of
> its maddest rioting--fettered, paralyzed and left to
> glower at heave in impotent rage for evermore.
> — Arthur Quinn

Some of the men questioned the campaign:

> ...For what? To drive a couple of hundred miserable aborigines from a desolate natural shelter in the wilderness, that a few thriving cattlemen might ranch their wild steers in a scope of isolated country, the dimensions of some several reasonable sized countries.

Inside the caves, Modoc leaders overrode Captain Jack's desire to sue for peace and voted to fight instead.

The attackers had planned to use howitzers, but a blanket of fog rendered them useless. The Modocs repelled the first assault without suffering any casualties, but the attackers retreated with twelve dead and twenty-five wounded. Defenders collected their clothing, food, and ammunition and prepared for the next assault.

Instead, they were offered a peace commission consisting of General Canby, Reverend Meacham, Reverend Thomas, L.S. Dyar, and two interpreters. Having been dealt with treacherously before, the Modoc leaders decided to turn this event to their tactical advantage. During the talks, the Modocs present pulled out concealed weapons and opened fire. Captain Jack shot and killed Canby and took his coat. Thomas died too. Meacham was shot but lived.

Canby's replacement, Colonel Jefferson C. Davis (no literal relation to the Confederate President), had helped General Sherman burn Georgia during the Civil War. On Sherman's march toward Savannah Davis had ordered the removal of a pontoon bridge built across a creek. He did this to prevent newly freed African Americans from following him. Many drowned; those who survived were rounded up by the Confederates. Davis now turned this steel-cold ruthlessness to the task of finishing off the Modocs.

He was able to fire his artillery during the second siege of the lava beds. Modoc casualties were relatively light, but one defender fell with his head blown off by a shell. Having bragged during the first attack about his powerful Ghost Dance magic, Curly-Headed Doctor lost what was left of his credibility when the attackers crossed the magic line he had drawn in the sand. The Modocs retreated. Although low on water, they turned to inflict further casualties in rapid ambushes; at Gillem's Graveyard, they killed twenty-two pursuers while sustaining one casualty. After they retreated, soldiers found an old man and woman in a cave, murdered them, and scalped the man.

Eventually the Modocs were bottled up, but only after the war proved the costliest in lives, money, and equipment of any fought by the U.S. against Native Americans. Four of the six peace commission assassins were hanged at Fort Klamath, and the other two, spared by a promise made by President Grant to Lucretia Mott, were sent to languish in Alcatraz. Despite the deep dread Modocs held for hanging, which they believed trapped the soul within the body forever, Captain Jack shouted a jaunty response from the scaffold when a heckler called out, "Jack! What would you give me to take your place?"

"Five hundred ponies and both my wives."

The surviving Modocs were taken to Redding before transfer to Quapaw Reservation in Oklahoma, where fifty died. Organized by the survivors, the Modoc Tribe of Oklahoma achieved federal recognition and grew.

After the war, Meacham became an advocate for Native rights. He wrote "The Tragedy of the Lava Beds," a play that would now be considered activist ethnodrama, went on a speaking tour with Modoc and Klamath representatives, attended the Universal Peace Union in Philadelphia and the U.S. Indian Commission in New York City, brought Chief Joseph to Washington, wrote two books on the Modoc War, and published the Native rights advocacy journal *Council Fire.*

According to Jennie Clinton, last survivor of the Modoc war, gold, saddles, and other valuables had been hidden in haste in a cave in the lava beds. Although blind, she thought she still knew the way and offered to show it. But when she brought her friends there, a blue sky filled with black clouds, the wind roared, and the party withdrew for another day. But the day never came because she died in 1950 at the age of ninety-one.

A century after the war another eerie sequel ensued. While writing his own account, *Hell with the Fire Out,* historian Arthur Quinn was diagnosed with a brain tumor. His symptoms reminded him of the rages, disorientation, double vision, deep depressions, fits of weeping, pitching forward out of balance so often suffered by combat survivors. Because of this, he came to believe the volcanic, quake-rattled, lava-burned Modoc Plateau to be "cursed." He died in 1997 as the final casualty of the Modoc War.

AFTER AN HOUR OF meditation below ground in the lava caves I removed my plastic helmet, put away my flashlight, and drove north toward Tulelake.

By comparison to other National Forests in California, the trees of Modoc seemed shorter, more pyramidal, and farther apart. This relative sparseness offered an earthly reflection of Vulcan's volatile ardency in Northeastern California. The myths say that when Vulcan desired Minerva (whose image graces the Great Seal of California) he tried to force himself on her. She fought him off, but as they separated he ejaculated onto her thigh. She wiped off the semen onto a wool cloth and threw it away. It landed on the ground and impregnated Gaia. When she had come to term, she gave birth to Erichthonius, first king of Athens. His name means "Troubles Born of the Earth." His symbol is the serpent.

Not that Tulelake's pioneers cared much for this symbol, not with so many rattlesnakes staked out around the lake under clouds of cattle-biting mosquitos. Dennis Cralwy and Henry Miller were probably the first settlers, the latter killed in a Modoc raid. The wool reappeared as herds of grazing sheep.

Troubles born of the Earth included the lake itself. Called Moatak by the Modocs, it had been created with the Lower Klamath from the conflictual action of shifting faults. As the original geologic upthrust that divided the Klamaths from the Modocs, the Sheepy Ridge fault pushed its way upward in between the lakes as well. One-thousand-square-mile Lake Modoc dried out at the end of the Pleistocene when the Klamath River cut deeper to form Tule Lake.

Muir saw it in 1874:

....Here you are looking southeastward and the
Modoc landscape, which at once takes possession
of you lies revealed in front....When I first stood
there, one bright day before sundown, the lake was
fairly blooming in pale light, and was so responsive
to the sky in both calmness and color it seemed
itself a sky. No mountain shore hides its loveliness.
It lies wide open for many a mile, veiled in no mystery but the mystery of light.

Among the first ranchers of Modoc County was Charles
Caldwell of Ohio. He arrived in 1885 to teach school, ranch in
Canby, and own the first Clydesdale in the county. He explored the
lava caves extensively enough to find a skeleton with a gold ring on
one finger. He wore this find for years until the day he washed his
hands in a basin and threw out the water. The precious went with
it and rolled downhill out of sight.

The landscape that reminded me somewhat of Mordor's was
softening into marshes and croplands. After fashioning the Modocs
out of old bones, the Creator had told them that in times of trouble
they should find shamans to ask the mountains for help. Where
were the shamans now?

In 1880, when the herds of Sacramento sheepmen tore up the
ground, stockmen petitioned President Roosevelt to establish forest reserves here (1904). These were later combined into the Modoc
National Forest. The lava beds gained National Monument status in
1925 after Judson Howard visited them and demanded their preservation. The roads there remained unpaved until the 1960s.

In 1906, the California Northeastern Railroad (absorbed eventually by the Southern Pacific) began building a railroad from Weed
into Klamath Falls. That year the Bureau of Reclamation erected
rock dams along Lost River and Miller Creek to drain Tule Lake.
The goal was to put homesteads on drained land here and in the
Lower Klamath. The Bureau also cut a drainage channel from Lost
River to Klamath River. This, however, was the altar of hot-blood-
ed Vulcan. Once drained and dried the Lower Klamath burned with
peat fires. The smoke and alkali dust sickened humans and birds

alike as botulism spread through the surrounding swamps. Schools were closed because of the dust and remained closed through the 1930s even after the Bureau abandoned a homesteading plan that seemed fine on paper but in actuality left no room for actual roads to actual homes. When seeping methane contaminated well water enough to make it ignitable, tank cars provided by the Southern Pacific were fitted to store potable water--where? At the bottom of the former freshwater lake, of course. With the lake's sump overflowing, the Bureau dug a mile-long drainage tunnel to the Lower Klamath to send water back to where it was supposed to have been drained.

In spite of all, the first Tulelake lots were auctioned in April 1931. The city incorporated six years later.

Camp Tulelake hammered together in 1935 by the Civilian Conservation Corps still stands. The Corps installed it to provide vocational training for young men left unemployed by the Depression. In March 1943, however, over a hundred "Disloyals"--Japanese Americans held in the Tule Lake War Relocation Center--were moved to Camp Tulelake after refusing to fill out a loyalty questionnaire. German and Italian prisoners of war were kept in tents to plant and harvest crops.

The smell of onions growing in volcanic soil followed me past marshes, cattle, and canals into Tulelake. Against the backdrop of distant, craggy buttes, squalid little homes and Keep America Beautiful trashcans only emphasized the poverty. Although it was Friday, most of the businesses on Main were closed. A truck hauling potatoes rumbled by. The Veterans memorial Park held more flagpoles than actual park. The official unemployment rate hovered near 16.9%, and it showed.

It's all of a piece, how we exploit each other with how we plunder the natural world. Elk, gray wolf, grizzly bear, sharp-tailed grouse, and California bighorn sheep have been hunted to death or wiped out through habitat destruction. Pronghorn herds have been decimated along with sage grouse, the endemic Modoc sucker, the Lost River sucker, redband trout, and the Shasta crayfish. Dozens of the three hundred and ninety-nine vertebrate species that live on the Modoc Plateau--birds, reptiles, amphibians, mammals, fish--are either officially endangered or on special watch lists.

Hunters seeking plumes for women's hats and ducks for San Francisco restaurants killed so many birds on the Lower Klamath that Theodore Roosevelt established a "Preserve and Breeding Ground for Native Birds"--now the Lower Klamath National Wildlife Refuge--in 1908. In 1910, an earthen dam formed Clear Lake Reservoir where pelicans nest on small islands and geese and ducks on shores visited by cormorants, mule deer, and pronghorn antelope. This was followed by a Tule Lake Wildlife Refuge established in 1928 to protect mallards, bald eagles, cinnamon teals, avocets, stilts, and geese, among others. In 1941 the Civilian Conservation Corps built the Lower Klamath Wildlife Refuge, and in 1961, seven thousand acres were set aside for the Modoc National Wildlife Refuge of wetlands just south of Alturas.

A sign at the Lower Klamath Refuge informed me that four hundred species of wildlife lived here in the Klamath Basin. Another sign described the region's "violent geologic past." On every side marshes swayed with autumn-brown tules. Around me prowled, crawled, flapped, and swam mountain lions, golden eagles, peregrine falcons, sandhill cranes, white pelicans, and various native fishes overseen joinitly by the Forest Service, the Bureau of Land management, Fish and Wildlife, State Fish and Game, and even the Department of Defense. Mount Shasta's white peak stared back from the horizon.

When asked why we need national parks, forests, and reserves, I sometimes point out the usual human-centered benefits such as aesthetic value, or education about nature, or even medicine. Where would we be today without penicillin drawn from fungi? What life-saving cures perish when natural landscapes go to ruin? Did the last rainforest felled to produce hamburger packages contain the cure for AIDS? Cancer? Dare we risk any further desolation?

Observing our non-separateness from these landscapes, ecopsychology and Deep Ecology warn that their destruction parallels the destruction of human sanity. The inflated conviction of our elevation above the natural world that evolved us is itself inarguable evidence of ecocidal hubris and madness.

The solitary arc of California just traversed--Hesperidean Inland Empire, border-crossed Imperial Valley, Trickstered Mojave and Death Valley, Owens Valley east of Eden, solitary Mono, reflective Tahoe, and now this northeastern workshop of self-directed Vulcan--suggests another reason for not sawing it all down or fishing it all up. Ever park still standing, every reserve we protect, every sanctuary of life announces that living things besides the human matter here. They enjoy what seems good to them, love as they would, observe the world through their own senses, set the world singing with their calls, chirps, and squeaks, and return to the dust when it's time to.

Such protected places push us past the self-destructive narcissism of viewing everything through the dim dual lenses of "What good is this to us?" and "How can we make money from it?" A lake restored, a hillside unsawed, a valley left in undisturbed green vitality serve as signposts along the evolutionary highway that genus Homo still retains a chance at sapiens. So proclaims what survives of the many-sided interior of California.

Part Two: Westward

Shasta: Mount Philosopher's Stone

"State of Jefferson" shouted a barn roof to Interstate 5 six miles south of Yreka ("why-reeka").

If I kept south on 5 for long enough I would reenter the Central Valley and pass Shasta Lake, Redding, and other places I had seen and written about. Instead, I would drop down into Yreka, Weed, and Mt. Shasta sixty miles below the Oregon border before turning north again to proceed west through the Klamath National Forest to the coast.

In 1852, citizens living near the border of California and Oregon introduced a bill in the California legislature meeting at Vallejo. The citizens were gold miners determined to avoid paying taxes. The miners tried again in January 1854 by meeting at Yreka Hotel to discuss how to carve "a new Territory out of certain portions of Northern California and Southern Oregon." Twenty-three men signed the resulting declaration that went nowhere, so they tried to redraw the state lines. These men floated "Jefferson" as a territorial name in honor of America's third president, drafter of the Declaration of Independence and advocate of states' rights, but even Jefferson had understood that the national government needed money to run.

In 1935, John Childs, a judge from Crescent City, protested badly maintained roads and other "injustices" by naming himself governor of the State of Jefferson. The movement gathered to the point of Governor Olson giving it a tepid nod. When Mayor Gilbert Gable of Port Orford, Oregon appointed himself interim governor of Jefferson on a platform of no sales taxes, no liquor taxes, no income taxes, and a prosperous red light district to generate revenue, Childs joined efforts with him. The Yreka Chamber of Commerce put the motion before the board of supervisors who liked the idea of Yreka's designation as capital of the forty-ninth state, so the Yreka 20-30 club drafted a patriotic proclamation of independence. Drivers on Highway 99 found themselves stopped and handed pro-Jefferson leaflets by men armed with hunting rifles. The leaflets bore as the new emblem of Jefferson a mining pan marked with two Xs to signify a double cross by both Oregon and California, but in actuality the new State Seal looked like a round face with crossed eyes.

In 1941, Del Norte, Trinity, Siskiyou, and Lassen counties merged with Josephine and Curry counties in Oregon and, as the state of "Jefferson," seceded from the Union. As local businessman George Wacker worked to bring the secession movement money by pitching for highways and road construction, Childs won the election to "governor." In December 1941, Yreka hosted an inauguration parade led by a bear named Itchy.

> You are now entering Jefferson, the 49th State of the Union. Jefferson is now in patriotic rebellion against the State of California and Oregon. The State has seceded from California and Oregon this Thursday, November 27, 1941. Patriotic Jeffersonians intend to secede each Thursday until further notice.
> — State of Jefferson Citizens Committee, 1941

The State of Jefferson might well have gained actual statehood-- plenty of Tea Party Movement forerunners supported it--but the Japanese attacked Pearl Harbor three days after the parade and Jeffersonians succumbed to the nationally fashionable vengeful patriotism. Still, today survives a Jefferson State Radio (JSR, first known as KSOR), Jefferson signs along I-5, memorabilia (as I saw on a visit to the Yreka Historical Society), and Etna Brewery, distributor of the official beer of Jefferson. The Pioneer Press, located in Fort Jones, CA, is the official HQ and flies its double-cross flag. "A lot of people who have survived the regulations of the past 20 years are frustrated and angry," stated Marcia Armstrong, Supervisor of Siskiyou County's fifth district. "Through a series of state and federal regulations such as the Northwest Forest Plan, Endangered Species Acts, Porter Cologne and Clean Water Acts, the economy of much of the area has been choked off. There are many pockets of real poverty and communities that are suffering." In other words, repealing the liquor tax must take priority over saving what's left of the biosphere. In 2001, Jeffersonians showed up to support the Klamath Bucket Brigade in Klamath Falls after environmentalist pressure suspended growers' water allotments.

I grabbed a copy of the free newsheet *Jefferson Backroads*. It informed that "the Mythical State of Jefferson is most definitely alive and well." Inside awaited ads for Mom & Pop Shoppes, Warner's Wagons ("Fine Used Cars"), Hi-Lo Cafe Motel & RV Park, Cortright's Market & Deli (the ad included the Great Seal of the State of Jefferson— "Locally Owned & Operated"), "a full line of products for all your farming, logging and agricultural equipment needs," a request for local business owners to attend monthly tourism meetings ("Heck, we may as well throw in a re-enactment of the State of Jefferson Patriotic Rebellion of 1941"), and an antique car show, motorcycle rally, and vintage trailer ad. "Variations Salon" sounded more like a San Francisco venue. To attend the "Lost Dutchman Mining Association Yearly Outing," contact Earl. The baking pie in an ad for Bob's Ranch House smoked as though someone had planted a bomb inside it.

Funny, I thought while walking around Yreka, *how often outsiders assume "Jefferson" refers to Jefferson Davis.*

It must be the rebellion motif rampaging through Yreka.

Historians claim that *Yreka* means "North Mountain," but it sounds like a parody of Eureka ("I Have Found It"). "Eureka" goes back to *heuriskein*, "to find," and contains the presence of tricky Hermes. Archimedes was said to have shouted "eureka!" upon realizing how to demonstrate that goldsmiths had mixed in silver to adulterate the metallic crown of Hiero II, king of Syracuse. In Yreka, a rebellious mining town since the first shanties went up in 1851, the shout might have been, "Why Find It?"

Mark Twain offered his own version:

> There was a bakeshop with a canvas sign which had not yet been put up but had been painted and stretched to dry in such a way that the word BAK-ERY, all but the B, showed through and was reversed. A stranger read it wrong end first, YREKA, and supposed that that was the name of the camp. The campers were satisfied with it and adopted it.

A year after a gold strike on a tributary of the Shasta River brought swarms of miners here, Bloody Point got its name when a wagon train of miners, although warned by riders from Yreka not to proceed eastward down the South Emigrant Road, did so anyway and were attacked by marauding Modocs. Everyone was killed except for a man named Coffin. As avenging vigilantes paraded through Yreka waving Modoc scalps, miners bedded down with Modoc women and their wives with Modoc men.

Acording to an old account, when Yreka competed with Deadwood (now like unto its name) for the Siskiyou County seat, a wagonload of whisky delivered to the swing-vote town of Etna on the eve of election adulterated voter turnout enough to ensure Yreka's victory. Robbers' Rock signals a road where the last stage robbery in the region blazed in the late 1800s. In 1885, a vigilante group hanged four men accused of murder right outside the court-house; folklore adds that the tree on which they were hanged died. The Yreka Railroad opened 1889; in 1920, when someone found several bullet holes in Engine 19, it was renamed Pancho. Dunsmuir, located below Mt. Shasta, had been named Pusher at first because trains on the steep canyon rails along the upper Sacramento River had to be pushed to their destinations.

Train tracks ran through Yreka behind the hotel I occupied. Upon them, behind an RV park, sat a line of empty hopper cars waiting to be loaded with coal. I read the graffiti on one car: "DAMS" and "KILL." Eight cars down the sprayer had written, "All Presidents Eat Shit." The hotel was off Montague. Where are the Capulets? Six feet under? I rode the elevator down with a gray-haired man and woman wearing black Harley Davidson T-shirts. In town, the courthouse held a large gold nugget on an altar all its own. Lotta Crabtree had started singing here, and John Heenan fighting. The Greathouse/DeWitt Building now advertised **THINGS FOR YOUR HEAD** with letters done up in smoke plumes. A rusted mining car planted with flowers sat parked in front of the Chamber of Commerce.

Signage confirmed the impression of tumult. CAPPS' SPEAKEASY. RICHTER SCALE REAL ESTATE. A giant Liquor Barn billboard had welcomed me into Yreka. Some of the retail signs bore stylized skulls. I walked past the Siskiyou County Jail and, on Miner Street, a Native American Heritage Park. Inside an octagonal redwood hut someone had added a grinning jester to the graffiti lining the walls.

Shouts, honked horns, squealing tires, pickup trucks with rifle racks, and a camouflage-colored VW parked in front of a Rite Aid that sold live crickets. At the pizza joint, the cell phone of the man behind me in line rang to Clint Eastwood's whistling "Man with No Name" refrain. A woman garbed in black stretched forth a hand bearing a black spider web tattoo and inserted coins into the jukebox. She selected AC/DC: "I'm on a highway to hell...." The terrapsychological question: Is one side of the San Andreas Fault grinding through this place, where the archetypal Outlaw held sway, more dominant than the other?

Off east along Highway 97 stood a very different kind of display. The Living Memorial Sculpture featured wiry metallic forms of combat veterans and helicopters surrounded by fifty-eight thousand replanted pine trees. Vietnam veteran Dennis Smith set up this haunting tribute to men at arms lost in war. Groupings bear evocative names: "Those Left Behind"; "The Refugees"; "The Why Group." A nearby labyrinth winding its mysterious way below the white immensity of Mount Shasta invites contemplation. Veterans' names are added to the granite Memorial Wall every Memorial Day and Veterans Day. I wondered if the ancient Romans ever paused to think about all the legionnnaires who never came home.

In rustic, pretty Weed I saw lots of Aphroditic touches--like an arch built out of railroad track replaced by one of pink brick, shops freshly painted in bright colors, many decorated with planters bearing flowers, in one park a metallic sculpture, "Vision," of a woman stringing a bow (Aphrodite and Eros rolled into one?), other sculpted art in windows and side lots, a Best Little Hair House, "Weed: A flower yet to be discovered," and old brick buildings carefully preserved. One had been the BLACK BUTTE SALOON AND BROTHEL.

> Nothing has been created as ultima materia — in its final state. Everything is at first created in its prima materia, its original stuff; whereupon Vulcan comes, and by the art of alchemy develops it into its final substance.
>
> — Paracelsus

ON THE SHOULDER OF Mount Shasta I sat listening to nothing in particular. Although the ground's chill crept through my jeans, my body felt light as though it had entered the heavens.

At eighty-five cubic miles, Mount Shasta is the largest volcanic peak in the continental U.S. Tall (fourteen thousand feet) and young (six hundred thousand years), the mountain rose in layers from four cones spewing andesitic lava. Hotlum, the last cone to form, appeared eight thousand years ago and last erupted down the mountain's eastern flank in 1786. The Comte de La Perouse spotted it from his ship while making for Monterey. From his log book for September:

> On the 7th the mist was still thicker than the day before. It cleared up, however, towards noon, and we saw the tops of mountains to the east, at a considerable distance...We then perceived a volcano on the summit of the mountain which bore east from us. The flame was very vivid; but a thick fog soon concealed it from our sight.

By the time Don Luis Arguello, future governor of California, passed through the area in 1817 in the company of Fray Narcisco Duran, the mountain had quieted temporarily.

Hudson Bay Company trapper Peter Ogden might or might not have seen, and might or might not have named, Mount Shasta in 1826 as he passed through what seems to have been Tule Lake. While there he glimpsed a mountain "high above all others pointed and well covered in snow." His Native guides named the locals "Sastise." On February 14, 1827, while heading northwest through the Rogue River Valley in Oregon Territory, he wrote, "I have named this river Sastise River. There is a mountain equal in height to Mount Hood or Vancouver, I have named Mt. Shasta. I have given these names from the tribes of Indians." Some think he actually named Mt. McLoughlin, although the mountain he had seen the previous year was probably Mount Shasta. His maps are missing, but historians speculate that the "Shasta" name for Mt. McLoughlin was cartographically teleported in 1844 to the tall white Cascade Range peak in California.

Jedediah Smith visited in 1828, and Fremont in 1846, but Elias Pierce made the first European ascent in 1854: "All the scenery beneath was the most beautiful that my eyes ever looked upon." A year later John Young painted the mountain during a railroad survey. By the 1860s, Mount Shasta's beauty eroded when climbers, hunters, and fishers arrived. Scientists too, like geologist James Dana and botanist William Brackenridge. When Josiah Whitney's survey party climbed the mountain in 1862, they found a newspaper, some broken bottles, a Methodist hymn book, a pack of cards, and other discarded items.

Not everyone who saw the great white mountain stayed that disconnected. Living in Castle Crags, poet Joaquin Miller wrote, "Lonely as God, and white as a winter moon, Mount Shasta starts up sudden and solitary from the heart of the great black forests of North America." John Muir saw the mountain in 1874: "When I first caught sight of it I was fifty miles away and afoot, alone and weary. Yet all my blood turned to wine, and I have not been weary since." After he climbed it he camped at the timberline to wait out a storm. In 1888, in the magazine *Picturesque California*, Muir suggested the preservation of Mt Shasta as a national park. Ronald Reagan signed the Calforina Wilderness Act in September 1984, but not before loggers cut lumber for California Bungalow homes built in the early 1900s. From the mountain's wood Louis Bedell carved violinis and violas. With demand for pine, fir, incense cedar, and hemlock peaking, the Forest Service began selling it in the 1940s, but the decline of old growth forest sent the industry into decline. The last mill, P & M Lumber Company, finally shut in 1990.

I had come up here onto the mountain after arranging to stay in a small boutique and tourist town huddling on Mount Shasta's western slope. Strawberries growing wild had suggested the name Strawberry Valley. The name changed briefly to Sisson after Justin Sisson, the town's first guide, innkeeper, and postmaster, before he sold most of his land to the Central Pacific in 1886.

What I saw of Mt. Shasta did not impress me at first. After scooping a cool, clean drink from the mossy rocks at the Sacramento Headwaters, I stepped onto a sidewalk that took me past kiosks, placques, and retail signs meant to be cute and spiritual: Sereni Tea. Shasta Rainbow Angels Gallery. The Crystal Room stocked with singing bowls. Soul Connections, complete with glowing salt rocks, chubby Buddhas, and Tibetan prayer flags. Someone had carved "UFOs heal" into a corner of the sidewalk.

I picked up a copy of the *Mountain Spirit Chronicles* and read, "Did Separation Get Lost in Separation?" "In This Issue" featured something called "soulchronicity," something else called "rainbow rays," "Heart of Satsang," and "Meth Recovery with Angels." Those must be some troubled angels. I read, "In the beginning we were one consciousness" and stopped reading.

Yet this was the town with the nerve to pass an ordinance prohibiting companies like Coca-Cola and Nestle from taking water from the local aquifer and PG&E from cloud-seeding with silver iodide. Going even farther, the ordinnance repudiated corporate personhood, elevated the rights of local community above those of multinationals, and recognized the rights of the natural world. This movement has leaped to Pennsylvania, New Hampshire, Virginia, and Maine. The Community Environmental Legal Defense Fund and Global Exchange are organizing to uphold this farsighted ordinance in court.

The Shasta, Klamath, and Modoc to the east, Achumawi, Atsugewi, and Wintun to the south, Karuk, Yurok, and other nearby tribes all revered the mountain on whose flank now I sat as a sacred domain. The Shasta Indian legends say the Creator, seeing the flatness of the land, raised up a sacred mountain that everyone could see and called it *Wyeka*, "Great White," which was also the name of the deity at the top. In other tales the Creator shaped Mount Shasta like a wigwam with a fire burning inside and, pleased with it, brought his family down from the heavens to live in it. The Winnimem Wintu call the mountain *Blum Phuq*, "Big Mountain," where Olelbes the Creators lives. They hold August ceremonies on the mountain and do not climb it because to do so would amount to climbing an altar. An altar frequently struck by lightning.

> For the mountain to know you, we sometimes introduce people to Bulim Phuq by introducing them to Sa'w Tip Mem, "Sacred Spring Water," at Panther Meadows. If one has shown Columa-Suk, respect for the mountain, and has not restricted the waters of the spring, the bubbles from the spring come to you. The mountain then knows you. You can take your sorrows there, your dreams and your prayers.
> —Jane English quoting Steve Vincent

A maiden (say the legends) once froze to death ascending the mountain, and her thumb is still visible as Thumb Rock. When it snows, drivers on Interstate 5 between Dunsmuir and Mt. Shasta can see the Lady on the Mountain's upturned face, hair, and breasts.

Coyote stories collect around the mountain too. When the Wily One built a fire on the peak, the waters that covered the world receded. This allowed Eagle to make people and send them forth from the heights. Coyote is Trickster counterpart to Hermes, god of alchemy and servant of the fabled Philosopher's Stone.

The alchemists suffered visions, some grotesque, some beautiful, and many deceitful in keeping with lessons taught by the dark light of Trickster's sense-twisting wisdom.

It is said, for example, that a race of beings from Lemuria, the Atlantis of the Pacific, burrowed into Mount Shasta after an undersea eruption sank their island. The early Romans told stories of ghostly *lemures* who moaned and walked the night with reflective eyes. Zoologist Philip Sclater transfered this haunting word to the small mammals whose fossils he unearthed in Madagascar and India. He surmised that both places had been part of one continent broken up long ago. For this continent, he wrote in 1864, "I should propose the name Lemuria!"

This name proved handy for projection onto other unknowns: onto a supposed missing evolutionary link, onto land bridges across the Pacific--and, in 1895, onto a mythic race living within Mount Shasta as told by Yreka resident Frederick Spencer Oliver and published in his book *A Dweller on Two Planets*. Oliver claimed to have been marking the boundaries of his family's mining claim during the summer of 1883 when his hand began to write uncontrollably. It would seem that Oliver had been chosen to channel the Lemurian spirit Phylos. (In Homer's *Odyssey*, Phylo is Helen of Troy's maidservant. In Greek *phylo* means "race.") Phylos had lived through several Atlantean incarnations before settling on Oliver as worthy of viewing what remained of the Poseidi, an advanced Atlantean society capable of antigravity, aircraft, submarines, wireless communications, aerial water generators, air conditioning, television, voice-activated typewriters, and high-speed rail. These devices no longer existed, but the souls of the Poseidi still did, and so did their polished jewels, fur carpets, and deep blue crystal pools hidden within Mount Shasta.

A Dweller on Two Planets and the writings that followed wove an elaborate tale of reincarnation (witness the lifetime of gold miner and occulist Walter Pierson), astral travel to Venus, karma, and hubris. The reader is warned sternly against repeeating mistakes that led to the demise of "Poseid, queen of the waves." The I AM movement, the Lemurian Fellowship, Elizabeth Claire Prophet, and Shirley MacLaine drew inspiration and audience material from this series of Shastean revelations.

The Lemurians were good for a few more epiphanies. Claiming to be a geologist, archeologist, and minerologist who had traveled the globe piecing together stories, legends, and anecdotes, Wishar S. Cerve wrote *The Lost Continent of the Pacific* in 1931. This book linking Lemurians to Mount Shasta grew so popular that Forest Service personnel claimed to have searched the mountain but found no evidence of any lurking Lemurians inside or around it. Nevertheless, a group calling itself Elan Vital bore greetings from Dugja ("DOO-jah"), Queen of the Lemurians, and Abraham Mansfield authored testimonies about a friend having slept in Lemurian beds of gold. During the last Ice Age, this mysterious race had assembled the Plates of Time to preserve their knowledge of atomic power for later "wise" use. Found worthy by them, Mansfield was appointed Chief of the Gods of the Lemurians, equipped with an Indian war bonnet to go with his promotion, and given a fourth of the jewels of Queen Etruceana. (The Etruscans were down inside the mountain too.)

Nola Van Valer climbed up Mount Shasta on the east side near Mud Creek and encountered none other than Phylos, only now Phylos was Tibetan. She founded the Radiant School of the Seekers and Servers, but it soon went under, or was vaporized to realms unknown. Mah-Atmah Amsumata (Norman Westfall) claimed to have been walking near the mountain when a dwarf offered his party some gold and a sack of black diamonds. Other dwarves appeared and, armed with hammers and anvils, began to sing.

Evidently the Lemurians had plenty of company. The Secret Commonwealth of the Yaktayians, for example, were a race of artisans who rang bells and chimes to chisel underground cities aglow with light and power. According to one Dr. Doreal of the Brotherhood of the White Temple, Inc, it's actually Atlanteans who live in the mountain. J.C. Brown reported a huge cavern with walls hung with golden plates and shields and floors strewn with the skeletons of prehistoric giants. Edgar Larkin looked through a telescope and saw golden temples on the mountain's east flank. Guy Ballard spoke with Saint Germain on the slopes of Mount Shasta in 1930 and founded I AM. In 1948, his organization--led by his wife Edna after his transmission off-planet--bought Shasta Springs, an old railroad resort between Dunsmuir and the town of Mt. Shasta, for reflection, revenue, and otherworldly pageantry. Witnesses say UFOs hide in the lenticular clouds above the snowy peaks.

Organizations devoted to peak experiences at Mount Shasta include various Harmonic Convergence gatherings, the Planetary Citizens, the Radiant School of Seekers and Servers, a Zen monastery, the Shasta Abbey Buddhists, the Dolphin Star Temple Mystery School, and a League of Voluntary Effort (LOVE).

"A new age is dawning," sang Don Henley in "Little Tin God," "on fewer than expected." It did not take long for the superegoic judgmentalism latent in Christianity to infect a New Ageism for which personal calamity, once interpreted as a sin of the victim, is now a sign of being "off the path." The puerile Divine Child overemphasis on light, ascension, and dematerialization conceals dark shadows no efforts at spiritual bypass can lighten. Nor need anyone possessed by the Child shoulder adult strivings for justice, equality, or sustainability because chanting and fingerpainting alone will conjure up the New Lemuria. As William James observed long ago, those who believe the world already good feel no need to make it good.

But why would the New Age scale the holy mountain?

Precisely because (as Native accounts attest down the centuries) this mountain embodies Spirit.

My book *Ventral Depths* uncovered alchemical parallels, images, and motifs brewing in the Great Central Valley of California. The hardpan-sealed depression in the middle of the Golden State works like an enormous alchemical retort to produce endless transformation: of soils, of crops, of communities and faiths, of mixes of human beings from everywhere. After two years listening in on the Valley, I found myself unable to name what every completed alchemical opus was said to produce. Where hid California's Philosopher's Stone? A dream gave me the answer:

> I am climbing over a pile of stones. When I finally reach the top after so much effort, I see what the pile had hidden from my view: the rising grandeur of Mount Shasta, not distant but giving itself to my senses with such glowing, radiating presentness that I could almost reach out and touch a snowy flank of the sacred mountain.

If California is an alchemical vessel scraped over millions of years from the floor of the Pacific, its Central Valley founded off the coast when the Farallon Plate pushed under the North American, then Mount Shasta, coagulated from lava streaming upward from these plate tectonics to raise the Cascades, must be the Golden State's radiant, glowing, and inhumanly emanative Philosopher's Stone. Had not Arabian alchemist Ab'l-Quasim al-Iraqi described the Prime Matter from which the Stone is worked as "found in a mountain which contains a measureless quantity of uncreated things"?

Vulcan struck Jupiter's head with a hammer and out thrust Minerva fully armed and armored. It occurred to me intuitively that, in some way I might never fully fathom, Mount Shasta as Philosopher's Stone represents even more than the grand opus of California. A geomythic peak forged in continuously creative volcanic fires, Shasta somehow represents California's entire purpose or point.

Did the Russian fur trappers who founded Fort Ross and named Mt. Saint Helena after Empress Helena of Russia ever see Mount Shasta? The Russian word for "white" or "pure" is *tchastal* (similar to "chaste"). Mount Shasta has also been named Shastasla, Sasta, Sasty, Satise, Shasty, Chaste, Chestet, Chasty, Shastl, Wyeka, and Blum Phuq. The Klamath and Modoc called the mountain Melaikshi, the Yana Wahkalu, the Achomawi and Atsugewi Yet. As every alchemist knew, the Philosopher's Stone's many names reflected its powers of *proiectio* and *multiplicatio* to send its presence outward to refine more of itself. Even if in the degraded form of crystal stores, bottled spirit shops, Soul Connections, and a Spirit service station in Mt. Shasta. Not far from the holy mountain, pyramidal, winged, circular, and double triangle petroglyph symbols endured etched in stone at Castle Crags. High above them, the Lapis of Spirit radiates white light at the top of the Central Valley.

If that Valley represented the inside of the chymical vat and Mount Shasta the Stone of the Wise, then the entire state must work as an alchemical vessel joined to but walled off from the rest of North America. Through this lens, first ground in the Valley, I saw California in a new light. *Separatio* in borderline San Diego, city of my birth. *Proiectio* in and above the City of Angels, *calcinatio* burning the eastern deserts dry, *circulatio* pouring through the vessel's largest inlet/outlet spout of San Francisco Bay....

> As I worked on the book [*Mount Shasta Reflections*] this week in the house of one of my former neighbors, the mountain stayed hidden among the clouds of the first big storm of the season. Then one evening after we had selected all the photographs and chosen an order for the various pieces of writing, the top of the mountain peeked out above the clouds at sunset, mirroring our sense of completion.
> — Jane English

The sun was setting, the air growing cold.

Thank you, I told Mount Shasta inwardly, patting the soil with my hand as I stood awash in new visions, *for this moment of realization.*

Serpents and Giants at Klamath

CRESCENT CITY
CITY LIMIT

Next to that sign, this one: TSUNAMI MARTIAL ARTS CENTER.

Del Norte County is as far north as you can go along the coast of California without entering Oregon. The Tolowa and Yurok lived here long before anyone else, and many still do. The county's only incorporated city takes its name from the crescent-shaped beach just south of town. I paused to look out over the Pacific at the Saint George Reef Lighthouse as a fog horn sounded its Triton notes. Dark, gnarled rocks jutted upward near the shore. Although the sun shone brightly, a curtain of fog hid the base of the forested hills down the coast from where I stood. To a man raised in Southern California, the absence of beach crowds on a sunny Saturday morning felt surreal.

The city had been founded to supply miners in the forests, but at times the weather had other plans. In 1925, a waterspout left the ocean, ran up Second and G Streets, and raced up the railroad tracks while hurling lumber into the air. 1955 brought floods and an Angus steer from Klamath into the harbor. After an earthquake struck Prince William Sound on Good Friday, 1964, three moderate waves washed in followed by a wall of water that pushed a lumber barge onto the dock before blasting away the dock itself. Cars and logs floated in the streets as Texaco tanks ruptured and exploded. A mother and baby were found still lying on their hotel mattress, but the mattress sat high in a fir tree.

For a fishing port subjected to periodic floods and storms, the city looked very tidy with its trimmed lawns, clean streets, and carefully ordered bunches of flowers here and there. Shrines *should* be clean, especially shrines to tempestuous Poseidon. Memorials to sunken ships dotted the park interspersed with remnants like giant anchors, a section of hull from the S.S. *Emidio* (a tanker sunk off the coast by a Japanese submarine during World War II), and even a fifty-two-ton redwood log. "The mainland," wrote second-century geographer Pausanias of Greece about another, but mythically similar, locale, "is skirted by a crescent-shaped beach and after the beach there is a spit of land up to a sanctuary of Poseidon...." Some things that never change go on recurring even without piety or memory. Who here would think of Poseidon, the might of sea and storm and quake personified?

> There is nothing unusual in my rendering trees honor--people have been doing this since time immemorial, and the thrust of the trunk, from roots beneath the earth, through our middle dimension, to the sky, where the leaves sway, has always lent credence to the division of existence into three zones. Trees were writing their own Divine Comedy about the ascent from hell to the high spheres of heaven long before Dante wrote his.
>
> — Czeslaw Milosz

The redwoods (Sequoia sempervirens) that have made this region famous sprout just north of the Oregon border and grow down to Big Sur along a belt ten miles wide. Living in sedimentary soil, refreshed by the coastal fogs, the trees soar to over three hundred feet in height. Fires and floods prepare the forest floor for the tiny seedlings. Unlike most conifers, redwoods can sprout new stems and roots from burned, cut, or felled trunks. I saw fairy rings of small young trees standing around the remains of fallen ancestors and thought for a time about my own. I was glad I had taken the trouble to find out who they were and where they came from. Knowing this gave me a feeling of continuity I had not grown up with and had not known how much I missed.

Redwoods make tall pillars of community, for round them live Douglas fir, Sitka spruce, and Western hemlock as companions in shaded microclimate zones of vine maple, California hazel, tanoak, and cascara. On these soils grow sword fern, wood fern, red huckleberry, salal, burning bush, and rhododendron in the company of flowering plants like fairybell, violet, trillium, redwood sorrel, false Solomon's seal, poison oak, and leopard lily. The Stellar's jay, spotted owl, thrush, chickadee, Roosevelt elk, Douglas' squirrel, marbled murrelet, black bear, and garter snakes are all found nearby.

The durability, pliability, and ruddy beauty of redwood suited it for lumber. Predicting the results of that, H.A. Crabb of the State Assembly insisted as early as 1852 for withdrawal of "all public lands upon which the Redwood is growing," but the lumber industries carried the day, which is why much of Del Norte County, where twenty-five sawmills cut wood for houses and furniture, is now logged out and, without tree roots to hold soil, badly eroded.

Miners and settlers came with the loggers. In the fall of 1853, as the Tolowa danced the Feather Dance of earth renewal, marauding settlers shot four hundred and fifty celebrants and burned their ceremonial gear. Some of the victims were cast into the sea with weights hung around their necks. Two men who hid under lily pads escaped. Hundreds more were shot at another earth renewal gathering at Achulet the following year, and seventy more at Howonquet the year after that. Beyond wanting land and somewhere to project their hatred, did the killers unconsciously envy the Tolowa their rich, ancient traditions? Their close affinity with the living earth? Is that why so many of the indigenous people whites kill, confine, enslave, bankrupt, and displace are earth-colored? Descendants of the survivors live at Smith River and Elk Valley.

By 1900, logging firms for which private parties filed dummy homestead claims had defrauded the federal government of almost all public lands on which redwoods grew. In theory the Homestead

Act limited each land purchase to a hundred and sixty acres, but in spite of this loggers controlled entire forests. Logging destroyed trees as an intentional consequence but also removed natural flood control, habitat, game, air filtration, rain (felling a forest reduces local rainfall), and salmon. Among the imperiled were seventy-nine species of birds and mammals depending on the standing snags of dead old-growth trees left intact. How loggers bought the land also made it much more expensive to protect because it removed the option of a simple government property transfer.

The establishment of Big Basin Redwoods State Park in 1901 near Santa Cruz represented the first significant official step taken to protect redwood ecosystems. Four years later William and Elizabeth Kent bought six hundred and eleven acres of redwoods under Mount Tamalpais in Marin County and sold half of what is now Muir Woods to the federal government. President Theodore Roosevelt established the woods as a national monument in 1908.

> I feel most emphatically that we should not turn into shingles a tree which was old when the first Egyptian conqueror penetrated to the valley of the Euphrates, which it has taken so many thousands of years to build up, and which can be put to better use. That, you may say, is not looking at the matter from the practical standpoint. There is nothing more practical in the end than the preservation of beauty, than the preservation of anything that appeals to the higher emotions in mankind.
>
> — Thoeodore Roosevelt

After Muir Woods indivduals and private groups like the Save the Redwoods League and the Sempervirens Club stepped up to protect other redwood forests. By 1964, protection extended to fifty thousand acres, but so much damage had been done by logging that in 1978, eroded hillsides and polluted pools scarred much of the lower Redwood Creek basin acquired by Redwood National Park. Rangers set to work on thirty thousand acres of watershed repair.

Any fool can destroy trees. They cannot defend themselves or run away. And few destroyers of trees ever plant any; nor can planting avail much toward restoring our grand aboriginal giants. It took more than three thousand years to make some of the oldest of the sequoias, trees, that are still standing in perfect strength and beauty, waving and singing in the mighty forests of the Sierra. Through all the eventful centuries since Christ's time, and long before that, God has cared for these trees, saved them from drought, disease, avalanches, and a thousand storms; but he cannot save them from sawmills and fools; this is left to the American people.

—John Muir

After MAXXAM of Houston bought Pacific Lumber Company in 1985, a transaction financed by Michael Milken's junk bonds, a legal decision at Owl Creek established two crucial legal precedents: that wrecking the habitat of an endangered species—in this case the marbled murrelet—constitutes a threat to that species and is therefore illegal, and that the Endangered Species Act was enforceable on private land. Pacific Lumber appealed to the Supreme Court, but in 1997 the origina ruling was upheld. Courts are supposed to be impartial, but it probably hadn't helped Pacific Lumber that a private party at which staff threw darts at a picture of a marbled murrelet became public knowledge.

When journalist Thurston Clarke drove through while researching his book *California Fault*, he saw a thin strip of remaining redwoods for tourists to gape at along the highway. This "Potemkin village" screened from their view the logging damage behind them.

Those photographs of a 1950s family driving a wood-paneled station wagon through a hole in a giant redwood had been among my first California icons, but when I finally eased my Tempo through the 315-foot-high Chandelier tree at the Leggett

Drive-Thru Tree Park to the accompaniment of
Waylon Jennings blaring from a loudspeaer, I felt
like a fool. My two dollars also bought the right to
carve my initials into a log, and patronize a gift
shop selling bathroom jokes carved into plaques
that, because they are made of redwood, will survive centuries without rotting.

— Thurston Clarke

Similar sights spoiled my own visit. I lost count of the carved
bears, wind chimes, and American flags sold in junk shops along the
highway.

The WE SUPPORT TIMBER signs in windows all
came from the same printer, like the slogans and
photographs of Kim II Sung in Prongyang. A psoter
in the coffee shop declaring REDWOOD SUM-
MER COST YOU THE TAXPAYERS $252,000-
$100,000 JUST FOR HAIRCUTS! referred to the
expenses of a lawsuit brought against the county
sheriff for shaving the heads of environmental pro-
testors.

— Thurston Clarke

I pulled off Route 101 at a turnout, locked the car, and walked
into the woods until the sounds of traffic had faded. With my back
to a giant tree that had probably been here when dinosaurs roamed
the planet I slipped into road-weary reverie.

We have lived with forest trees for millions of
years, yet how little we understand of them. We
only very recently have realized that, in their way,
they are as alive as we are. If their lives seem rudimentary and simple, this only reflects the rude sim-
plicity of our knowledge. It would be a greater
thing than talking to dolphins really to understand

the slow life of a forest tree as it passes its millenni-
um of steadfast silence.

— David Wallace

The Yurok practice was to never burn redwood but to make homes and boats from it. However, a fire pit lined with stone, and a round knob a few feet back from the bow, acknowledged the living spirit in the wood. We could learn much from such simple acts of respect. To live in an enspirited world is to treat its objects and crea-tures like persons or subjectivities in their own right lest they object and assail us with what we fail to anticipate.

There is little reason to feel optimistic about the fate of the red-woods. Global warming is steadily drying up the coastal fogs they need to live. The volume of fog has already decreased 30% over the past century. In time not even a Potemkin village may mark where the giant trees once towered.

What is true on the surface, though, may not be so underground. Redwood seed pods can survive in the soil for hundreds of years while waiting for their chance to sprout upward. And the trees don't manage themselves without help. Fifty-one percent of the biomass in a forest is fungi. Clear-cutting and brushfires in piled-up tinder can kill it, but its nerve-like threads are resilient enough to reach across regions, perhaps even continents. This mycelium, which recycles dead organic matter and connects the trees to each other, also shuttles nutrients back and forth across ecosystems. If a stand of trees is undernourished, fungi know to divert minerals to com-pensate. We are only beginning to understand how naturally this brain-stuff in the ground coordinates the life of entire forests.

No, what worries me is that forests make oxygen, scrub the air, call down the rain, and provide other good things too numerous to list. To take one for an example: although 70% of our pharmaceuti-cals derive from plants, only 1% of the world's trees have been explored in modern times for their medicinal potential. Taxol from the bark and needles of the Pacific Yew treats ovarian cancer but was thought of as a nuissance by loggers who cut it for padding to break the fall of large conifers they sawed down. Trees on Junipero Serra Peak show an unusual resistance to blister rust, and trees from

Sierra San Pedro Martir in Baja carry blue foliage useful for fighting drought. What other treasures hide all around us in plain sight?

If the forests disappear, so will we, having sawed off the branches we all live on.

AT THE VISITOR CENTER on the eastern side of the Klamath National Forest, the Klamath River had spanned perhaps two hundred feet as it passed within several hundred yards of Interstate 5. Its green-gray murmur needed the protection of stone and metal fences. By the time the river ran west of the forest to Requa, it had broadened by several hundred feet, grown colder, and acquired various mollusks, otters, and lampreys. The Karuks said the Creator wept the river in fear that his people would not have enough to eat.

Requa crouches wind-blown but stoic on the coast where the Klamath River enters the Pacific. Now part of the Yurok Reservation, the small community with a post office, an inn, and a beach for fishing is one of fifty-four ancient Yurok villages along the river between this estuary and the confluence with the Trinity River. The Hupa dwell along the Trinity, the Klamath in the Upper Basin, the Wiyot to the south, and the Karuk south and also here. At the village of Waulkau near the southern end of the sand spit covering the estuary, the Brush Dance invites healing for babies. At other sites alongside the Klamath and Trinity Rivers, Karuk dancers perform the Pikiawish ("World Renewal") ceremonies to bring Earth back into balance.

When I came to Requa I smelled burning rubbish and saw people camped out in trucks and patchwork tents, but the forested hills and the shining arc of water within the spit of sand reminded me that this place was holy. It was from here that the Creator called to Pulekukwerek, the River Spirit, to feed the forthcoming humans with fish, but, wisely, not all at once. So the River made eels for the winter run, candlefish for spring, sturgeon for summer, and salmon for fall. Then he made people and showed them the two large rocks he had placed on either side of the river mouth to protect them. The northern rock Oregos is a female guardian shaped like a woman carrying a basket on her back. Her sister just south of the river carries the burden when the mouth of the spit moves to her side.

The spit itself provides a protective barrier as well as an initiatory threshold. Smolts (juvenile salmon) must wait for high tide to beach the sand barrier on their journey to the sea. Mature salmon returning from the Pacific to spawn inland need tidal pushes over the spit and into the waters of the Klamath.

"I have created you in this place," the River told the humans after teaching them to fish and cook. "I have left the fish, the acorns, and all the things you need to eat." *Rekwoi*, the community's original name, derives from the act of singing and speaking to Nepewo, the salmon leader, during the First Salmon Ritual. The Yurok and Karuk never captured any salmon until enough had swam upstream to ensure plentiful spawning for years to come. Echoing Yurok wisdom stories, biological science suggests that salmon and human arrived here together.

Yurok is a Karuk word for "downriver," and *Karuk* is Yurok for "upriver." In contrast to "Native American" rituals conducted by workshop graduates who point their feathered rattles north, south, east, and west, people living here think primarily in the two directions of upstream and downstream. Both were held as holy until Native children were forced into boarding schools and, with 90% of the reservation in non-Yurok hands (Simpson Timber's, for instance), their parents were forced into canneries until depletion of the chinook by the early 1920s rendered canning them unprofitable.

The Klamath River contains more water than any river in California but the Sacramento. It flows two hundred and fifty-four miles through four California counties to the Pacific from Oregon's Klamath Basin. Upon the Basin, a ten-and-a-half million acre miracle of biodiversity, depend over four hundred and ninety species of animals. Among them thrive salmon, steelhead, mule deer, river otters, pond turtles, and three hundred and fifty-three species of birds like the cormorant, the Western grebe, the short-eared owl, the bald eagle (who flies in around February to comprise the largest grouping of the species in the continental U.S.), the tricolored blackbird, the white-headed woodpecker, the white pelican, the yellow-bellied marmot, the mountain bluebird, and millions of ducks, swans, and geese drawn to the freshwater marshes.

All this changed, of course, when the dams went up in 1918, followed by more pumps, canals, reservoirs, and dams installed by power companies that preferred not to invest in fish ladders.

The first dam cut the runs of spring chinook, and canning and fishing declined. Yet sport and industrial fishers blamed the Indians rather than the dam-builders. In the 1930s, then, the state set up a forty-year ban against all Native fishing. Arrested as an adult for tribal gill-netting, Yurok fisher Raymond Mattz refused a judge's officer to go free in exchange for paying a $1 fine. The case went to the U.S. Supreme Court, and the Yuroks won back their fishing rights. But another seasonal ban was imposed in the 1970s because of a drought. The Yuroks, who caught less than 5% of the running salmon, were blamed again by non-Indian commercial and sport fishers pressuring the federal government into letting *them* fish. The Yuroks' refusal to comply with such blatant hypocrisy brought the Secretary of the Interior to Klamath. As a result, the government imposed a moratorium on all fishing near the estuary. Police in riot gear came in by boat to beat Yuroks who defied the moratorium. The resulting publicity pressured the government to finally let the Yuroks manage their own fishery as they had wanted to do all along.

Unlike sport or commercial operations, the Yurok, Karuk, and Hupa tribes depend on the salmon, suckerfish, and lamprey for their livelihood, culture, and sustenance. *Nepu*, the Yurok word for "salmon," also means food itself; the Karuk word *am* is both noun and verb for "salmon" and "to eat." The mechanized agriculture that drains the Klamath River of its vitality to support fourteen thousand growers on two hundred and ten thousand acres of the Bureau of Reclamation's Klamath Project remains unsustainably onerous in its demand for subsidized, once-plentiful water.

The year 2002 was disastrously dry for the river and its fish. The Bureau of Reclamation turned down the Yurok Tribe's request for more water released from Iron Gate Dam. Growers got most of it for irrigation—as personally promised by incoming President George W. Bush—and at least thirty-eight thousand juvenile and spawning salmon died off in a massive fish kill. Although the Bureau maintained that dieoffs happen all the time in confined natural systems, the Yurok, Fish and Game, and the National Oceanographic and

Atmospheric Administration all confirmed that the catastrophe was unprecedented. The Bureau also argued that more available water does not guarantee that the fish will come, but the culture observing this ecosystem carefully for millennia disagreed.

When the furor escalated, Bush's policy adviser Karl Rove called a consultation meeting to emphasize the administration's pro-grower posture to the Bureau and NOAA biologists. One scientist quit to protest this political pressure as unethical. Offstage, Vice President Dick Cheney made phone calls to middle managers in both agencies. The content of these calls was never disclosed, but the result made it plain when the growers received their full water allocation. Temporarily, anyway, because in October a federal appeals court threw out the Bush plan to deliver more water to upriver growers.

Predictably, 2005 marked the lowest number of spawning salmon on historical record. Commercial fishers suffered as well. In 2007, the Klamath Riverkeeper filed a citizens' enforcement lawsuit in U.S. District Court against PacifiCorp, owner of the dams along the Klamath, for river pollution leaking from the Iron Gate Dam hatchery. In 2008 the Chief Executive Officer of PacifiCorp signed an agreement-in-principle to remove the company's four hydroelectric dams, but in 2011, Republican Congressman Tom McClintock sent an amendment into the House of Representatives to cut $1.9 million from the budget of the Department of the Interior. The targeted budget contained a dam-removal study for the Klamath River. After comparing Interior funding to excesses under the Soviet Union--"We know of many cases where massive government spending and borrowing has destroyed economies and brought down great nations"--McClintock showed up with a ceremonial shovel to celebrate the opening of the Center for Hope. This drug rehab clinic in Grass Valley depended on a sizable injection of federal stimulus money.

Tired of being set against each other, growers, fishers, and Californian Indians have been forming alliances--confluences, one might say--to overcome cultural and political divisions so reflective of those cut by dams in the Klamath River. All parties agree on this: The dams must go.

In 2011, a forty-five-foot gray whale swam into the estuary and remained there for two months before beaching herself and dying. Yurok Tribe member Janet Wortman saw her. "She would just swim back and forth right in front of you and at one point go like this, like she was waving at us. Silly me, I waved back. It was like she was there to see people. She went back and forth. It was almost like she was going, `Here I am, you guys. Can you see me?'" Many did, like those who played flutes and violins for her as she floated under the Highway 101 bridge spanning the river. After she died, her calf swam out to sea.

Wortman and tribal chairman Thomas O'Rourke interpreted the whale's visit as a sign of a dangerous loss of balance in a world of failing relationships and ecologies. In legend this had happened once before when the world tilted over so far that the sea decanted a mighty creature into the river.

Yurok storytellers still speak of Ninawa, the Inland Whale. After swimming into the estuary, she spoke in the dreams of the young hunter Toan. *Like you*, she told him, *I too am an exile, a fatherless child whose mother was cast out of her family. Yet the outcast winter wind ushers in the budding and blooming of spring.* The hunter, she predicted, would grow up great and strong. *And never forget that you walked on Ninawa's back.*

Recently, young men of the Yurok, Karuk, and Hupa have resumed building fish weirs for use where the Trinity meets the Klamath. Astounded parents watch their almost-adult children sewing together a sacred technology not seen in generations.

It is said that when the young swim the cold Klamath River for their initiation into adulthood, the palms they place on the river's bottom often bear the marks of scales visible after the ritual. The scales belong to Ka'mes ("kah-mess"), the mysterious serpent who swims in the Klamath and his brother rivers. In the stories of many lands, the serpent's initiatory knowledge rejoins the unmoored mind to its earthly sources. Upon the snake in Eden the Gnostics ("Those Who Know") bestowed the title of Instructor. In their view the exile from innocence and effortlessness meant the gain of coming consciously home to a verdant world.

Where the Klamath River meets the Pacific, a sand-
spit narrows its channel. Like a tongue, the peninsula of sand reaches almost entirely across the
mouth of the river. From year to year, even from
month to month, that tongue moves, opening to the
ocean in a different place.

— Stephen Most

Studying the waters of the Klamath from a hillside turnout at
Requa, my eyes revealed what had gone unnoticed on my way up.
The river's supple curves, magical, sinuous, patient, and confluen-
tial, were undeniably serpentine.

SEVEN WILDERNESS AREAS, SIX national wildlife refuges, six national
forests, two national parks, and two national monuments reside
within the Klamath bioregion. Where did this canopied terrain
packed with so many stories, serpents, and giants originate?

Most of the heights started forming during the Jurassic at the
bottom of the sea. Klamath rocks are older than those of the
Cascades or Coast Ranges; the oldest surround Mt. Eddy. They are
also more jagged, faulted, and folded. Early explorers like Jedediah
Smith (who came through in 1828 to trap) had trouble scaling the V-
shaped canyons. Cherts, conglomerates, and schists line the
Klamath and Trinity Rivers.

Klamath rocks don't sit idly under white sand as do
Florida limestones, or roll gently under deep loam
as do midwestern sandstones and shales. They are
athletic rocks, at times prankish. They like to stand
on their heads and play practical jokes, pranks
unappreciated by a hiker who finds a trail ending in
a landslide or a roadbuilder who sees a steel culvert
tipping into a gully. As with all pranksters, it is
hard to get a straight story from Klamath rocks;
they prefer to speak paradoxes, obscure codes, or

apparent nonsense. This is why geologist call them
a "knot," a nightmare.

— David Wallace

Even older than the mountains around them, the Klamath and
Rogue Rivers keep their own counsel by running backwards. Bass
go upstream, trout downstream, and salmon swim upriver against
the current. Temperatures range from icy to bathtub in rivers whose
floods can scour the hillsides. Serpentine outcroppings host arnica,
Indian Paintbrush, lomatium, leather oak, white pine, tank oak, and
California Bay.

So far, Klamath's relative geographic isolation has prevented
glaciation, desertification, and urbanization from disturbing two
hundred and eighty-one species found nowhere else: Port Orford
cedars, Brewer's spruce, weeping spruce, Siskiyou Mountain sala-
mander, Kalmiopis leachiana, Humboldt marten, and a host of
unique goshawks and owls, silver-haired bats, marbled murrelets,
blacktail deer, black bear, coyote, bobcat, Roosevelt elk, mountain
lions, and feral pigs. In meadows see and appreciate the startling
profusions of larkspur, wild onion, crane orchids, blue gentians,
asters, geraniums, sneezeweeds, and coneflowers.

Giants live here too. The Klamath and Trinity Forests contain
climax stands of redwood, Ponderosa pine and Douglas fir. Sugar
pine, white fir, madrone, Western yew, Sadler's oak, mountain hemlock, Shasta red fir, and noble fir cast their shadows over the puls-
ing forest floor. On steep ridges grow vine maples, oxalis, salal,
phantom orchids, man-sized sword ferns, rhododendrons the size
of houses. Legends describe a huge salamaner in the Trinity Alps
known locally as the "belly-whomper." The chinook is "king
salmon." Trees stand so high that microstorms flicker in their upper
branches. At Klamath, just below Requa, giant statues of Paul
Bunyan and Babe the ox gaze out over the highway. Billboards
depict UFOs shedding beams of light like those cast from automobile headlamps on foggy evenings.

Within this land of giants and serpents, somehow Time itself
has buckled or stopped. Seventeen conifer species growing in one
square mile at Russian Peak stage multiple plots in an ancient tale

of evolution. Tree fossils twelve million years old look like some of the trees now standing. Mammoth bones have been uncovered near Douglas City. Temperatures are similar to what they were during the Eocene Epoch. Horsetails go virtually unchanged from their Devonian ancestors, and the sturgeon's tail, fin, and jaw resemble those of fossils three hundred million years old. Here grow kalmiopsis, the oldest living relative of azalea and rhododendron, the ancient weeping spruce, and the rare foxtail pine. The redwoods are virtually ageless because they clone themselves.

To this contrary landscape of ancient forms belong salanders that breathe through their skin, a tailed frog living in near-freezing water, water ouzels that fly underwater, salmon traveling from sea to rivers and back, springtails that mate on water or snow but feed and lay eggs on land, six-inch newts that spend spring and summer in lakes to breed before spending winters underground. Like the man-faced serpent Ka'mes, all these living things represent hybrid forms connecting present with mythic past, landscape with soulscape, human with nonhuman. Even bodies of water bear dreamy names like Spirit Lake, Man-Eaten Lake, Secret Lake, Lost Lake, Deadman Lake, Wild Lake, Devil's Punchbowl, Lonesome Lake...Will-o'-the-wisps hang over them at night.

And then there's Bigfoot.

Giant footprints seen in the Klamath Knot, the Bluff Creek watershed, in 1958 prompted Jerry Crew to emerge from the forest with a giant plaster cast. The Associated Press, United Press International, newspapers in San Francisco and Sacramento, and varioius national radio networks picked up the strange story. Logging crews dubbed the mysterious creature Big Foot--eventually shortened to "Bigfoot"--after finding their equipment vandalized and more giant tracks circling nearby. As he confessed before his death, logger Ray Wallace laid the tracks. His co-conspirator, Scoop Beal, was editor of the *Humboldt Standard*.

At the time Roger Patterson and Bob Gimlin claimed to film Bigfoot in the Six Rivers National Forest in 1967, the hoax had not yet been revealed. This allowed Patterson to make sure that new editions of his Bigfoot book coincided with sightings and reports of fresh tracks. He was terminally ill with cancer and might have been trying to make money to leave for his family. However,

> Faking Bigfoot tracks or running across a road in an
> ape costume is harmless fun. But the particulars of
> Patterson's story raise questions about his mental
> health. To produce a facsimile of what a Bigfoot
> might sound like, he recorded himself screaming on
> audiotape while sitting in the bell tower of a church
> with a bucket over his head. On another occasion,
> he had an enormous metal cage fabricated and
> hoisted into a tree as a Bigfoot lookout. Witnesses
> recalled him sitting in the cage at night blasting his
> recorded Bigfoot screams into the dark, hoping to
> attract the beast.
>
> — Michael McLeod

Before his death Patterson succumbed to a hoax himself when he spent much of his remaining money to prepare for a trip to Thailand to take charge of a Sasquatch supposedly held in a Buddhist monastery. There was a precedent for this adventure: when explorer Charles Bruce stopped on his way to Mt. Everest to ask at the Rongbuk Valley monastery about the yeti, the lama informed him that five of the beasts lived in the upper valley. Mountaineers who came to search for them provided the valley with tourist income.

News of Bigfoot did not surprise local Natives. Karuk legends told of a couple that when exiled for marrying outside their village lived alone at Bluff Creek until they evolved into large, shaggy beings. The Yurok even had a name for their version of a giant hominid: *Oh-Mah*. According to the white man's evolutionary science, humans branched off from tree-dwelling mammals six million years ago. When we walk on two legs, we throw the giant shadow of creatures who went before.

My ancestors based the story of Beowulf and monstrous Grendel on the older Sumerian myth of Gilgamesh and Enkidu. Unlike dangerous Grendel, wild and hairy Enkidu was no killer. In a sense he was the natural half of Gilgamesh. When Enkidu died, his heroic friend dived to the ocean floor (much as youths now do in the

Klamath River) to seek the herb of immortality. He found it, but a serpent stole it from him. Mythically imagined, it is the footprint of Enkidu--the signature of our lost connection to our animal self-- that seekers find in these dark forests.

> It was in the Kalmiopsis that giants are supposed to have sacked a mining town. If forest giants can express a human desire for linkage with wild nature, they also can express a fear that what lies at its heart, in its deepest, most secret parts--the night, the wilderness, the earth's core--is alien.
> — David Wallace

Serpents and giants at Klamath, Trinity, and Six Rivers confronted me with a question: Do the myths that play out in places like this one emanate from the land, or does the land somehow rest within the myth and whatever archetype projects it? Either way of asking presents a problem. When I spoke once at a conference about the protective feel of maternal San Diego, someone in the audience had evidently read Jung: "Oh yes, you mean the Great Mother." "No," I replied, resisting this psychification, "I mean San Diego." But reducing myth and archetype to landscape would prove equally reductive in the other direction. I doubt that the fantasy of Bigfoot inhabits these forests just because big trees grow here.

When Goethe began writing about the archetypal or *ur*-plant he saw in in the leaves and stems he observed, Schiller accused him by letter of advocating a Platonic realm of ideal essences. Not so, replied Goethe. The primal form lived not behind or above the material plant, but *within* it as a motion, gesture or presence. In other words, the *ur*-plant did not blueprint the tangible plant like a kind of DNA at work, but lived as a potential or virtual form of which the plant represented one expression. Many decades later, zoologist Adolf Portmann came up with the similar idea that animal bodies carried a gestural or representational value beyond anything selected for by evolutionary forces. A particular zebra's stripes, the curve of a particular antelope's horns, the shape of a particular goat's beard communicate an animal's essence, style, or inwardness beyond what purely empirical considerations can detect.

When Jung first wrote about archetypes, he emphasized their imagistic expression in dreams, art, and culture. Even as early as 1912, when he theorized about "primordial images," he insisted that they manifested in instinct as well. By the time he wrote *On the Nature of the Psyche* (1947), he had learned from synchronicity that archetypes are transpsychic, or *psychoid*, suspended between the material and the mental until the moment they constellate. The analogy with the collapse of a measured quantum probability into either particle or wave is apt if overdone. Neither entirely material nor entirely mental, archetypes must be part of the world beyond human consciousness, Jung surmised.

As potent archetypal images, mythoi must be too. Inhabiting the imaginally liminal between land and lore, mountains and meanings, they dream themselves forth into recurrent protostories that bind interiority and exteriority (human and nonhuman alike) into the fantastic shapes and ecological complexes looming up in our mythologies and folklore.

To note that something uncanny inhabits the Bluff Creek water-shed, then, is to note that the creek, trees, and hollows align mean-ingfully with legends of invisible mountains, lost villages of ancient spirits, and shamanic healings at Doctor Rock. No wonder David Wallace found the place so strange:

> There was a tension in the ridges that departed rad-ically from conventional notions of the irregularity and relaxation of wide open spaces. It was almost an attention...The ridges seemed not only vigilant, but reticent, as though hidden within them might be the most extraordinary things.

Wallace got sick there one night:

> ...My mind started reeling through history--tribal youths starving on mountaintops for totem visions, Taoist sages living on nettles and mushrooms in Chinese caves, Hebrew prophets eating locusts and

wild honey on the Sinai peninsula, elderly Brahmins leaving comfortable estates to wander the Bengali jungle.

He saw "intensely vivid faces" speaking "incomprehensible words."

> The rational explanation was that I was sensitized to my experience in the forest, but I couldn't dismiss the possibility that I was sensitized to something in the forest.

Wallace was reminded of a similar encounter in Wyoming happening to Edward Drinker Cope. After taking ill while hunting fossils in 1872, Cope wrote, "I had terrible visions and dreams, and saw multitudes of persons, all speaking ill of me, and frustrating my attempts to sleep."

Indeed. While hunting fossils he evidently forgot the voice and presence of the land he dug about in. It did not forget him.

> ...I cannot help feeling, on seeing a tan oak or chinquapin that is nurtured and watered by fungi, pollinated by insects, and propagated by jays and squirrels, that the evergreen forest is much more than an aggregation of competing entities. People often feel, on entering a forest, that they have encountered something with integrity and volition, with consciousness. I would be more comfortable about dismissing such feelings, which I hae experienced, if we understood how our own consciousness arises from the tangle of neurons in our heads.
>
> — David Wallace

The deep encounters produced by the collision of human thought with the presence of some specific, living, and awakened place can manifest as symptomatic and even nightmarish. But if creatures like Ka'mes of Klamath wear a human visage, something within the human mind remains archaically forested over.

Fortuna at Humboldt Bay

From Highway 101 Orick looked to be stuffed with carved redwood. My eye tried unsuccessfully to avoid statues of Indian chiefs, bears, horses, and windmills turning in the fog-laden sea breeze. Ancient Yuroks believed that money came with its own personality and was difficult to get along with. Ancient Greeks believed that hamadryads--arboreal nymphs--punished people who cut down their trees. Remember the fate of greedy Erysichthon. What imaginal figures struggled to come to life in carved wood twenty-four miles south of windswept Requa?

I passed Humboldt State Lagoon. Farming and agriculture had tried to grow and breed things here without much success. The three lagoons might have been named more imaginatively than Big, Stone, and Freshwater. Birds negotiating the Pacific Flyway stop here to eat and rest where the Little Red Hen motel and restaurant once did business.

Here came Trinidad, a small city fifteen miles north of Arcata. The Yuroks had lived along the bluffs above the bay. Sebastian Cermeño sailed the galleon *San Augustin* by the harbor without stopping in 1595 before wrecking his ship at Point Reyes. Bruno de Heceta and Juan Francisco Bodega anchored their ships here in 1775 and on June 11, Trinity Sunday, named the harbor Saint Trinidad.

Hudson Bay Company trappers wandered through during the 1820s.

Further inland, Major Pierson B. Reading struck gold in 1848 on a river he mistakenly believed flowed from this place and named the river Trinity, which not only stuck but spread to an entire forest. In 1850 settlers founded Warnersville and opened a post office a year later. Trinidad grew into a modest fishing town, then a tourist destination, then a member of the California Coastal National Monument created in 2000 to protect cliffs and rock outcroppings all down the coast. The city also contains a small cemetery with Native and settler graves and a tombstone planted in honor of Edward Schnaubelt, the gold-panning relative of two men accused of the Haymarket Riot bombing in Chicago. After he lost the sawmill he had opened, he snuck in one night to gather up his tools and was shot by a security guard. For an epitaph his wife chose "Murdered by Capitalism."

The same might have been said of the trees in these forests. Over three hundred sawmills cut wood in California by 1875. By then, a third of the forests had been logged. "...Our immense forests of timber, as a source of wealth, are as valuable as the best gold mines in the State," bragged the *Humboldt Times* in 1858, "and they are equally inexhaustible." The fantasy of inexhaustibility soon fell to the logger's ax. With sugar pine almost gone, loggers turned to redwoods. In the 1950s only 4% of the original stands survived, with the plant and animal species dependent on them dead or dying.

East of Eureka, which was settled just below Arcata, rise the Trinity Alps, so named in the 1930s by a resort booster. Although they were added to the National Wilderness Preservation System in 1984, some grazing and mining is still permitted there. Twenty species of conifers have survived the saws, and red alders that grow in damaged soil are fertilizing it. Over three hundred plant species live above five thousand feet. Clouds are rare upon the eight-thousand-foot peaks. Wildflowers bloom in February. In 1999 a lightning fire burned almost a third of the old growth. It continues its recovery.

The county is named after naturalist Alexander von Humboldt: "Nature herself is sublimely eloquent." Sentiments like this got him accused by positivist professors of romanticizing the natural world, but he had been over much of that world studying it carefully, appreciating its beauties and terrors, and documenting what he found. He was working on *Cosmos*, a multi-volume compendium of naturalistic knowledge, when he died in 1859. Although he never saw the bay and county named after him, he certainly would have appreciated what endured of their freshness and natural vigor.

The sandbars of Humboldt Bay (called Wigi by Native people) curled around it like protective arms that concealed it and its Wiyot, Yurok, Hupa, and Karuk occupants from passing sailors, including Russian fur traders who had trouble entering the bay, but in 1849, the starving Gregg Expedition walked in and found food and greetings from Wiyot leader Ki-we-lah-tah. In another year the *Laura Virginia* sailed in and named the bay. Arcata, Eureka, and Trinidad reinvented themselves as rowdy ports and supply centers for mines at Orleans, Willow Creek, and other northwestern locations willing to purchase lumber, crab, oysters, salmon, whale oil, dairy products, and apples. Seth Kinman, a local mountain man dressed in buckskin and moccasins, supplied elk and deer meat to the soldiers at Fort Humboldt (1853-65) and entertained them by playing a banjo crafted from the skull of a favorite mule. Ulysses Grant was posted at the fort where, when bored, which was often, he took long horseback rides by day and drank in James Ryan's saloon at night.

On February 26, 1860, immigrants armed with guns, clubs, knives, and hatchets invaded Tuluwat, a Wiyot ceremonial center now called Indian Island, and butchered between eighty and a hundred people preparing for a World Renewal celebration. The victims were mainly women, children, and old men. Few survived. None of the attackers was ever brought to account, nor was any motive established. Given the projective paranoia endemic to colonialism, however, Native nonaggression has never guaranteed any safety. Bret Harte wrote an article about the massacre and was promptly run out of Arcata.

Meanwhile, the assault on the surrounding forests rolled forward as well. Between 1889 and 1893, six hundred and seventy million board feet of redwood were sawed in Humboldt County.

Twenty-two sawmills cut lumber in and around Eureka. Redwood and spruce had once grown near the water's edge, but now they vanished from the hillsides too. Once this insanity had run its course, Bartlin and Henrietta Glatt set aside land for Sequoia Park, Eureka, as early as 1894 to give seventy-seven acres to coast redwood, Douglas fir, Sitka spruce, grand fir; rhodododendrons, ferns, redwood sorrel, salmonberry, huckleberry, many native plants, and Mirror Lake, now a duck pond. In 1923, Zipporah Russ, wife of pioneer Joseph Russ, donated a hundred and sixty-six acres of redwood forest for protection within the Prairie Creek Redwoods State Park.

Work is also under way to rejuvenate habitats in Humboldt Bay. Eelgrass that grows in shallow water feeds incoming waterfowl while weaving a nursery for many species of fish. Halibut, cabazon, English sole, rock fish, Pacific herring, pipefish, sea hares, leopard sharks, and gill sharks rely on the eelgrass beds. Birds also depend on mudflats exposed at low tide, as do clams, ghost shrimp, polycheate worms, and inkeeper worms. Anaerobic bacteria inhabiting the mud tinge it with the smell of rotten eggs. Eelgrass and muflats belong to the bay, but the non-native cordgrass infesting its salt marshes and estuaries does not. Like many who have arrived here uninvited, though, the invasives, having been welcomed in, make themselves right at home.

ARCATA IS A COLLEGE town, and its jubilant mood made it feel like one. Youngsters in tie-dye colors and shabby jeans reminded me of the Flower Children. Some of them, presumably, went to school at Humboldt State. Innumerable dredlocks, sandals, sneakers, backpacks, and very baggy pants made me feel like an ancient. Turquoise footprints painted on the sidewalk lead up to the Humboldt Natural History Museum.

"We don't have a free will!" someone insisted in the central plaza while walking by the bronze statue of President McKinley. He had run his office as a corporatist, ignorer of monopolies, and igniter of the imperialistic Spanish-American War. Why celebrate him of all people? Flyers posted on utility poles called for urgent action. So, in their own way, did the signs hung in shops around the plaza: "Sandal Sale," Solutions, Yoga, "Health Fair," Organic Soup and Salad Bar.

Arcata is Wiyot for "Over There," which makes sense. "Arcata" resembles Arcadia, a pastoral Greek countryside named for a son of Zeus and Callisto who taught his people to bake bread and weave. Wild Pan liked to romp and chase nymphs there. As for Arcata, or Goad-la-nah to the Wiyots, its American incarnation rose in 1850 because of a land settlement firm called the Union Company. Bret Harte was far from the only citizen to be ejected from Paradise. The Chinese were too after a Eureka city councilman was killed in a tong battle crossfire in 1885. Italians were not permitted to live west of G Street and could visit only with a police escort. As more immigrants arrived, including Portuguese, Yugoslavs, and Swedes, tolerance and a new delight in cultural variety gradually took root. The plaza, always town central, has often served as a commons.

Environmental awareness has burgeoned in the city whose council became the first in the nation with a Green Party majority. At the northern end of Humboldt Bay, where an old landfill once reeked, the Arcata Wastewater Treatment Plant ("the Marsh") also provides a wildlife sanctuary and an outdoor laboratory for student research. A sign hung on a fence above a block-circling mural dotted with woodlands, deer, and farmer's markets announced a Coastal Cleanup Day.

Between Arcata and Eureka stretches a Safety Zone announced by several road signs punctuated by suggestions to "Please Be Courteous." The signage, the hospitality to newcomers, the sheltering sandbar arms, the childlike spirit loose in Arcadian Arcata. Was Humboldt Bay an overprotective mother?

By the time I reached F Street, it was clear that Arcata and Eureka were the bay's twin boys, the first dreamy and introverted, the second dramatic and extroverted. One long mural featured cats, dogs, lions, bears, and birds clothed in suits. Another, at the Performing Arts center, splashed a ballerina, Shakespeare, a clown, and two musicians across an entire wall. The "historic" section--1st through 7th streets, with 1st at bay's edge--operated as one big trinket arcade run from within old-fashioned wooden buildings daubed in yellow, purple, green, turquoise, orange, red, and yellow. The State Theater wore a Spanish Colonial Revival persona done up with ornate red trimmings. A red brick walkway spiraled around a gazebo decorated with purple-leaved trees. A bump in the sidewalk had been sprayed bright pink to prevent tripping. At the Eureka Theater: "Duck and Cover, Here Comes Gallagher."

The Wiyots knew this area as *Loleta*, "pleasant place at the end of the water." City founder James Ryan supposedly shouted "Eureka!" when he sailed into Humboldt Bay.

Inside a glass case sat Zoltar under a gold turban. One brown hand held a playing card as the other hovered over a crystal ball. This place made me feel playful. I dug out some coins and drew forth my fortune:

> Now is the time to start that new project you have been contemplating. Your deliberation will pay off in the long run because doubt is the father of invention and the key to knowledge.

As I made my way to the edge of town, the impression that creative children had designed Eureka lingered. The sign for Sole-Savers Used Cars displayed talking shoes. Ky's Hair Design parked itself in what appeared to be a domed spaceship. A remarkable mural right next to the courthouse/post office was half courthouse brick and half an animated facade with costumed people and animals popping out of it. A bird wearing a hat perched on the hatted head of a passerby carrying a newspaper tucked under an arm.

Even the Victorians on M Street wore eye-catching colors. The most subdued, the Ingomar Club ("Members Only"), stood in elaborately carved and furnished pride behind a filigreed wrought-iron gate just up the road from the exuberant Carson Mansion otherwise known as the Pink Lady.

I began to understand the presence here at the 14th Street Food Bank. While driving by, my eye was caught by a colorful mural of a smiling, motherly woman. I got out for a closer look. One of her hands held what looked like a round apple, the other a cornucopia so full that fruit dropped from it. Behind her lay cultivated fields fringed with sunflowers.

She seemed familiar, but I could not name her until driving far enough south of the bay to spot a road sign welcoming me to Fortuna. I saw her again, cornucopia in hand, on a mural that placed her in a fertile meadow touched by a rainbow. A butterfly sat on her shoulder. I nodded.

Fortuna--Tyche to the Greeks--often found depiction with a cornucopia, a ship's rudder, a ball (in this case a piece of fruit), some grains, and the wheel I had seen echoed in large four-point compasses etched into sidewalks in Eureka. The Indo-European root of her name means "to carry" and also links to the round of seasons (*vortumna*). This cycle gradually reinvented itself in the Wheel of Fortune imaging the samsaric rise and fall of luck. A reminder, perhaps, of how much of our real luck depends on aligning our efforts within the circle of natural rhythms.

Fortuna's sacred day was June 11, the very day Humboldt's first European explorers landed at Trinidad.

Our English word "luck" is related to the German *glück*. not only luck but good fortune, joy, prosperity, cheer. Hermann Hesse loved this word and wrote a poem around it in 1952:

> If luck you chase, you have not grown
> enough for happiness to stay,
> not even if you get your way.
> If, what you lost, you still bemoan,
> and grasp at tasks, and dash and dart,
> you have not known true peace of heart.
> But if no wishes are your own,
> and you don't try to win the game,
> and Lady Luck is just a name,
> then tides of life won't reach your breast—
> and all your strife
> and all your soul will rest.
> (translation by Walter A. Aue)

"Don't try to win the game" could be misunderstood as an ideal of nonattachment, and in fact Hesse had flirted with this ideal earlier in his life during his Buddhist studies phase. Nonattachment has ever seemed a balm to tempestuous souls. But the Hesse of 1952 understood the difference between timid noninvolvement in one's life and losing one's soul to competition. Joseph Knecht, the hero of Hesse's last novel *The Glass Bead Game*, plunges into life even while fully aware of its transience. It isn't that life is unreal, it's that life's motions, like seasons and lunar cycles, ebb and pulse, wax and wane. One root of "samsara" is "wandering through." Enjoying the game instead of trying to win. Meeting each phase gladly while knowing it will end one day. Living in the spirit of play ("eureka!") the way Creator-Trickster intended it.

Zoltar was right, and Fortuna too. It was time to wrap up these Californian journeyings and move on to my life's next phase.

Mendocino and Clear Lake: Altared States

The westernmost point on California's coast looks on a map like a small bump jutting into the Pacific. That is Cape Mendocino. Its name derives from that of a Spanish viceroy and means "Cold Mountain," an appropriate appellation along the inhospitable Lost Coast of southern Humboldt County. Inhospitable because inaccessible by any but mountain roads, lost because depopulated during the Great Depression and never heavily populated to begin with. The beaches of this coast are composed of black sand overseen by severe dark cliffs.

The sand is black because the Mendocino Triple Junction located offshore of the cape keeps things seismically active. The Pacific, North American, and Gorda Plates grind and clash at this junction out of which zigzag the Mendocino Fracture Zone and the San Andreas Fault. Three large earthquakes rumbling in April 1992 reminded witnesses of the power of movements in the depths.

> At sea and air, monotonous gray
> lingers way past memory.
> Isn't there just one other human being,
> like a tangled mass of kelp or a styrofoam cup,

floating toward dry land?
— Virginia Sharkey, from "Walking on the Ocean
Floor"

My drive southward along Highway 101 brought me through Humboldt Redwoods State Park east of Cape Mendocino and down into Piercy, home of the roadside attraction Confusion Hill. The house George Hudson built in 1949 incorporated clever tilts to produce dizzying optical illusions. The site suffered its own imbalance, a fiscal one, when engineers realigned 101 away from it to avoid ongoing mudslides.

At Leggett I faced a fork in the road. Below the Drive-Thru Tree Park, Highway 101 buds off Interstate 1, which keeps to the coast through Fort Bragg, Mendocino the city, the Iverson Indian Rancheria near Point Arena and its marine preserve, and on down to Fort Ross, Bodega Bay, and Marin County, rejoining 101 at the southernmost tip of Mill Valley. Highway 101 continues inland, paralleling the Mendocino National Forest at a distance while passing through a number of small towns, Willits, and Ukiah (seat of Mendocino County), before bypassing Clear Lake on its way to Sonoma County and points farther south. Eventually I would go that way but leave 101 for Lake County, Harbin Hotsprings, Napa, and, finally, Benicia, our former state capital.

Fort Bragg, which is fifty miles south of Cape Mendocino, was originally a Pomo place. The fort was opened on twenty-five thousand acres by Lieutenant Horatio Gates Gibson on June 11 (that day again! Yet another turn of Fortuna's wheel), 1857 to keep an eye on the Mendocino Indian Reservation set up a year earlier. He named the fort after Mexican War veteran and Confederate Captain Braxton Bragg. The fort was closed in 1866. Came lumber mills, ranches, shippers, and settlers, and a railroad to haul logs up Pudding Creek. The town incorporated as a city in 1889.

Although the 1906 earthquake damaged Fort Bragg, revenue for reconstruction flowed in once the local mills were hit by demands for lumber from San Francisco. Commercial fishing and tourism also brought in money, as did a new railroad track to Willits. A four-hundred-acre lumber mill owned by Georgia Pacific Lumber

Company is up for sale as a possible future conference center, marine research facility, or college campus, depending on who purchases it.

The family name Bragg points back to Bragi, Norse god of eloquence. *Bragr* means "poetry." This coast and county have heard the tones of poetry both before and after Whitman:

> A California song,
> A prophecy and indirection, a thought impalpable
> to breathe as air,
> A chorus of dryads, fading, departing, or
> hamadryads departing,
> A murmuring, fateful, giant voice, out of the earth
> and sky,
> Voice of a mighty dying tree in the redwood forest
> dense....
>
> Thus on the northern coast,
> In the echo of teamsters' calls and the clinking
> chains, and the
> music of choppers' axes,
> The falling trunk and limbs, the crash, the muffled
> shriek, the groan,
> Such words combined from the redwood-tree, as of
> voices ecstatic,
> ancient and rustling,
> The century-lasting, unseen dryads, singing, with-
> drawing,
> All their recesses of forests and mountains leaving,
> From the Cascade range to the Wahsatch, or Idaho
> far, or Utah,
> To the deities of the modern henceforth yielding,
> The chorus and indications, the vistas of coming
> humanity, the
> settlements, features all,
> In the Mendocino woods I caught.
> — "Song of the Redwood Tree," 1876

Back in the early 1900s, Fort Bragg residents were in the habit of throwing their garbage over the cliffs above a beach where glass, appliances, and even car parts accumulated. Attempts to clean up "the Dumps" began in 1967. But decades of waves washed away some of the trash and, in time, wore the glass into small, smooth baubles that cover what is now known as Glass Beach in a carpet of naturally crafted gemstones. The California State Park System bought the thirty-eight-acre beach in 2002 for incorporation into MacKerricher State Park.

> The clock moves a slow few moments
> beyond the seductive second
> when I would have lain tangled in kelp
> showered in bloody shatter of glass
> rolled by blue white waters
> sloshing and pulling
> at the foot of the sacrificial cliffs.
> — Lourdes Thuesen, from "Presences: On the Closeness of Almost Driving Over An Ocean Cliff Under The Full Moon After A Poetry Reading"

Mendocino clings to a small peninsula ten miles below Fort Bragg and a few miles south of the Jughandle State Reserve. Each of its five Ecological Staircases rises as an uplifted terrace a hundred thousand years older than the next. As the only coastal Californian town designated a Historic Landmark, Mendocino stirred in the 1850s as a seaside settlement and grew modestly into a collection of Saltbox and Victorian cottages. Flowers cover planters, fences, and beaches as the goddess Flora's response to the gemstones gathered just north of here. Most of Mendocino's forty wineries lie along Highway 128 further inland, but five along the coast offer tastings and tours. The town of Little River tried to be a port three miles south of Mendocino, but the Wheel of Fortune turned again and the town subsided into a pygmy forest of Bishop pine, Monterey pine, and cypress acquired by the State Park System in 1934.

We shall have to listen
as the rasping wind searches out
the corners where we hide, scouring
every angle of our too-bright days

And wonder each time we recall
the crack and thunder of their falling
if the trees said: Yes, we are done
and gave thanks to every creature
as they fell.
— Susan Maeder, from "If the Trees Say Yes"

Entering Willits brought me into a cacophany of yelling pedestrians, revving engines, squealing tires, and barking dogs. At a service station a youth blasting rap music backed his beater out of a parking space straight for my front end until I added to the noise by honking. At this he halted and looked bewildered.

Willits was once Willitsville after Hiram Willits of Indiana. Black Bart (mining engineer Charles Bolton) liked to stop here in between encounters with Wells Fargo stage coaches intimidated by his nonfunctional shotgun and polite requests for money.

he wants to know
about me and bikes
and do I like that
buzz they say
gets girls off
— Susan Maeder, from "Danger"

This altar of Idunn, "Rejuvenator," elvish wife of Bragi and patron of apples, nuts, woods, dales, and youth, is also home to biointensive farmer and experimenter John Jeavons. He has made a lifework of how to produce as much food as possible from very little space. The title of one of his books reflects this regenerative passion: *How to Grow More Vegetables, Fruits, Nuts, Berries, Grains, and Other Crops Than You Ever Thought Possible On Less Land Than You Can Imagine.*

Like the morning glories in the field
common as weeds, however lovely
radiating their potent messages back to the sky
something forgotten suddenly blooms in your
memory
and the snow thaws around your heart
and the world becomes alive in you
as you rise up in your meadow and shine....
— Liz Haapanen, from "Morning Song"

Triple Junction, Confusion Point, Pygmy Forest, Mendocino Wine Country, alluvial soils and gravel loam of stupendous fertility: such influences mix thematically and perhaps terrapsychologically to readily alter the mood. No surprise, then, that two-thirds of the county's income derives from the growth and sale of cannabis. Once voters in the county approved Measure G in 2004 to legalize ownership of pot plants, $1 billion a year entered the county instead of being spent battling South American drug lords. However, those same lords have staked out secret plots here in the Emerald Triangle to grow their own pot illegally. Measure M also passed to make Mendocino County the first to ban genetically modified crops.

Glancing over place names around the county, I noticed how many invoked nature in an idyllic mood. Rivendale. Longvale. Steelhead. Hardy. Grove. DeHaven. Marble Place. Four Pines. Twin Rocks. Fair Oaks. Bell Springs. South Fork. Ridge....In addition to grapes and cannabis, Philo Gold and King David apples flourished here.

In Ukiah I paused in a plaza with no art in it. Same story at the red-tile-roofed Civic Center. Square functionality. Yet at the corner of North State and Henry, a mural illuminated the drab side of a sushi bar with flames, waves, forests, frogs, roses, planets, stars, and an egg-shaped Earth breaking open to birth a DNA strand of butterflies emerging from cocoons. Malakai Schindel had gathered young artists to paint and name it "Transformation."

THE WPA GUIDE TO California refers to Lake County as "hermit-like." The county kept its introverted feeling even after waves of retirees moved there in the mid-1980s with younger geothermal industry job-seekers.

I departed from Highway 101 by transitioning to State Route 20 and driving eastward until I reached Upper Lake settled at the top of Clear Lake in 1854 when William Elliott opened his blacksmith's shop. A red metal arch over the road bore the city name and date of founding.

A little south of these boutiques in barns, Clear Lake had breathed and pulsed for 2.5 million years. The largest natural fresh-water lake in California (nineteen miles by eight, with a maximum depth of sixty feet), it was also one of the oldest on the continent. The Pomos called it *Lypoyomi*, "Big Water," and went there for fish, visions, and healings in nutrient-rich waters ever-renewed by cold and hot springs. The lake is home to bass, Sacramento perch, chan-nel and white catfish, black and white crappies, carp, bluegill, brown bullheads, and the once-abundant Clear Lake hitch. Its out-let is Cache Creek.

Reflections from the surface seem to have bounced into place names. Four years after acquiring a post office, Upper Clear Lake changed its name to Upper Lake (1875), then to Upperlake (1905), then back to Upper Lake (1906). Upper Lake shares Clear Lake with Clearlake, Clearlake Oaks, Clearlake Highlands, Lakeport, North Lakeport, Borax Lake, Thurston Lake, and Lower Lake. There was also an Eastlake, but it closed.

The purity of the lake's reflections began to dim during World War II when flying boats from Alameda Naval Air Station landed on the surface. Throughout the 1940s, insecticides were dumped into the lake to kill off clouds of swarming gnats, but fish and birds like the Western grebe died too. From the Sulfur Bank Mine working steadily through both World Wars dripped so much mercury that the abandoned mine was declared a Superfund site in 1990. To this day Fish and Game caution children and pregnant women against eating fish caught in the lake.

Polluted reflections make for polluted visions, and especially in Meth Central of Northern California. Upon entering town I stopped to make a call and found that my cell phone, though fully charged, had blacked out. Rebooting it did no good. It did not recover until I reached Napa. My eye kept running into ads for psychotherapy--Mental Health Services here, Family Health Services there--until I reached Lakeshore, where they gave way to signs hung up by men running for sheriff or city council on fenceposts guarding barren lots and yards full of dry grass. An Enjoy Clearlake! sign announced a run-down lounge, trashed apartments, consignment stores, check cashing business, and cheap hotels like Paradise Cove. Reflections Resort was closed, and enclosed by a tall metal fence.

Driving east, I expected from the map to find a 22nd Street, a 23rd Street, and so on, but in the real world dirt roads with no sidewalks sat forlornly in hot sunlight. Police shook down a young Latino ordered out of an old green car. His sagging pants exposed white underwear. A bumper sticker on the back of a black pickup parked in front of a trailer intoned, "Praise the Lord and Pass the Ammunition."

> We are God's clothes; without us God cannot be
> seen...
> Our lives are the little soap operas to fill the bore-
> dom
> Between earthquakes, hurricanes and another year.
>
> Our songs of praise and thanksgiving grate on
> God's ear.
> Patient as parents at the piano recital of the privi-
> leged.
>
> Like a clothes closet run amok, we philosophize,
> Iron the ruffles and pad the bras of being.
> — Jane Reichhold, from "Dressed to Kill"

Kelseyville, formerly Kelsey Creek, Kelsey Town, Peartown, and Uncle Sam, was named after Andrew Kelsey. From the Vallejos he bought a rancho in 1847 beneath Mt. Knocti just south of Clear Lake. Kelsey and his partner Charles Stone built an adobe in Pomo

territory and treated the Indians so badly--enslavement, rape, starvation, murder--that in 1849, Pomo warriors killed them. In retaliation, the U.S. Army under Captain Nathaniel Lyon came upon a
group of anywhere from forty to four hundred Pomo on May 15th,
1850, and massacred them on Badon-napo-ti ("Old Island") a quarter mile west of today's Highway 20 and a mile and a half south of
Upper Lake. After shooting women and old men and smashing the
heads of babies against rocks and tree trunks, the dragoons marched
onward to kill another seventy-five Natives at the Russian River
before retiring. Lyon was eventually promoted to the rank of general and died in the Civil War.

Six-year-old Ni'ka (Lucy Moore) survived the Bloody Island
Massacre by hiding underwater while breathing through a tule. Her
descendants founded the Lucy Moore Foundation to educate the
public about Pomo history and culture, organize annual May 15th
gatherings at sunrise to remember the massacre, and obtain five
hundred acres of Bloody Island and its marshland to protect ecologically sensitive habitat, preserve archeological finds, and, following
a dream that visited Sage Runningbear, found a museum and cultural center roundhouse, a research laboratory for studying traditional nutrition, a counseling center for abused children, an
amphitheater for concerts and powwows, and a healing center to
offer indigenous healing practices and herbal treatments. "If we can
do this together, to know and learn from each other, to accept the
truths of the old world and the new," stated Clayton Duncan of the
nearby Robinson Rancheria, "perhaps our children will not see the
colors of skin, the manners of our worship, our cultural heritages as
characteristics that divide us. Perhaps they will see them as the
attributes that unite us so we can all work together to fix, mend and
heal the Earth, our mother." A tragedy thus alchemized into community visioning might finally restore a balance between cultures
and communities and, beyond them, between us and the more-
than-human world.

To my growing list of consciousness-altering influences in
Mendocino and Lake Counties I found one more to add from roughly twenty miles below Clear Lake.

A magma chamber under Mt. Hannah twelve miles to the north

heats all the springs around here, but the Lake Miwoks called this one Eetawyomi, "Hot Place." The seven primary springs at Harbin--sulfur, iron, four cold soda springs, and one warm spring of weak arsenic used for a footbath--bubble with water stored below the ground for twelve million years. The Miwok came here to heal, to dance songs dreamed by shamans (who also learned about cures by dreaming at this site), and to trade with Clear Lake Pomos, Wappos, Wintuns, and other Native travelers passing through.

So did other visitors with less beneficent agendas: Luis Arguello in 1921 with soldiers "recruiting" Natives for guides; the Vallejo brothers to grant Laguna de Lupi-Yomi in 1840; Captain Archibald Ritchie from Delaware to buy ranch land in Lake County and see the springs in 1856 before being found dead after falling from a horse and having a stroke on the road between Napa and Sonoma. Which James Harbin, father or son, bought the property next, or whether a formal sale was made before or after Ritchie died, is still unclear. James the younger, whose nickname was Mat, married a woman named Sarah (as had his father), but she died, and Harbin was thereafter trailed by shady real estate auctions and failed business dealings. It could be that he and his brother Cal jointly founded the hot springs as a business. Take note of the pairings that flap like wingbeats through the entire history of Lake County's first resort.

Richard Williams of Wales brought his wife Mary to the springs, but she died anyway three weeks after the birth of their third, and short-lived, child. Williams decided to build a resort there anyway, and he and fellow Welshman Hugh Hughes applied for a grant in 1867 to do so. To prevent either from selling out to a third party, each sold half of his interest to the other. The property was just a rough log cabin near the springs, with no road. Hughes eventually sold out.

Health-seekers arrived at Harbin Hot Springs Health and Pleasure Resort by 1872. Middletown, located on the stage route between Calistoga and Lower Lake, was growing despite Lake County's reputation as "walled-in" and "hidden." The sulfur water soaks at springs around the county were advertised as good for gout, rheumatism, arthritis, and gunshot wounds, although Witter Springs in northern Lake County was forced to close after its fame as a cure for syphilis proved unfounded.

> One old gentleman from Sacramento who was paralyzed for seven years was cured here...His complete recovery was sudden, after the first favorable signs commenced. And when at last one morning he was able to throw his crutches away, half wild with delight and excitement, he set off on horseback for home in such haste that he rode the horse to death.
>
> — from a testimonial

By 1881, Harbin was a small village of twenty-five buildings. A year later Williams contracted pneumonia, was delirious for two days, and died without a will.

Evidently something warlike came with the resort package. *Harbin* thrusts like a dragon's tooth from "Herbert," which means "famous army." In Belgian Harbin means "glorious warrior." By the end of the 1800s, so many boxers arrived that a gym was equipped for them. Police from the Mission District in San Francisco took the cure as well.

In 1907 the next owner, Jim Hays, was thrown from a buggy and died two years later--without a will.

After that the place took a break, closed, and was auctioned to Newton Booth, his wife Lela, and his brother and brother-in-law. They cleaned and reorganized and changed Harbin from a spa into a family resort. Newton and his son worked as its primary managers until the senior Booths left in 1957 to live in nearby St. Helena because of ill health.

Real estate investor Robert Ramsey bought Harbin but could never make it work, so he wisely sold out before it injured him. In 1963 East Bay developer Maurice Abend bought it and made the mistake of hiring Art Blum as an executive. They ended up suing each other. The property was deeded in 1965 to CKB Corporation of Los Angeles headed by Bob Schneider, who also wanted to profit from the place but never did. He defaulted, and Harbin became a temporary halfway house for boys who wrecked it.

Having been told on a flying saucer trip that he had a mission to enlighten the world, Donald Hamrick, founder of the Frontiers of Science Fellowship, took over in 1968. His first headquarters had been in San Rafael, but neighbors objected, so they ended up in Harbin just as a candle fell off a table there and burned up a cabin. In spite of this signal, or perhaps unconsciously because of it, Hamrick changed the business name to Harbinger and set up Harbinger University to usher in a new age for man. A "laboratory" for research occupied a former cocktail lounge. Visiting Lake County officials received a taste of the IQ-boosting machine, with unknown results.

Soon Harbinger University degenerated into a kind of LSD country club. Swarms of hippies came to Harbin to live for free and usher in the New Age by trashing the grounds, breaking the windows, and leaving behind a car graced with bullet holes to greet visitors at the front entrance. After this and a heptatitus outbreak, Health and other agencies shut down the party.

To this wreck came Robert Hartley, a Gestalt Therapy advocate and Miami real estate developer. With two fellow Gestaltists he sought a place to birth a non-hierarchical New Age community. After an argument the partnership dissolved, but Hartley bought the place anyway and recruited workers to clean up and to manage another fire that sprang out. The Heart Consciousness Church incorporated 1975 to take over ownership from Hartley.

After a noisy split in leadership, several dissenters went off to form their own community a few miles away and to grow pot and mushrooms until they were arrested. In 1977 the Utopians ascended from San Francisco to do workshops at Harbin for revenue, but when they started taking over, even printing up notices identifying Harbin as their new rural base, they were asked to not come back.

Hartley changed his name to Ishvara ("Lord" or "Supreme Being") and embraced Yoga after meeting and being inspired and instructed by Yogeshwar Muni (Charles Brerner). Harbin now evolved to offer meditation and macrobiotics. Guests could go naked and natural. In Ishvara's words:

> Thirty-eight years ago for the first time, I took off
> my clothes and ran in the sun and breeze. Never
> before had I felt so free! I was claiming my ecstatic
> human birthright--to be in nature, free from limita-
> tion.

Free or not, Harbin still needed to pay the rent. Dick Price, cofounder of Esalen, desired to set up a Spiritual Emergency center for schizophrenic patients, so Aurora House was built, but no hospital or doctors would refer anyone to Harbin, so this project too went nowhere. Aurora was built on the same parcel previously set aside for personal growth guru Ken Keyes.

The century-long pattern of unfortunate events peppered with occasional successes suggests that human activities involving authentic and not ersatz healing can work well here. Watsu, water-dance, massage, art, holistic sexuality, and many other therapeutic modalities bring eager participants to stay in a non-WiFi center long enough to rejuvenate while enjoying the natural beauty all around. Some of it reveals itself with varying degrees of shyness or exuberance in the clothing-optional spas. A health-conscious cafe provides nourishing meals. Of the Holy Lands Preservation Trust formed to oversee Harbin Hot Springs, most of the sixteen trustees are Native Americans committed to protecting sacred land.

Although I appreciated the beauty at the spas and elsewhere at Harbin, I came away with two unexpected gifts. The first was an insight about this land's organic wisdom, the second an idea about what fiery myth might be active here.

The insight caught me at the edge of sleep. Awakening to daylight in the windows of the guest house, I grasped the faint remnants of a dream in which Something about or within Harbin itself was teaching me a form of meditation.

There are dreams that instruct and dreams that rebalance the psyche from outside of awareness. The first kind are worth remembering in the morning, the second need not be. A third kind mixes them. Most of the details of my dream at Harbin faded as soon as I woke up, but for my conscious mind the important image to recall was that of being taught a spiritual science by the spirit of the land.

I sat with this image all morning. What if it were true not only here, but elsewhere? Everywhere? What if a large body of what we thought of as divinely inspired spiritual activity--not only meditation but prayer, revelation, guidance, and even religion, myth, and mysticism--came to us not from only within or above, but from the sacred ground from which plants that change consciousness have been eaten by us and by other animals since we all had legs to walk on and mouths to browse with?

> ...Why should all the major religions of the modern world include a crucial encounter with wilderness--Moses, Jesus, and Mohammed in the desert mountains, Siddhartha in the jungle? And why should the predominant modern view of the origin and development of life have arisen from the five-year wilderness voyage of a Victorian amateur naturalist named Charles Darwin? There evidently is more to wilderness than meets the eye--more than water, timber, minerals, the materials of physical existence. Somehow there are mental trees, streams, and rocks--psychic raw materials from which every age has cut, dammed, or quarried an invisible civilization--an imaginative world of origins and meanings--what one might call a mythology.
>
> — David Wallace

So Who was here at Harbin?

According to the *Prose Edda*, the giant Thiazi desired Idunn, but she was already spoken for. So Thiazi bullied Loki the Trickster into luring her into an isolated wood with the promise of delicious apples. Thiazi soared down in the form of an eagle, snatched her from the wood, and took her home. Shapeshifting into a falcon, Loci found her, turned her into a nut to disguise her, and returned her to Asgard, where she assumed her normal form once again. Thiazi flew in pursuit, but the gods knew he was coming and built an enormous pyre. When the eagle neared it, the gods ignited it, and Thiazi burned. Removing his eyes, Odin placed them in the heavens to serve as stars.

Lake Miwok stories mention the creation of humans warmed by stolen fires from the feathers of a sacred bird.

The Assyrians called that bird the Phoenix. Living on incense, it liked to dwell near a well in Phoenicia. At dawn, when it bathed there, the beauty of its song prompted mighty Helios to halt his sun chariot long enough to listen and to admire the light shining on its purple and crimson feathers. When the Phoenix had lived long enough, it collected fragrant branches, built a nest, set it afire, and burned on this pyre until a young Phoenix emerged from ashes into new life.

Perhaps the presence of Phoenix/Thiazi is why all the odd pairings recur here, why the occasional fires light near these pools, why times of order alternate with spells of chaos, and why the forking road leading to Harbin Hot Springs recalls the lobes of the heart or the spread, flaming wings of the Phoenix.

Napa, Vineyard of Saturn

State Route 29 led me south from Middletown to Calistoga. "Calistoga" is what happens when you mix a California with a Saratoga Hot Springs, New York, as the ever-enterprising Sam Brannan did while mapping the town in 1859 and installing a "grand hotel" plus guest cottages. His goal, to build "the great resort spa in the west," proved unachievable, especially after he let his imported sheep run free, found himself accused of ruining pasturelands, and came away partially paralyzed from a gunfight over ownership of a sawmill.

Nevertheless, people showed up in Calistoga, especially the Chinese who arrived to work in fields and as servants, builders, carpenters, and diggers in the Calistoga Silver Mine--for a brief quicksilver boom in 1870-71--and the tunnels of a local winery. Robert Louis Stevenson showed up to inspect the Petrified Forest--giant redwoods turn to stone by volcanic ash three million years ago--and to have an affair with Fanny Osbourne. To pitch the hot springs, a tourist guide reported in 1881 that "There is evidently some mysterious agency at work underground at Calistoga not quite comprehensible to visitors...." Evidently, because in 1928, a geyser at Pacheteau Baths that blew drilling equipment high into the air took days to contain. Today things have grown much calmer. Tourists can sample wine instead of digging for it, or emulate the redwoods by sinking with blissful sighs into hot mud baths.

The highway leads farther south through St. Helena past its Culinary Institute and numerous wineries. Lack of parking on the narrow, often-congested highway forces the visitor to pass miles of boutiques to buy and eat from. Behind them, rows of planted wine grapes race away into the distance like an optical illusion gridded over the fertile ground. Wine suggests Bacchus, but this highly structured and dynastic region could never be taken for an altar of the Ecstatic One. The Mayacamas, mountain site of redwoods and Douglas fir, sit on the west of the valley, the Howells of conifers and thick chaparral on the east. This valley thirty-five miles long and a few miles wide from Calistoga to San Pablo Bay had been a Wappo and Miwok place, but today a quarter of California's eight hundred wineries operate here. Valley grapes sell for 10-20% more than from anywhere else in the Golden State. Wine concocted in Napa Valley fiefdoms fuels the engines of financial empires.

It started, albeit rather innocently, when North Carolina trapper George Yount showed up in 1838 to settle and to plant a few Mission vines bought from the Vallejo family. He had swept through Napa in 1831, worked for Mariano Vallejo in Vallejo, killed some rebellious Indians for him, gotten baptized at Mission San Rafael as Jorge Concepcion, and in 1836 received a grant from Vallejo for twelve-thousand-acre Caymus Rancho in Napa Valley. There Yount built a log cabin and blockhouse, planted crops, kept cattle, hunted bears, and planted the first grapes in Napa Valley.

Little came of this, at first, so Yount sold off his estate and it became a farm named *Konig* ("King"). But next door in Sonoma County, Agoston Haraszthy bought five hundred and sixty acres in 1856 and, hiring Chinese laborers to build Buena Vista, expanded it to five thousand acres of the first commercial vineyard in California. His sparkling wine Eclipse sold widely in San Francisco. When his winery departed for Nicaragua, only the aroma of inspiration lingered--long enough for John Patchett to start making wine by 1858 and Charles Krug from Prussia three years later. Krug had worked in Patchett's winery. Now on his own, he sold commercially, eventually making wine for the family of "Doctor" Edward Bale, master of the Carne Humana ("Human Flesh") grant where Americans,

Indians, and Mexicans had fought. Bale had renamed Rancho Calajomanas as a sick nod to the amputations he had performed as an inebriated army surgeon. The Beringer brothers worked for Krug.

> Wek-wek the Bullet Hawk, grandson of Coyote, stole fire from the heavens one day and brought some down to give to human beings. For a while after this Thunder hunted and ate people until the warrior Wild Oats killed him with his arrows. Then Wild Oats began to hunt and eat people until his sister confronted him, at which point he stopped.
>
> — Miwok legend

When phylloxera from the Mississipi River Valley crossed the ocean to descend upon and destroy many of the best vineyards of France in 1882, this calamity gave California winemakers an opportunity to distill something besides bulk vintages. That year vineyard acreage in Napa reached twelve thousand, up from thirty-five hundred acres just two years before, and up once again to almost seventeen thousand by 1887. Who was doing all the planting?

William Watson, secretary and cashier of Bank of Napa and son-in-law of George Yount, had acquired the Konig farm in 1871 and renamed the property Inglenook. Gustave Niebaum, a Finnish captain and fur trader, bought Inglenook in 1880, expanded its acreage, and built a three-story winery right into a hill for temperature control. Niebaum was passionate about winemaking. After collecting hundreds of books on enology and viticulture and on the work of Louis Pasteur, father of germ theory, he ran the cleanest winery anywhere while grafting phylloxera-resistant root stock from cuttings he collected in France and Germany. In 1882 Inglenook made eighty thousand gallons of carefully prepared wine. When Niebaum died in 1911, his widow Susan took over both the estate and her husband's commitment to quality.

Krug's winemaker Jacob Beringer established Beringer Brothers in 1877 in a three-story winery up against a hill. The hill held pipes through which grape juice and skins flowed downhill to second-floor fermentatino tanks, then to first-floor casks shaded in long tunnels carved into the hillside like mining sluices. This operation produced palatable if rather sweet wine.

Georges de Latour of Bordeaux came to Napa after mining in Nevada left him all but broke. Trained in chemistry, he set up Beaulieu Vineyards and began importing and selling phylloxera-resistant Rupestris St. George roostock. He also supplied wine to churches and brought up fine varietals that by 1934 won medals in state wine competitions.

The Salmina family of Switzerland took over an old vineyard and made it into Larkmead Winery in 1892 while Battista Salmina bought the William Tell Hotel in St. Helena. Felix Salmina and his sons produced a hundred thousand gallons a wine of year. Christian Brothers started up in Napa and Martini in St. Helena. By 1933, Martini, producer of cool-fermented varietals, was state-of-the-art even if its metal roof had been cut from a dog-racing track in Southern California.

After buying several hundred acres of the old Jerome C. Davis farm in 1905, the University of California founded the University Farm School at the future site of UC Davis in Yolo County. Soon the College of Agriculture founded in 1922 graduated hundreds of expert enologists to be hired as winemaking consultants at vineyards interested in turning out competitive brands.

When Larkmead, Inglenook, and Beringer wines won a Diplomma of Honor from the Paris Exposition in 1937, the world began to realize that Californian wines could compete with French. At Beaulieu Vineyards, Andrew Tchelistcheff introduced updated winemaking technologies like cool fermentation and controlled malolactic fermentation to soften the natural tartness of wine grapes. These methods circulated through Napa Valley and beyond.

The penchant of California winemakers for experimenting with hybridized European-American vines outside the bounds of enological tradition continued to pay off. Able assistance by the University of California and the Napa Valley Wine Technical Society Technical introduced storage containers of glass or stainless steel, blanketing of wines with carbon dioxide or nitrogen, infusing bentonite to ensure protein stability, and early bottling with sterile filtration and low-oxygen-pickup systems. At a 1976 tasting in Paris, the highest-rated wines were a cabernet and a chardonnay from Napa Valley.

> The Golden Age was that first age which uncon-strained, with heart and soul, obedient to no law, gave honor to good faith and righteousness. No punishment they knew, no fear; they read no penal-ties engraved on plates of bronze; no suppliant throng with dread beheld their judge; no judges had they then, but lived secure...No battlements their cities yet embraced, no trumpets straight, no horns of sinuous brass, no sword, no helmet then--no need of arms; the world untroubled lived in leisured ease. Tellus [Earth] willingly, untouched, not wounded yet by hoe or plough, gave all her boun-teous store; men were content with nature's food unforced, and gathered strawberries on the moun-tainside and cherries and the clutching bramble's fruit, and acorns fallen from Jove's spreading tree.
>
> — Ovid

The reputation of Napa wines would have ripened without expensive advertising, but it ripened much quicker because of it.

As the University of California armed vintners with shiny new methods, the St. Helena Chamber of Commerce published brochures, flyers, window displays, magazine articles, and even newsreel footage to promote staged rounds of tours, tastings, parades with suitable floats, and a Labor Day "village festival" in 1934 complete with an allegorical play, barrel-rolling contests, a petting zoo, floats, a Festival Queen, and a grand ball for Her Majesty. The play's exotic title was "Il Sogno di Sant'Elena": "The Dream of St. Helena" in which a vintner comes home after a hard day's work to fall asleep in a chair while dreaming about the histo-ry of winemaking in Napa. His dream staged colorful costumes and folks songs. For this event the Napa Valley Cooperative Winery constructed a replica of the Golden Gate Bridge out of white and black grapes with wine standing in for the Bay.

The show must go on, and it did. At the Golden Gate Exposition in 1939, thirty vintners participated in an immense Wine Temple exhibit two stories high. Premium Wine Producers of California staged tastings around the nation in 1955 to prove a widespread preference for Californian wines even though the tastings most often came to a split decision. The Napa Valley Vintners Association invited Harvard students to a free lunch and sponsored the 1958 film *This Earth is Mine* starring Rock Hudson and Jean Simmons.

Some of the promotion depended on psychological tricks like selling Napa wines by varietal label instead of by brand. Edmund Rossi, manager of the Wine Advisory Board, supported the use of "group psychology" to influence consumer behavior. Holding tastings in "exciting, colorful and unusual surroundings" where tasters could "witness others, more knowledgeable than they, interested, even enthusiastic about the event" raised sales. Howard Williams, Gallo's Vice President of Marketing, believed consumers wanted a "luxury product" that would express and reinforce the buyer's self-perception (read: narcissism). They wanted "to live better and to exhibit their success." Someone certainly did. New back labels on bottles told rustic winemaking stories with text placed in scenic settings out in fertile fields.

By 1965, premium wine sales had topped five million cases to reach a 245% escalation of sales in ten years.

A sign placed to greet potential consumers to Napa Valley refers to "bottled poetry," Robert Louis Stevenson's reference to wines made in France, not California. Stevenson did write about California winemaking, however: "The beginning of vine-planting is like the beginning of mining for precious metals: the wine-grower also 'prospects.'"

> When Saturnus fell to dark Tartara and Jove reigned upon the earth, the Silver Race replaced the Gold, inferior, yet in worth above the tawny bronze.
>
> — Ovid

The Saturnine shadow of the dynastic struggle for dominance fell heavily over Napa Valley.

Wineries produced dry varietals to fight back against Gallo's cornering of the sweet (and cheap) wine market. Cesare Mondavi bought out Charles Krug. After his death, Robert Mondavi left the family over a feud about who would be king of the Mondavi empire --his mother Rosa had already anointed brother Peter and waged a costly court battle to keep the winery from Robert--and, having toured European wineries, based his chardonnay, cabernet, and fume blanc on French vintages aged in oak. They competed well as Mondavi fell behind in both quality and technological innovation. Beaulieu sold to Heublein, Beringer to Nestle, Larkmead to Solari, and Solari to still other buyers. Quality didn't always suffer, but....

Neibaum's widow Susan had raised engineer and Inglenook heir John Daniel Jr., the son of her niece and, eventually, husband to Betty. Why he sold Inglenook remains under argument. Some say he found himself unable to either leave or care for his abusive, pill-popping wife even after she ordered laborers to board up the window to her bedroom. His doctor was worried about his rising blood pressure. When he died, officially of a heart attack, his blood contained a large quantity of barbiturates. Suicide?

In what wine editor Jon Bonné called "one of the greatest branding takedowns in history," United Vintners took over Inglenook in 1964 after agreeing to maintain the deceased owner's high standards of quality and cleanliness and, instead, sold them off in 1970 to Heublein, producer of Smirnoff Vidka and acquirer of BV. Heublein's idea of winemaking involved pesticides in the formerly pristine vindeyards, termination of salesmen uninterested in pushing Inglenook as jug wine, relocation of the winery to Oakville, and, for a finale, selling it to R. J. Reynolds (now RJR/Nabisco) in 1982 to raise cash to avoid a hostile takeover by KFC. Reynolds sold out to Grand Metropolitan, the British company that owned Pillsbury, Haagen-Daz, and Burger King. In 2008 the winery belonged to The Wine Group, the world's third largest wine company, for $135 million.

Saturnus received this oracle: "Best of kings, you shall be knocked from power by a son." Jabbed by fear, he devours his offspring as each was born, and entombs them in his bowels. Rhea often complained of much pregnancy and no motherhood, and mourned her fertility.

— Ovid

This intensity of commercial struggle was, of course, what many moved to Napa to get away from. Hildegard Flanner, for instance, whose name June recalled Juno and whose husband was architect Fred ("peaceful ruler": Saturn in a harvest mood) Monhoff:

The San Gabriel Valley had been wiped out with bizarre speed and ease. Now in the north we were shaken to hear vineyardists heatedly contending for the too familiar privilege to convert their rich and productive land into building lots and cash. Strangers though we were, we stood up boldly in these public meetings and solemnly, loudy told them that they did not know what they were doing. "You will lose the valley," we cried, "it will be one big subdivision." And we told them, "We come from Southern California," as if that were the same as saying that we were escapees from a fate that gave us a desperate vision.

They landed in Calistoga. Monhoff had Saturn's green thumb and could grow vegetables even on hilltops. He designed their house in a scenic locale. Nevertheless,

There is a knoll in the middle of the valley facing our property. We watched in distress and bewilderment as huge mechanical equipment attacked the crown of this knoll and gradually reduced it to flat areas. On this flat ground slowly rose a mammoth building of a blank white, a new winery.

Other disturbances haunted the night. They were alone one evening watching meteors fall across a summer sky:

> But suddenly there was a cry from the bushes, the trees, the earth below, a cry of terror and supplication…Somewhere near at hand a predator, in quiet fury, was tearing and biting through a soft furry throat while the victim, perhaps a voiceless rabbit screeched in agony big enough for an elephant and died too slowly.

On another summer evening she heard from inside the house a horse and wagon clopping by. The sound stopped when it reached the woods. Just then her husband showed up: "Did you hear it?" She thought he meant the horse and wagon, but he hadn't heard them; instead, he had come to a fence along the woods in the dark, drawn there for no reason he could name, when, just before the moon rose, a scream hit him full in his face: "It was pain, anger, hatred." Aside from Saturn's dark connection with death, "Hildegard" identifies one of the Valkyries whose job was to escort the dead to Valhalla. For years she had kept in a special box a child of hers born dead. Without telling anyone, she buried the small body beneath a Napa Valley tree to whom she confided, "His body was born dead, but his soul was born alive. It is still alive."

> For a long time I stand in my garden and look across the Napa Valley to the opposite hills. In this rich scene there must be a meaning that is special and about to become an image of this place, a legend of this earth. But it is finally with disappointment, although always with desire, that I turn from the view of vineyards and hills and come into my home. It might be that from inside and looking out, as through a lens, I will catch the haunting image for which I search, floating before the stony Mayacama Mountains. Could I trust its reality?

Difficult to catch a glimpse of that image when you live inside it.

On a morning after her husband had endured an "existential" depression, a mist or rain a rose vine hung with "liquid gems" resembling rubies, sapphires, emeralds, topaz, like gems from the Roman treasury of Saturn.

> We should take care how we talk about legends
> and that sort of thing. They are rife in a time when
> the old faith of men has been renounced, and the
> new certainties are terrifying, and it is easy to settle
> our belief on a destructive image. Ever beyond the
> vine and its fruit and the pouring of the wine, the
> heart still waits for a sign. May its meaning be gen-
> tle and familiar; above all, may its meaning be close
> to the earth.

One October, as farmers bent to harvest from their fields, Flanner came home to find her husband dead. "Take me with you!"

> The young lovers at the next table
> Are very hungry ones.
> Their deepest cups run over.
> They laugh and languish in their spoons,
> They boast of sweet, they boast of sour.
>
> We call to them gently, Come to our
> Table, here the truly happy, the passionate
> Sit down to a shrug of salt
> By cold potato light,
> And only the empty platter can excite.
> Blessed be hunger, we say,
> For love must learn to starve before it eats.
> Give us no more, we say,
> Of sour, of sweets.
> Take the cup, take the cupboard away.

It is richer fare and richer sleep tonight
To know that honey longs for honey
In the empty comb of twilight.
— "The Feast" by Hildegarde Flanner

IN THE LATE 1960s, Napa Valley, home of many vineyards, remained a collection of small ranches raising walnuts, grapes, prunes, and cattle. But the scythe of Saturn was already at work in wide fields set aside by the Napa County Board of Supervisors for viticultural development. When growers sought to sell their vineyards, many went to Andy Beckstoffer. He was happy to them to a grape-growing empire whose mission he summed up proudly as "stewardship."

Carneros, which means "sheep" and also refers to meat (*carne*), began in Napa Valley as a collection of wooly beasts before the name transferred to a plot of land just north of the bay at the valley's outer edge. Although cool and foggy, this patch of land held potential. Louis Martini bought the Stanly Ranch there in 1942. Over thirteen hundred acres of vineyards wound through Carneros by the 1970s. Its chardonnays and pinos drew investors in the late 1980s as acreage under cultivation doubled.

Napa growers waxed blissful over newsworthy medical research in favor of moderate wine drinking. For international tastings they made sure the streets of the city-turned-resort were empty of the poor escorted off the busy thoroughfares.

Today Artesa (owned by Codorniu) and Premier Pacific propose to increase their pinot production by removing two thousand acres of redwoods and Douglas firs from Annapolis in Sonoma County to make way for what they dare to call Preservation Ranch. "There forests," stated Tom Adams, a Ranch official, "can be cleared and preserved at the same time."

> The owners of wineries themselves would be celebrated as a new class. These self-made baronets—formerly real estate speculators, developers, academics, brokers, dentists, oilmen, and purveyors of products as varied as frozen food and feature films

--would put their names on bottles, tacitly associating themselves with an older order and an endeavor above ordinary commerce. They would invite the public into a romantic association not unlike that involving movie idols and real royalty.

— James Conway

Downtown Napa is what happens when you build an enormous mall and turn it inside out. I parked in hot fall weather and strolled about looking through clothing store windows and wine shop doorways. Giant lamps guarded the doorstep of the post office. Clusters of tall buildings looming over clean, straight sidewalks punctuated by quaint street lamps wore gantries or platforms that looked for all the world like crowns. Saturn, after all, had headed the ambitious Titans until Zeus disposed of them in Hades.

Along NapaArtWalk glittered a huge metal sculpture of a fish about to swallow a frog on a hook. "Barrel of Fun," a mixed media work assembled by Gordon Huether to make fun of parking garages, hung on the side of a parking garage. His immigrant father had designed a window for a department store demolished to make room for such a garage. I wondered what his father would think of his son's artistic placement and the purposes it now served.

There were moments in Napa Valley when I felt that I was in a budding theme park, where the activity was orchestrated by unseen wizards in far-off places. The crunch of businesses devoted to yielding a return was so stultifying that I soon became numb to the humor I might ordinarily have extracted while passing the Vintage Inn or the Chablis Lodge or, worse yet, the John Muir Inn, where the rooms looked out on Marie Callendar's House of Pies.

— Bill Barich

I grew aware of what felt like a bottomless sadness about this place. It emanated from someone besides me or even the damaged land. It felt as though Saturn himself felt regret over how things had gone here. *I gave you magnificent growth and the means to harvest it...in my desire to serve what procreates, I had no idea the results would be so ruinous.*

In Napa Valley as elsewhere, some rose up to oppose overdevelopment, but the shadow of an unseen mythology wields a mighty scythe. Dorothy Erskine, who lived in San Francisco but owned a house in the valley, started People for Open Space one dinner party at a time to stop sprawl from ruining Napa. One result of this effort, the California Land Conservation Act (Williamson Act), allowed counties to tax agricultural land at a lower rate than adjacent residential areas. To qualify, owners had to agree not to develop their land for at least ten years. Advocates met in the back of the Sweet Shop in St. Helena. For a time they made a dentist's office their headquarters. The Saturnian imagery of eating proved even more appropriate when lower agricultural taxes offered incentives for building still more vineyards.

Along Highway 29, Rutherford hosts thirty-six wineries. Hearing about the dismal fate of Inglenook, Francis Ford Coppola bought the estate in 1975 and acquired the rest of the business in 1995. He bought the Niebaum home and property with profits from *Godfather II* and the rest of the property with help from *Bram Stocker's Dracula.* From The Wine Group he purchased the Inglenook name for an undisclosed sum. He is on a mission, he says with characteristic enthusiasm, to restore Inglenook's good name. The winery purchases fruit only from growers who farm sustainably, many organically, relies on Integrated Pest Management, and recycles cardboard bottle carriers and grape and water waste. Coppola's flagship cabernet bears the kingly name of Rubicon.

What if the harvest god who wears the crown had actually come to care about the effects his presence wrought? And what if, on our side of the conversation, the unseen mythology that always seems to emanate from the ground underfoot were cultivated with more conscious attention to the story that surrounds our efforts precisely here? Cultivated perhaps under the power of Rhea, called by the Romans Ops, whose name forms the "opus" of the Great Work done by Earth and her creatures alike? Isn't the agony of Napa Valley exactly the agony of Ops under the yoke of Saturn when both should work freely together toward a Golden Age and State?

Recently the smaller Napa winemakers have shown an interest in what the French call *terroir* ("tear-WAHR"). The untranslatable word points to how flavor depends on local qualities of soil, microclimate, mesoclimate, wind, rainfall, and personal care. A vintage carries a particular taste because of where it comes from: this place and no other. Terroir can never be duplicated, displaced, or mass-produced on some Titanic scale because it remains unique to particular landscapes. Wine distilled from grapes grown in accord with the natural cycles of Napa bear, therefore, an unmistakable, unrepeatable touch of Pacific fog, Napa River, oak woodland, chaparral, volcanic soil, and Coast Range.

And who knows? Perhaps the microscopic remnants of plants harvested by the Coast Miwok and Wappo show up too, and the sweat of their labors, and even the love they felt for the place, its spirit, where the long struggle against cool, fog, wind, and exploitation crowns the fruits of Napa with their uncopyable ripe uniqueness.

Overshadowed Benicia

When the Americans arrived in force in California, Mariano ("dedicated to Mars") Guadalupe Vallejo occupied Sonoma and its far-flung surroundings as Mexico's Director of Colonization for Alta California. This profitable post had given him thousands of acres and heads of cattle and ranch homes built by Native laborers subjected to the rule of Chief Solano. That, his baptismal name, was bestowed at Mission Dolores in San Francisco; his Suisunes name had been Sem Yeto, "Mighty Arm."

He wielded it on Vallejo's behalf through the smallpox epidemic of 1837, from which a vaccination saved him, until 1850, when incoming gold miner and squatter Samuel Martin found him dying in Suisun Valley. Vallejo would outlive Solano, to whom he had granted a Potter's Field named Rancho Suisun, by forty years before dying in relative poverty. The spent war god who'd considered himself an agricultural guardian lost his cattle and lands to American squatters.

Follow the Napa River southward sixteen miles and you will find on its east bank the town named after General Vallejo. This surrounded city, with Mare Island stationed on the west, streets named after states, and freeways on every side, has always served as a transitional site, even for the Suscols to the north, the Suisuns to the east, and the Karkins along the straits who came to gather tules, hunt, and fish.

Lieutenant Padro Fages saw the straits in March 1772. In three more years Jose Canizares, of the de Anza Expedition, drew a map of the area and called the river's west bank Flat Island. Vallejo came through in 1833 buying grants as he went. John B. Frisbie married Vallejo's oldest daughter Epifania and laid out Vallejo's first city streets. He also donated land for settlement.

Thanks to maneuvering by Captain David G. Farragut, the Navy bought Mare Island--so named when Vallejo's lost white mare showed up there--in 1854 to found the first U.S. naval base on the Pacific coast. This brought sailors (one of whom built the octagonal Ink Bottle House on Florida Street) and many ships. Although he called Vallejo town a "blunder," Robert Louis Stevenson berthed his yacht *Roamer* at the Vallejo Yacht Club. In 1867 the California Pacific Railroad put its southern terminus at Lemon Street. A Chinatown grew along Marin Street between Georgia and York. Progress seemed assured.

Stevenson's "blunder" remark may have jabbed intuitively at a recurrent truth: Vallejo has been unlucky. Manuel Viera owned the Old Stone House (building with stone occupies a prominent place in town history) until he shot a squatter and was himself killed in the street by vigilantes. The undertaker ran a livery stable. A warehouse replaced the former state capital building from which a photograph shot from the second story--the first shot ever taken of Vallejo, and so an origin story clue perhaps--revealed fenced, boxy houses with no trees and bare hills beyond. The warehouse burned in 1859. Closed in 1922 because of a murder and sex scandal, the Good Templar's Home for Orphans subsided into a golf course, then a subdivision. Frisbie's third home, a hill mansion on the corner of Virginia and Sutter, eventually became a girls' school, then a private residence again, then an Elks Lodge, then burned down in 1933, killing five.

Vallejo's lack of luck stands in odd relation--compensatory?--to the industry so long evident in the town of forges and smithies. The Carquinez Bridge opened on May 21, 1927 with governors of four states attending. During the celebration, newsboys shouted that

Charles Lindbergh had reached Paris to finish in triumph the first solo trans-Atlantic airplane flight. Lake Dalwigk was named for automobiler George Dalwigk after he sneaked his 1927 Dodge onto the new bridge for a quick photo very different from Vallejo's first grim portrait.

Having evolved into a trade and transport hub sending lumber through the Carquinez Strait, Vallejo expanded throughout World War II and beyond because of the Mare Island Navy Yard and dry-docks. The yard constructed over five hundred ships--cruisers, destroyers, submarines, and a battleship--and repaired many other vessels. In the 1950s the yard built and overhauled nuclear submarines. A second bridge parallel to the first went up in 1958 to spur construction of small airports, a lumber yard, carriage, bike, and automobile shops, and Sperry Mills, where Boris Karloff was hired to drive a truck. Of the monuments carved by Pioneer Marble and Granite, one graced Vallejo's grave site in Sonoma.

In May 2008 Vallejo, the "City of Opportunity," was forced to declare bankruptcy because of decreasing tax revenues combined with rising costs for basic services like firefighting and police. Homes in newly built neighborhoods found themselves in foreclosure. In three years, though, the city emerged from bankruptcy partially reorganized. Streets still ran cracked and neglected, buildings sagged, and gangs roamed the streets, but small victories sprang up here and there. One of them, the People's Garden, teaches organic gardening and community leadership at the former Navy Yard on Mare Island. This was the vision of Vilma Aquino:

> I have lived on Mare Island for over two years. During my walks around Mare Island, I would see the empty lot behind the Global Center for Success and each time I would pass the barren, empty lot, I would say to myself: "Wouldn't it be nice if this barren, empty lot were alive with people: clients of GCS, senior citizens, school children, community members all interacting with one another and growing fruits, vegetables, and flowers?"

A clue to the myth of Vallejo receives utterance every time residents call the city "Valley Joe." The gospels say Joseph, husband of Mary and father of Jesus, worked not only carpenter but an artisan skilled with wood, iron, or stone. That is why Joseph is the patron saint of laborers and of those in search of work. He had lived in Nazareth but traveled to Bethlehem to comply with the Roman census. After Jesus was born, the family moved back to Nazareth (possibly from "watch, guard, keep") once Herod had died.

What happened to Joseph after the death of his son remains unwritten. I like to imagine he went back to work, and prospered.

WHEN THE SPANIARD SOLDIERS and priests reached the breast-shaped northern bank of the Carquinez Strait, they saw what must have seemed, to the priests at least, like the astonishing religious parable of Native fishers casting nets from canoes and rafts of tules. Unlike the Spaniards, these Patwin, Wintun, Karkin, and Suisun fishers of fish did not take Sunday off.

Jose Sanchez and his men crossed the strait in 1817 and were attacked by Suisunes armed with bows. On land Sanchez fought them near Fairfield until the Suisunes met defeat by burning themselves to death in their huts.

Something about the Strait resists invasion. Fur traders and trappers who neared it were stung by insects and weakened by malaria. Later Americans complained about the fleas. Ewing Young tried to cross several times in 1834 and lost many cattle while doing so. The corral he built the surviving steers was the first structure built by non-Natives in Benicia. Robert Semple, a paranoid dentist from Kentucky, lashed some tules together with his lariat and tried to cross but only got halfway. He was lucky to be rescued because he couldn't swim and the ferry meant to pick him up didn't. William Tustin tried to make his own raft after waiting for Semple to show up to accompany him to the gold fields, but the current carried him back to where he launched. Another man who asked to use that raft found himself swept into Suisun Bay. When Captain R. Robbins lost an entire team of horses when they backed off McKay's Wharf and drowned in the strait, the generous town of Benicia reimbursed him $350. That year (1856) a telegraph cable laid across the bottom of the strait failed to operate on the very first attempt. In 1896 a train engine fell over the end of the ship *Solano* and plunged into the strait. Jack London nearly downed in it after a three-week bender but got lucky. On her last cruise the *Encinal* ran into the center span of the Carquinez Bridge. On the other hand, Captain O.C. Coffin of the steamer *Carquinez* carried quite a few passengers--if at exhorbitant prices--across the moody strait.

Robert Semple, Thomas Larkin, and Mariano Vallejo stood in long enough for the three Wise Men to found the city named after Vallejo's wife's middle name. She had received it in remembrance of Saint Philip Benicio. The saint had visited a convent and found both great piety and great hunger. The monks refused to beg, but a prayer of Benicio's to Our Lady (so the legend goes) made loaves of bread appear on the monastery doorstep. Mary then became known as the Mother of Divine Providence.

Generosity has characterized this place and its people for as long as industry has stamped those of Vallejo across the strait. The first American settler, William Isaac Tustin of Virginia, set up a general store that also served as a center of community. Marshall's discovery of wealth at Sutter's Fort first leaked in Benicia thanks to Charles Bennett. Captain Von Pfister, owner of the El Dorado Saloon, charged famously moderate prices for drinks. Semple gave away lots to city-builders like Landy Alford and Nathan Barbour, as did enterprising Larkin. The Navy, Army, and Merchant Marine landed in Benicia to stay because of Larkin's offers of lots to top officers. Alex Riddell gave the Masons a lot as well as the Presbyterians. One day a third of the tanned goods in California would arrive from the seaside city whose artisans sold plows of high quality internationally. Benicia itself hung southward sheltered by the wind and protected by bays on either side that moderated hot inland air and cold ocean currents.

Although one of the city's founders, Semple would have done best to emulate the Wise Men and drift off the page of local history. Instead, he stayed in a place whose spirit proved contrary to his suspicious nature. Having given away lots to make special friends, he kept his bidding prices high for newcomers'. Those who did not agree with his development plans found themselves accused by him of being secret enemies. After chastising Larkin for not investing enough in Benicia, the former chair of the California Constitution Convention was forced to move out of town while giving away his land almost for free. Like most paranoiacs, Semple came to a bitter end after falling off his horse. Worse still, onlookers who disinterred his body for reburial found it contorted and with splinters under the fingers. Evidently he had been buried prematurely and tried to claw his way out of the coffin.

Like Nazareth under the Romans, Benicia found herself under military occupation but proved much more resistant than Vallejo to this martial presence. On its way to becoming a restored wetland of the twenty-first century, Southamptom Bay, named after a Navy storeship grounded there by accident, collected enough silt from hills blasted by gold-seeking water cannon to be a graveyard for old ships like the *Toronto*. Of ships built in Benicia, the *Congress* was destroyed by the *Merrimac*, the sloop *Vandalia* vanished in a hurricane, the transport *Fredonia* was wrecked in a tidal wave, the *Levant* went missing between Honolulu and Panama, Semple's scow--intended as a step up from his raft--was sent into the tules by a freak high tide, the *Colusa* steamed in circles on her maiden voyage, *Amazon* burned at sea, as did *Geneva*, *Ariel* fell in Japan, *Pitcairn* went down in the Philippines, the *Nome*, the *Seven Sisters*, and the *Courtney Ford* sank in Alaska, the *Antelope* ran astray in Oregon, the *Eureka* ran out of luck at the Coquille River, and the *Berwick* ended at the Columbia bar. The Chilean bark *Confederacion* wasn't built in Benicia but ran aground there. However, the *Galilee* and *Amaranth*, built in Benicia under Matthew Turner, enjoyed long careers. *Galilee* decomissioned in 1936 to retire as a clubhouse off Sausalito.

On land, troops manning the new (1851) arsenal at Benicia built by Stone out of stone (bricks being in short supply) complained about fleas and the lack of trees. Joseph would have sympathized, if not his son. The arsenal and the old fort commanding the strait blew up. As cattle and game drifted over the oak forests and grass-covered gorges, an attempt to dig for artesian wells struck natural gas, which expoded. Soldiers and settlers were short of water ("I thirst"?) until Milo Passalacqua's timely spring gave access to an abundance of sweet, life-giving water. *Passalacqua*, an occupational nickname for a ferryman or boatman, derives from *passa l'aqua*, "one who crosses the water." The first permanent shop in town was that of a carpenter who trimmed it in stone.

Tradition has it that Mary was placed in the service of the Temple when very young. Later, she found her son conversing with the learned there. Sophia, Athena, Minerva, Brigid, Sekhmet, Fatima, Saraswati, White Buffalo Calf Woman, Guinevere, Kundry, Andraste, Sulis, and the rest of Mary's archetypal Wisdom Goddess sisters all involve themselves in providing an education. In Benicia, General Ethan Allen Hitchcock wrote books on alchemy, Swedenborg, Christ, fiary tales, Shakespeare, and Dante. Colonel Julian McAllister, in whose honor a Clock Tower was installed after the Arsenal blew up, owned an extensive library and knew more about English poetry, according to Berkeley's English instructor Leonard Bacon, than most poets and professors. Colonel James Benet also knew English poetry as well as history. The Young Ladies Seminary, forerunner to Mills College, opened in 1852 with Susan Lord as principal.

Mother Mary Goemaere brought her Santa Catalina convent from Monterey to Benicia and opened St. Catherine's in 1854. The curriculum required reading, writing, arithmetic, orthography, grammar, geography, history, composition, mythology, botany, bookkeeping, chemistry, astronomy, sewing, embroidery, and tap-estry (weaving). St. Mary of the Pacific opened in 1870 on the later site of the Benicia High School and, still later, City Hall. One stu-dent, Gertrude Atherton, wrote about Maria de la Concepcion Arguello, a widow who became California's first nun, established the charity La Beata ("The Blessed One"), and helped open a Dominican convent in Benicia.

The Protestants had a hard time setting up a church in Benicia--as late as 1923, a bolt of lightning struck the spire of the First Congregational Church on West J Street--but the Dominicans came right into the city linked by a strait to San Pablo Bay.

As with Vallejo, World War II brought ships, supplies, and occupants to the waterfront city. Speculation about Mary's out-of-wedlock pregnancy, for which righteous Joseph prepared to "put

her away," hints at the dual nature of Wisdom's feminine personifi-
cations: Sophia and lower Sophia, Durga and Kali, Athena and
Medusa, Inanna and Ereshkigol. Perhaps the lower pole of this dual-
ity manifested in Benicia to counterbalance the higher as fifteen
brothels gathered around the First Street/waterfront axis. A secret
door from the Alamo Rooms opened onto the Mayor's Closet. Next
to the Arsenal, prostitution brought in the most revenue. After
attending St. Dominic's on Sundays, the ladies gave sacks of gro-
ceries to the poor to feed them through the Depression. When the
brothels closed, the girls got married.

Benicia was intended to be the state capital, but it was not in her
mythology. Being put away and overshadowed was. Although the
state legislature approved the site of the new capital, Governor
Bigler, who seems to have possessed the cleverness of a Pontius
Pilate, made back-room deals to relocate the capital to Sacramento
even while saying otherwise in public. His deals summoned forth a
steamboat, *Empire*, filled with food and liquor for the lawmakers.
They made for Sacramento but encountered such severe flooding
that *Empire* landed in Vallejo.

Benicia had tried to lure them by promising them the town's
most marriageable ladies plus land and buildings for free, and it
worked from 1853 to 1854, but after the capital wound up in a
Central Valley floodplain and Bigler had washed his hands of all former agreements, the city faced an onslaught of bypasses and depar-
tures. A planned Benicia-Marysville railroad (sunk after the engineer drowned on his way back from England), the deepwater ships
docking in San Francisco instead (even five-dollar gold coins mint-
ed in Benicia unexpectedly displayed the imprint of San Francisco),
the Pacific Mail Steamship Company, the closure of the arsenal, the
county courthouse, the loss of the county seat to Fairfield.....so many
presences were unexpectedly converted into absences that on
Sunday Sep 10, 1880, a student of St. Mary's fainted in church and
hit her head on the register. She soon revived, and Benicia too. But
rivals Vallejo and San Francisco rose to prominence.

After staring out over the Carquinez Strait toward Martinez, I
turned from the dazzling sunlit water to find the Greek Revivial /
Paladian structure of red brick with white trimmings still standing

by itself on West G Street. Shortly before this visit I had awakened from a dream in which a voice said to me, "Mary really likes you." That had given me the key to the mythic nature of Benicia.

Two tall columns guarded a door opening onto a hall with a pinewood floor upon which had paced lawmakers debating the future of California. A placque set into the brickwork told me of the State Capitol's dedication to TRUTH - LIBERTY - TOLERATION. Another placque listing the Founders of Benicia included the often-forgotten fourth, Francisca Benicia Vallejo, "for whom Benicia was named."

I wondered how California might have turned out differently had its capital abided here. Instead, what was born here--an expansive innocence, an educated idealism, a vision of edge-of-continent democracy as yet unseen in the world--had been apprehended and marched off, like the Redeemer himself, to the city named after his final sacrifice.

This thought greatly saddened me until I realized that because cities other than Benicia had swelled to Titanic proportions, this place had never suffered overdevelopment, pollution, or thick banks of smog. Unthreatened by acid rain, its monuments, and memories, were left intact, as though Mary's bright, wise quietness protected this overshadowed place.

For a time. After centuries of watching the faithful pray to Mary, the Catholic Church finally agreed with the force of tradition and made it official:

After dying, Mary, like her sister Sophia, had ascended into heaven again to join her son, attain to final glory, and become one at last with God. Exiled from the masculine heaven, Feminine Wisdom had returned on high to assume its rightful station.

Modest down so many centuries, Mary finally rose. So, at last, will Benicia. Maybe California too.

"Our Gold is Not Ordinary Gold."

> And the wild oats and poppies still come up pure
> gold in cracks in the cement we have poured over
> utopia.
> — Ursula K. Le Guin

From West Berkeley I watched seasons pass while I read and wrote to the loud accompaniment of honking horns, car alarms, screaming schoolchildren, spitting pedestrians, and cell-phoned arguments bobbing down the street behind my oft-closed blinds toward busy San Pablo Avenue a block away. Yet the streets around me bore the names of poets.

Before the settlers came, the Ohlone people who lived here mounded empty shells near the sea. Later, Americans living in the city forming around the university did likewise with their trash. In fact, they heaped up enough to reach from what is now the Aquatic Park to the seaward edge of the Marina. By doing this, inhabitants of Berkeley were participating in the ancient activity of the estuary, a site where toxins and wastes undergo transformation into nutrients; but by the end of the 1950s, smoke from self-igniting heaps of garbage rose over a troubled city.

Estuaries are also what permaculturalists think of as edge places: overlapping ecozones that unleash productive biodiversity in novel biotic and abiotic configurations. Led by Save the Bay founders Kay Kerr, Sylvia McLaughlin and Esther Gulick, citizens concerned about the waste heaps that comprised their shoreline, and about Army Corps of Engineers plans to double the size of Berkeley by adding still more landfill, set in action a plan to convert that entire smoking twelve-foot-thick mass into meadows, parks, and even a marina. Native plants grow there now.

When I came to Berkeley I knew it was an edgy place, but wrappers and boxes left in my yard by some nocturnal passerby prompted me to reflect a little deeper. The sheer quantity of litter here staggers the imagination, as does the quantity of graffiti scrawled on walls, sidewalks, street lamps, store fronts, and road signs. The booming music, the fading tie-dyes, the loudness of it all, and the scrawls (and the street names near my temporary home: Browning, Chaucer, Byron) bring to mind the mad poet and musician Orpheus, that wandering charmer destined to be dismembered by the maenads of Dionysus. Behind the property where I lived, a homeless addict in his early thirties drank and strummed a guitar. After he had moved on I saw him walking the streets--chin puff of hair, dirty sneakers, sports cap turned backwards--with his skeletal waif of a Eurydice. If the mythic pattern held, she would die before he did.

Next door awaited Albany, Morrigan's place, if the powerful red-haired Celtic goddess addressing me in dreams were any indication. I had missed, I saw, or perhaps just needed to make a detour before arriving in the city whose name meant "Scotland." I was introduced to Albany, I remembered, by a woman whose name was pronounced "terra." While walking in the streets we heard bagpipe music wailing from St. Mary's College. It made my blood pump and ancestral hackles rise. In 1908, a group of Albany women armed with rifles and shotguns turned back a wagon driven by men attempting to dump Berkeley trash here. The Albany Bulb had been trashed as well until citizens took the initiative to make it an art colony and then a park. Stands of eucalyptus on Albany Hill recall the dynamite factory that planted them to contain accidental explosions.

I had dreamed of sitting in a pub looking out at the Berkeley Hills while puffing my briar pipe and tipping brews in the company of hobbits. Desiring to move to this side of the Caldecott Tunnel, I had landed in West Berkeley. Only later did I connect the dream to the English pub in Albany where I had bought my pipe tobacco and sat for a smoke on a cool summer evening or two. Just as well I had overlooked this, for I carried a staggeringly heavy emotional, historical, and imaginal load of California to be finished with. Better to compost it safely here in edgy Berkeley than try to in tidy Albany.

Because nobody had ever done this before, I wasn't sure what to make of the mixture of disappointment, emptiness, and relief now assailing me. I have visited, spent time in, dreamed with, felt into every one of California's fifty-eight counties, every one of her major cities, most of her minor ones, and various unincorporated areas, mountains, valleys, deserts, rivers, creeks, and points in between. Yet I hadn't seen but a fraction of California. Every highway I had traveled ran next to culverts and canyons I would never enter. Every meadow I had walked through stretched away into distances I would never be acquainted with.

During the writing I had found myself back in all those places so completely that after each session at the keyboard I needed to give myself time to remember where I was. Again and again over the past eleven years I sat in the low places of drained and damaged neighborhoods, felt the cut of saw blades, cried dam breaches of tears, awakened sweating from nightmares about massacres long past but never properly mourned and accounted for. I stood once again in sewers and poisoned fields where farmers had once grown crops to feed early townsites. Yet I still have not written a tenth of what I saw and heard and felt. The rest of my life would not suffice for it.

I sat and thought back over where I had been. How had old Montalvo written it in his sixteenth-century novel?

I tell you that on the right-hand side of the Indies there was an island called California, which was very close to the region of the Terrestrial Paradise....

For me and for California's conquest, it all started in San Diego, city of my birth, named after a saint who had fought a border war and after the ship that brought conquistadors into its natural sheltered harbor. They founded San Diego as a military outpost. Split by canyons, positioned above Mexico, it lays out a natural altar for Hecate, fiercely maternal goddess of crossroads, borderlines, and borderlands. From the air, the shape of San Diego recalls her witch-like face with its Mission Bay eyes, downward-pointing Point Loma nose, and watery frown glaring out over the Pacific. Above this face, the volcanic giantism and sprawling industrialization of Orange County (where the giant Crystal Cathedral is being sold to the Catholic Church) recall Hephaestos, conservative blacksmith of the gods, with oil derricks for hammers beating away at the ground. The aboriginal Kumeyaays, Luiseños, Gabrieleños, and Juaneños must have known these mythic presences well and spoken of them by other names.

In Los Angeles, materialized out of a site viisited by Native ritualists seeking jimson-weed visions, angels continue to rise and fall as celestial messengers transformed into projectors, movie stars, airplanes, and theosophers. Like Venus from the waves, the entire Los Angeles Basin rose from the depths of the sea millions of years ago as a clamshell-shaped stage rotating into view. The channeled LA River either lies dry or flash-floods. Here where the image often matters more than what it images as Oz thunders intoxicated by expansionary, water-powered imperialism. Centuries of violence in the City of Angels remind us that where Venus resides, Mars is never far away. The native Tongva people might have called her Chehooit. Naturally, for she was beautiful...

Ventura and Santa Barbara once shared a county, but the presence of Artemis in wild Ventura, where developers strive to imprison her in gated communities, clashed with that of St. Barbara, a Christian version of Sophia. Just as Barbara, locked in a castle by her wealthy father, gazed down on the lands below her window, so the mansions of the Butler Belt in the Santa Ynez Mountains overlook a city crafted carefully into a Mission Revival resort. Gnostic Sophia lived in a timeless heaven reminiscent of, say, Carpinteria and Summerland. The former is an idyllic beach town, the latter named after the realm of dead spirits. Its founder disappeared down an oil well. According to the Chumash, who have lived here for millennia and who referred to their Barbara/Sophia as Hutash, Point Conception, site of numerous shipwrecks, is a gateway to another world.

San Luis Obispo County holds the geographic midpoint between Southern and Northern California. The place is named after a bishop who died halfway to old age. So many pendulum swings at play so far back--Salinans to the north and Chumash to the south, the frequently-burned mission located between two heights of rock, conservatives arguing with liberals, William Randolph Heart's rise and fall--recall torch-bearing Nemesis stepping forth to act as restorer of the balance. From her territory, Highway 101 winds upward into Monterey County and the deepest underwater canyons along the coast just offshore like a watery Hades. On land, the fertile Salinas Valley conceals the longest underground stream in the nation.

Turning inland, we come to the ceaseless janglings of earthquake-prone San Benito County. Here Themis, named Justitia by the Romans, stands astride the San Andreas Fault with a sword in one hand and scales in the other. Collisions of law and lawlessness, of Hells Angels pilgrimages and county histories written by a judge, never end here. On the coast, forested Santa Cruz hosts all the airborne intensity of the archetypal Divine Child. Where Iacchus flies by turns inspiring and reckless, the story has been one of high-velocity cruises and Highway 17 crashes. On the other hand, new things grow rapidly here, whereas in labyrinthine Santa Clara County to the north, they tend to grow luxuriantly, as befits the altar of spring goddess Persephone, whether fruit orchards of times gone by, silicon yesterday, or cleantech startups today.

Proceeding up the peninsula toward San Francisco, we encounter Redwood City, Burlingame, and other sheltered sites whose introversion contrasts strongly with the City's extraverted exuberance: surely that of transsexual Dionysus, vine-wrapped god of drama, ecstasy, and wild celebration. Keeping to the east brings us into Alameda County and to Fremont, Union City, Hayward, Livermore, Oakland, Berkeley, and other cities busy with the construction sounds of talented carpenter Daedalus. He must feel at home in a county named after its groves of poplar trees, for Oakland's first mayor was Carpentier, and the nearby mission named after Joseph the Carpenter.

Running till farther northward, El Camino Real ends at Sonoma and the top of the old Mission Trail. The last mission rose briefly and collapsed in the county of fruitful Demeter. Under her all-giving influence, Sebastopol and nearby rural arenas play out the tale of the Garden of Eden.

From Contra Costa County and its Avalonian heavens and hells I sought the ventral depths of the horizontal Central Valley, and I found them in strong contrast to the vertical, living inwardness around the edge of the state.

In the end, back here again to the Bay Area, where I live now and where, perhaps, a significant chunk of California's future waits to be refined, reinvented, reconstructed, or reborn.

I still have questions about California, Golden State, west of the west, Land of the Sundown Sea, edgy culmination of so many destinations. How do these places I've known relate to each other and to the planet as a whole? Notice Who is next to Whom: Francis and Clare in the Bay Area, San Diego near Tahquitz, Tahquitz near Mars, Yosemite and Tahoe like Zeus and Narcissus. Why these groupings? I do not know. And what of places more distant from another? All of them must represent complexes or subplots in the story-mind of California. Her protectiveness she harbors at San Diego, her projections elevate from Los Angeles, her ecstasies adorn San Francisco, and the Sierra gives her a backbone.

California in turn expresses the edge of America where plates and politics collide with each other. The name "America" first appeared on Martin Waldseemüller's 1507 world map known over time as the baptismal certificate of the surprising New World. *America* derives from Amerigo, which comes from the Gothic name *Amalrich*: "work ruler" or "master workman." Although Calvin Coolidge might have been more or less correct to say that "the business of America is business," our real "work," extending north and south to both continents, follows the alchemical ideal of a Grand but unfinished Opus. We are here, North and South Americans, to get things done. Gaia's things: the work of She who dreams us.

And what will become of California?

Our state consistently ranks near the bottom of national "worst places to live" surveys because of its broken budget, divisive politics, violent crime, underfunded education, overfunded prisons, deteriorating ecosystems, and hosts of other troubles. As monocrop agriculture salts itself out of the Central Valley, where a third of the nation's food still grows, predictions range from statewide desertification to superstorms that could drown the heart of our near-bankrupt empire. I can't worry about California anymore. My focus must concentrate steadfastly now on the Bay Area, on the inflow and outflow of the great estuarine chamber of alchemical California.

I remember the sign I saw on some store or other in Santa Rosa when I first reached Northern California and decided to stay a while: JOURNEY'S END.

To what end, for me? What was all this journeying really about?

I know where I came from, and where I ended up, and why.

I know my ancestry, the gods of my ancestors, my past, my myth, and my place.

I know that we are always within the discourse of the lands on which we work, play, dream, and dwell.

That geology, ecology, climate, and meteorology *are* deep psychology.

That what we seek to dominate in nature returns to us as wild shadow.

That the rootless uproot until they heal their wounds of dysplacement.

That as members of cultures in ongoing evolution, indigenous people here and elsewhere wait for the rest of us to grow up enough to hear about our troubled history together and respond heartfully by moving beyond the mentality of objectification, control, and war.

That Thales was correct-- "All things are full of gods"--and that things go better when we relate to these gods from the hard-won standpoint of responsible, aware respondents come of age.

That Story joins us to the living presence of Earth, place of places, and to her manifold local sentiences.

That to tend the presence of the land is to fully rouse the soul.

In my mind's eye California flares numinous, auriferous, and animated in her entirety, an illuminated self with many facets and quirks of personality, but perceivable at last as an integrated soul. I feel like a small branch given the gift of insight, however limited by my own mortality and fallibility, into the mighty being of the multi-armed tree to which it finds itself attached. To grasp the psychic depth of any particular feature--a hillside, a neighborhood, a coast-line, a county--is to listen in on what California, the world's alchem-ical retort, is brewing, stirring, thickening, coagulating, dreaming, decanting, thinking about.

FOR SOME TIME NOW a Sophia figure has been showing up in my dreams. In one dream I asked her whether we could save ourselves, each other, the planet and its creatures. "Yes!" she said firmly: "There is still so much light in the world!"

I was born on July 6th, the day Juan Cabrillo became the first European to spot the Californias. For the past eleven years I had supposed this connection (Jungians would call it a synchronicity, but I think of it now as a gesture or a motion) the emblem of a kind of geomythic parentage. I was California's child, I believed, although to what end I did not know. As I neared the terminus of my journey, however, a version of Hera appeared in a dream to inform me that my birth had been arranged for purposes beyond those of my home-land. Much for me to ponder there...

Hera upholds the rightful order of things. Mary and Guadalupe are bright siblings of Sophia; Llorona is Sophia fallen, and from there Sophia creates and redeems the world. We all share a divine parent-age that joins us to the dreams of animate Earth. *Anima Terrae* abides as planetary source of all our myths and the relations they enliven.

What happens in California becomes true everywhere, not as a first but as an extreme, in either direction: where to go, where not to. And, in my case, how to begin to envision Terrania, the just and sustainable and Earth-loving civilization humanity must build to survive and, beyond that, to flourish and achieve our full stature as a responsible species among many other species.

> Throughout my whole life, during every minute of
> it, the world has been gradually lighting up and

blazing before my eyes until it has come to sur-round me, entirely lit up from within.

— Pierre Teillard de Chardin

For the past eleven years I had dreamed of California as a black woman--black like Queen Calafia--giving me work, gesturing impa-tiently at the piles of paper on my desk, asking me how the writing was coming along. In a final dream here at journey's end, I walked out of my old workplace, a psychic collage of offices, desks, and cubicles gone by, while saying goodbye to imaginal coworkers.

The last, none other than Queen Calafia, hugged me so strongly that I woke up tingling. The hardships, terrors, and psychic shocks had been worth feeling the warmth of that lingering embrace.

"You're welcome," I said aloud. Before my morning coffee no less.

In the song of Earth Horizon man wanders in search of the Sacred Middle from which all hori-zons are equidistant, and his soul happily at rest. Once the Middle is attained, all the skyey rings that encircle earth's six quarters dissolve into the true zone of reality, and his spirit, no longer deflected by the influences of false horizons, swings freely to its proper arc.

— Mary Austin

How long could we keep up fighting each other if we thought Someone Else was watching from near at hand? What new commu-nities might we build, what new sciences might we found, splits overcome, projects undertake, once meeting our Earth as a sentient, mindful being? Such questions distill the gold I found, neither mined nor vulgar, but alchemical gold. "Our Gold Is Not the Ordinary Gold," said the alchemists who sought the soul of matter. Gold turned over, looked into, and treasured along my California way.

From my home in the Bay Area I take my leave of the trail with the satisfaction that, in my hands and those of the thirty or forty others now tending Terra deeply from wherever we live around our vocal world, the human translation of the speech of place, nature, and Earth has begun. We find ourselves addressed by terrestrial powers we have scarcely begun to understand, let alone decipher. Powers more ancient and far more comprehensive, if less focused and differentiated, than our own. So far it is proving a lively conversation.

Epilogue:
El Cajon and Pandora's Jar

"Oh hell, I dropped my truck."

According to my parents, this, my first sentence, popped out of my mouth when I dropped a toy pickup. I was a late speaker, which worried them; yet here I came with a full sentence.

I didn't have much to say growing up, in part because my surroundings baffled and grated on me. I grew up in a box: El Cajon, the "Big Box" Valley about fifteen miles east of San Diego as the beer bottle flies. Settlers bringing cattle named the Valley this (they thought) because the enclosure prevented the herds from roaming. I add "they thought" because our terrapsychological work has shown us that place names spring forth from the interactive field between the namers and the place itself: its ecology, its geology, its shape, size, color, history.

Case in point: San Diego, named after a militant monk who defended a border in Spain centuries before the murderous split of the International Border divided California from Mexico. Crevices and cleavages run through the heart of the city. Mythically speaking, it's as though San Diego were an altar to Hekate, borderline goddess of borderlands, crossroads, initiations, medicinal plants, magic, dreams, and moonlight. Perhaps she brought her two torches together on July 4, 2012 to detonate at once all the fireworks stored up for the Big Bay Boom. From space San Diego turns a witchlike face eastward.

The ancient Orphic tales put Hecate together with another powerful goddess: Pandora, the first woman, created by Hephaestus and Athena at the command of Zeus to serve as bride to Epimetheus ("Afterthought"), backward brother of Prometheus ("Forethought"). Pandora's name, All Gifts, refers to those given her so lavishly by the Olympians before sending her down with her famous box or jar. When she grew curious and opened it, out flew hardship, poverty, disease, death, and other "evils" that make us mortal. In some versions of the tale she slammed the lid down to contain Hope; in others Hope flew into the world as well. From one point of view, Pandora is an Eve-like figure who brought trouble into the world; but from another, she gave us both the gifts of necessary limitation and the means to bear up under them. Maybe the gods knew what they were doing.

In 1845 Rancho El Cajon was granted to Maria Antonia Estudilla, wife of Miguel Pedrorena. Amaziah Lord Knox (1833-1918), a transplant from New England, started a hotel on the ranch to provide for travelers heading from San Diego to the gold mines in Julian. He charged $1 a night for room and board, and gave his name to Knox Corners before it was renamed El Cajon.

How a container functions depends on what we make of it. The tallest building in El Cajon is a jail: that's one kind of box. The Jack-in-the-Box restaurant chain started in El Cajon. (I worked there for a few weeks one summer and quit after a drunken Marine knocked the cash register off the counter.) UFO sightings have been frequently documented in the Valley, and El Cajon serves as the earthly headquarters for the Uranius (UNiversal Articulate Interdimensional Understanding of Science) Academy attempting to send messages to hovering Space Brothers. Now and then followers form a circle of chanting bodies in some field or other in Jamul, but nobody from on high ever shows up. A more sinister presence rose from Pandora's jar in the 1970s as a TV repairman named Tom Metzger represented the Ku Klux Klan when he ran for various public offices.

I grew up in a former olive orchard that succumbed to a subdivision forming around what neighborhood lore said was a haunted house. Ours was a relatively well-off neighborhood compared to many in El Cajon, where even now it's common to see pregnant teens pushing strollers, drunks reeling through motel parking lots, and white trash drug dealers staking out street corners. Time does not advance in Pandora's jar, it only goes in circles. The last time I visited my parents, who still live in the same small house I grew up in, I was lucky enough to land in the only hotel in the city not infested with crack dealers and petty criminals.

Many of us dislike our home town and wish we had grown up somewhere else. I used to be one. I never felt at home with the redneck vulgarity, the in-your-face racism, the hands-on conservatism (my first grade teacher threw a chair at a noisy kid), the giant crosses posted on people's lawns, with the cross on Mt. Helix overseeing all. Behind my obedient son facade I threw rocks and sniped with my BB rifle and blew up pumpkins on Halloween. I couldn't wait to escape the box and go to college, and once there I seldom looked back, although I did work for a time in an ice rink that stimulated good memories of skating my way through my junior high years.

During my days as a doctoral student living in Escondido in northern San Diego County, I faced poverty severe enough that my Chevy pickup got repossessed. On the morning I watched the tow truck drive away with it, I heard myself say, "Oh hell, I dropped my truck." This loop in time seemed like one more reason to loathe where I'd been raised.

As I studied the witchlike "soul" of San Diego for my doctoral work on psyche, history, and place, I wondered what part El Cajon played in Hekate's story. On a visit home I was walking my old neighborhood (the place looks the same) and thinking about the boxlike nature of the Valley when I spotted something new in a neighbor's yard: a sculpture of a woman, perhaps a goddess, stooping over a large jar. I thought about time loops, about the shape and name of the Valley, about Knox as a place of strife and gold, about the name Pedrorena, which means "stone" (as does "Craig") and "reborn," about Halloween (my favorite holiday as a child), and

about my parents--my Hephaestus dad who was handy at everything, my Athena mom who had run a hospital laboratory--and the
image of Pandora walked into my imagination.

From that moment my relationship to El Cajon began to change.

It's an odd thing, being born on Hekate's altar and growing up in
Pandora's jar. At the time I couldn't stand the confinement of it; but
over the years, with my roots still in El Cajon, I came to realize how
much psychic stabilty this town gave me as my travels took me all
over California and to places across the nation and beyond it. Even
when I did not visit, I knew I could come back at any time to see my
parents, walk around the neighborhood, swim in the pool in our
backyard, and rest in a timelessness that offered a brief respite from
my overactive life. Renewed, I could spring back out of the box and
dive into the deadlines and schedules and commitments.

It's an odd thing, allowing yourself to love your home town. Not
the racism or the jail mentality, but the place itself.

On my last trip to El Cajon I noticed a minivan truck parked in
my parents' driveway. I liked the gold tint, compact profile, and
sturdy wheels. When I asked my parents about it, they said they
wanted to sell it because they seldom drove long distances anymore.
A pity, because the van was in good shape with relatively little
mileage on it.

Because my weary car was on its last legs, I offered to buy the
van from them. They agreed, then called me the following day to say
they were giving it to me.

I hung up the phone and thought:

Oh good, I found my truck.

Bibliography

Anzaldua, Gloria. *Borderlands (La Frontera): The New Mestiza.* Aunt Lute Books, 2007.

Armand, Dione. *Eureka and Sequoia Park.* Arcadia, 2008.

Austin, *Land of Little Rain.* Modern Library Classics, 2003.

Bachand, Thomas. *Lake Tahoe: A Fragile Beauty.* Chronicle Books, 2008.

Barich, Bill. *Big Dreams: Into the Heart of California.* Pantheon, 1994.

Barnett, Loretta, and Farnbach, Rebecca. *Temecula.* Arcadia, 2006.

Bean, Lowell, Vane, Sylvia, and Young, Jackson. *The Cahuilla Landscape: The Santa Rose and San Jacinto Mountains.* Ballena Press, 1991.

Beckley, Timothy, Tessman, Diane, Lee, Regan, Gorightly, Adam, Roberts Paul, Parzanese, Joe, Cactus Jim and Swartz, Tim. *Secrets Of Death Valley: Mysteries And Haunts Of The Mojave Desert.* Global Communications, 2010.

Beesley, David. *Crow's Range: An Environmental History of the Sierra Nevada.* University of Nevada, 2004.

Bellamy, Stanley, and Keller, Russell. *Big Bear*. Arcadia, 2006.

Buckley, Christopher, and Young, Gary. *The Geography of Home: California's Poetry of Place*. Heyday and The Clapperstick Institute, 1999.

Bussinger, Julia, and Phelan. Beverly. *Benicia*. Arcadia, 2004.

Campbell, Eileen. *Carneros: Travels along the Napa-Sonoma Edge*. Carneros Quality Alliance, 2000.

Carle, David. *Mono Lake Viewpoint*. Artemisia Press, 1992.

Casey, Ed. "A Matter of Edge: Border vs. Boundary at La Frontera." Presented at UCSB, May 10, 2011.

Casterline, Renee, and English, Jane. *Mount Shasta Reflections*. Bluestar Divison of Amber Lotus Publishing, 2003.

Chalquist, Craig, ed. *Rebearths: Conversations with a World Ensouled*. World Soul Books, 2010.

Chalquist, Craig. *Terrapsychology: Reengaging the Soul of Place*. Spring Journal Books, 2007.

Churchwell, Mary Jo. *Palm Springs: The Landscape, the History, the Lore*. Ironwood, 2001.

Clark, Galen. *Indians of the Yosemite Valley and Vicinity Their History, Customs and Traditions*. Nabu Press, 2010.
Conway, James. *Napa*. Avon, 1990.

Conway, James. *The Far Side of Eden: New Money, Old Land, and the Battle for Napa Valley*. Mariner, 2002.

Cummings, Martha. *Mono Lake Stories*. Rowbarge Press, 1995.

Cuncannon, Delcie. *Joshua Tree: The Story Behind the Scenery*. KC Publications, 1999.

Curtin, Jeremiah. *Myths of the Modocs: Indian Legends of the Northwest*. Benjamin Blom, 1971.

Danelo, David. *The Border: Exploring the U.S.-Mexican Divide*. Stackpole Books, 2008.

Dear, Michael, and Leclerc, Gustavo, eds. *Postborder City: Cultural Spaces of Bajalta California*. Routledge, 2003.

Despain, Joel. *Hidden Beneath the Mountains: Caves of Sequoia and Kings Canyon National Parks*. Cave Books, 2003.

Dillon, Richard. *Great Expectations: The Story of Benicia*, California. Benicia Heritage Book, Inc., 1980.

Dilsaver, Lary, and Tweed, William. *Challenge of the Big Trees: A Resource History of Sequoia and Kings Canyon National Parks*. Sequoia Natural History Association, 1990.

Doubiago, Sharon, Baker, Devreaux, and Maeder, Susan. *Wood, Water, Air and Fire: The Anthology of Mendocino Women Poets*. Pot Shard Press, 1998. [Sharon: "fertile plain." Susan: "lily." Devreaux: "bank of a river" - the Muses of Mendocino?]

Ellingwood, Ken. *Hard Line: Life and Death on the U.S.-Mexico Border*. Pantheon, 2004.
East, Claudia, Cleland, Karen, East, Donald, and East, Yale. *Yreka*. Arcadia, 2007.

Ewan, Rebecca. *A Land Between: Owens Valley, California*. The John Hopkins University Press, 2000.

Farquhar, Francis. *History of the Sierra Nevada*. University of California, 1965.

Faulkner, Jessie. *Arcata*. Arcadia, 2004.

Fiddler, Claude. *Yosemite Once Removed: Portraits of the Backcountry.* Yosemite Association, 2003.

Fitzpatrick, Linda, and Conkle, James. *Needles*. Arcadia, 2010.

Flaherty, Dennis, and Schlenz, Mark. *Mono Lake: Mirror of Imagination.* Companion Press, 1996.

Flanner, Hildegard. *Brief Cherishing: A Napa Valley Harvest.* John Daniel, 1985.

Fleck, Richard, ed. *A Colorado River Reader.* University of Utah, 2000.

Forstenzer, Martin. *Mammoth: the Sierra Legend.* Mountain Sports Press, 2002.

Glazner, Allen, and Stock, Greg. *Geology Underfoot in Yosemite National Park.* Mountain Press, 2010.

Holsinger, Rosemary. *Shasta Indian Tales.* Naturegraph Publishers, 2006.

Houk, Rose. *Mojave Desert. Southwest Parks and Monuments* Association, 2001.

Huber, N. King. *The Geologic Story of Yosemite National Park.* Yosemite Association, 1989.

Irwin, Sue. *California's Eastern Sierra: A Visitor's Guide.* Cachuma Press, 1991.

Isenberg, Andrew. *Mining California: An Ecological History.* Hill and Wang, 2005.

James, Cheewa. *Modoc: The Tribe that Wouldn't Die.* Naturegraph, 2008.

Jones, Ray, and Lubow, Joe. *It Happened in Yosemite: Remarkable Events that Shaped History*. Morris, 2010.

Johnson, Steven, producer. *Battle for the Klamath*. Veriscope, 2005.

Johnston, Verna. *California Forests and Woodlands: A Natural History*. University of California, 1994.

Johnstone, Peter, ed. *Giants in the Earth: The California Redwoods*. Heyday, 2001.

Journal of the Modoc County Historical Society, No. 18, 1996: "The Tule Lake Area, Twentieth Century Development."

Kern, James. *Vallejo*. Arcadia, 2004.

Kingston, Maxine Hong. *China Men*. Young Adult, 1989.

Klages, Ellen. *Harbin Hot Springs: Healing Waters, Sacred Land*. Harbin Springs Publishing, 1993.

Klett, Mark, Solnit, Rebecca, and Wolfe, Byron. *Yosemite in Time: Ice Ages, Tree Clocks, Ghost Rivers*. Trinity University Press, 2005.

Kolpan, Steven. *A Sense of Place: An Intimate Portrait of the Niebaum-Coppola Winery and the Napa Valley*. Routledge, 1999.

Laflin, Patricia. *Coachella Valley California: A Pictorial History*. The Donning Company, 1998.
Laflin, Patricia. *Indio*. Arcadia, 2008.

Lankford, Scott. *Tahoe Beneath the Surface: The Hidden Stories of America's Largest Mountain Lake*. Heyday, 2010.

Lapsley, James. *Bottled Poetry: Napa Winemaking from Prohibition to the Modern Era*. University of California, 1996.

Laufer, Peter. *¡Calexico! True Lives of the Borderlands*. University of Arizona, 2011.

Lang, Julian, ed. *Ararapíkva: Traditional Karuk Indian Literature from Northwestern California*. Heyday, 1994.

La Pena, Frank, Bates, Craig, and Medley, Steven. *Legends of the Yosemite Miwok*. Heyday, 2007.

Lee, Gaylen. *Walking Where We Lived: Memoirs of a Mono Indian Family*. University of Oklahoma, 1998.

Lingenfelter, Richard. *Death Valley & the Amargosa: Land of Illusion*. University of California, 1986.

Lukacs, Paul. *American Vintage: The Rise of American Wine*. Houghton Mifflin, 2000.

McBride, Peter, and Waterman, Jonathan. *The Colorado River: Flowing Through Conflict*. Westcliffe, 2010.

McCormack, Cheryl. *Susanville*. Arcadia, 2008.

McLaughlin, Mark. *Sierra Stories Vol. 2: True Tales of Tahoe*. Mic Mac, 1998.

McLeod, Michael. *Anatomy of a Beast: Obsession and Myth on the Trail of Bigfoot*. University of California, 2009.

Merchant, Carolyn, ed. *Green Versus Gold: Sources in California's Environmental History*. Island Press, 1998.
Moss Wayne. *The Trinity Alps Companion*. Ecopress, 2009.

Most, Stephen. *River of Renewal: Myth & History in the Klamath Basin*. Oregon Historical Society Press, 2006.

Most, Stephen, producer. *River of Renewal: United by Water, Divided by*

People. Pikiawish Partners, 2009.

Murray, Keith. *The Modocs and Their War*. University of Oklahoma, 1959.

Navez, Ren. *Palm Springs: California's Desert Gem*. Westcliffe, 2006.

Newland, James. *Cleveland National Forest*. Arcadia, 2008.

Niemann, Greg. *Palm Springs Legends: Creation of a Desert Oasis*. Sunbelt, 2006.

Normal, Bob, Whitney, Mary, and Sisk, Gordon. *Hemet*. Arcadia, 2008.

Patencio, Francisco, and Boynton, Margaret. *Stories and Legends of the Palm Springs Indians*. Palm Springs Desert Museum, 1943.

Purluss, Betsy. "Climbing the Alchemical Mountain." In *Psychological Perspectives*, Vol 51, Issue 1, 2008.

Quinn, Arthur. *Hell with the Fire Out: A History of the Modoc War*. Faber and Faber, 1997.

Richard, Ellis. *Lassen Volcanic: The Story Behind the Scenery*. KC Publications, 1993.
Reisner, Marc. *A Dangerous Place: California's Unsettling Fate*. Pantheon, 2004.

Reisner, Marc. *Cadillac Desert: The American West and Its Disappearing Water*. Penguin, 1998.
Rohde, Jerry, and Rohde, Gisela. *Redwood National & State Parks: Tales, Trails, & Auto Tours*. MountainHome Books, 1994.

Round, Phillip. *The Impossible Land: Story and Place in California's Imperial Valley*. University of New Mexico, 2008.

Runte, Alfred. *National Parks: The American Experience.* Taylor Trade, 2010.

Sawyer, John. *Northwestern California: A Natural History.* University of California, 2006.

Service, Pamela, and Hillman, Raymond. *Eureka and Humboldt County California.* Arcadia, 2001.

Schoenherr, Allan. *A Natural History of California.* University of California, 1992.

Scott, Edward. *The Saga of Lake Tahoe. Crystal Bay.* Sierra-Tahoe Publishing, 1957.

Sharp, Robert, and Glazner, Allen. *Geology Underfoot: In Death Valley and Owens Valley.* Mountain Press Publishing, 1997.

Shelton, William. *Towns of Mount Lassen.* Arcadia, 2007.

Smith, Genny, ed. *Deepest Valley: A Guide to Owens Valley*, Its Roadsides and Mountain Trails. Spellbinder, 1995.

Smith, Genny, ed. *Sierra East: Edge of the Great Basin.* University of California, 2000.

Solnit, Rebecca. *Savage Dreams: A Journey into the Landscape Wars of the American West.* University of California, 1999.

Soltys, Richard. *Coachella Valley Yesterday, Today, and Tomorrow.* Solyts Productions, 2005.
Snyder, Gary. *The Gary Snyder Reader.* Counterpoint, 1999.

Stillman, Deanne. *Joshua Tree: Desolation Tango.* University of Arizona, 2006.

Stillman, Deanne. *Twentynine Palms: A True Story of Murder, Marines, and the Mojave.* Angel City, 2008.

Stringfellow, Kim. *Greetings from the Salton Sea: Folly and Intervention in the Southern California Landscape, 1905-2005.* Center Books, 2005

Strong, Douglas. *From Pioneers to Preservationists: A Brief History of Sequoia and Kings Canyon National Parks.* Sequoia Natural History Assocation, 2000.

Storytellers of Lassen County, California. *Small Moments in Time: Memories of Lassen County.* Lassen College Foundation, 2009.

Swinchatt, Jonathan, and Howell, David. *Winemaker's Dance: Exploring Terroir in the Napa Valley.* University of California, 2004.

Tetley, Rhea-Frances. *Lake Arrowhead.* Arcadia, 2005.

Tevis, Yvonne. *The Coachella Valley Preserve: The Struggle for a Desert Wetlands.* Borgo, 1995.

The Redlands Institute. *Salton Sea Atlas.* ESRI Press, 2002.

Tweed, William. *Sequoia & Kings Canyon: The Story Behind the Scenery.* KC Publications, 2003.

Tweed, William. *Uncertain Path: A Search for the Future of National Parks.* University of California, 2010.

Vollman, William. *Imperial.* Viking Adult, 2009.

Wallace, David. *The Klamath Knot: Explorations of Myth and Evolution.* University of California, 2003.

Warneke, Jack, and Holtzclaw, Kenneth. *San Jacinto.* Arcadia, 2008.

Watkins, Mary. "The Shame of Forcibly Displacing Others: 9/11 and the Criminalization of Immigration." Unpublished article, 2011.

Wattaway, Gayle, ed. *Inlandia: A Literary Journey through California's Inland Empire*. Heyday, 2006.

Waterman, Jonathan. *Running Dry: A Journey from Source to Sea Down the Colorado River*. National Geographic, 2010:

Webb, Robert, Fenstermaker, Lynn, Heaton, Jill, Hughson, Debra, McDonald, Eric, and Miller, David, eds. *The Mojave Desert: Ecosystem Processes and Sustainability*. U of Nevada Press, 2009.

Wessels, Tom. *The Granite Landscape: A Natural History of America's Mountain Domes, from Acadia to Yosemite*. The Countryman Press, 2001.

Wehrey, Jane. *Voices from This Long Brown Land: Oral Recollections of Owens Valley Lives and Manzanar Pasts*. Palgrave Macmillan, 2006.

Zanger, Michael. *Mt. Shasta: History, Legend & Lore*. Celestial Arts, 1992.

www.ingramcontent.com/pod-product-compliance
Lightning Source LLC
Chambersburg PA
CBHW031501270326
41930CB00006B/190